A Computational Biology Strategy For Deciphering The Biomolecular And Genomic Mechanisms Of Aggressive Cancer

Yam Chaim Nasi

A Computational Biology Strategy For Deciphering The Biomolecular And Genomic Mechanisms Of Aggressive Cancer

First Edition March 2025

Written by Yam Chaim Nasi

Contents

Chapter 1: Review of Literature

1.1. Leukemia

Abnormal Clonal Proliferation of cells of the hematopoietic lineage in the bone marrow leads to blood cancer, known as Leukemia. These abnormal white blood cells (WBCs) are not fully developed and are clinically referred to as blasts. In addition to a well-known genetic predisposition, there are other environmental risk factors such as exposure to Ionizing radiation, benzene, formaldehyde etc. Based on the lineage of origin, Leukemia is broadly categorized into four types; acute myelogenous (AML), chronic myelogenous (CML), acute lymphoblastic (ALL), and chronic lymphoblastic (ALL) and 95% of all leukemias are acute. ALL is more common in children than in adults [1][2]. According to Globocan statistics, Asia is the most significant contributor to Leukemia cases (48.6%), with India having the 3rd largest Incidence rate (~10.2%) worldwide [3] (**Figure 1.1**). Myeloid leukemias are common in India and lymphoid in the Caucasian population, along with an uneven distribution of the percentage of cases between adults and children[4,5].

A

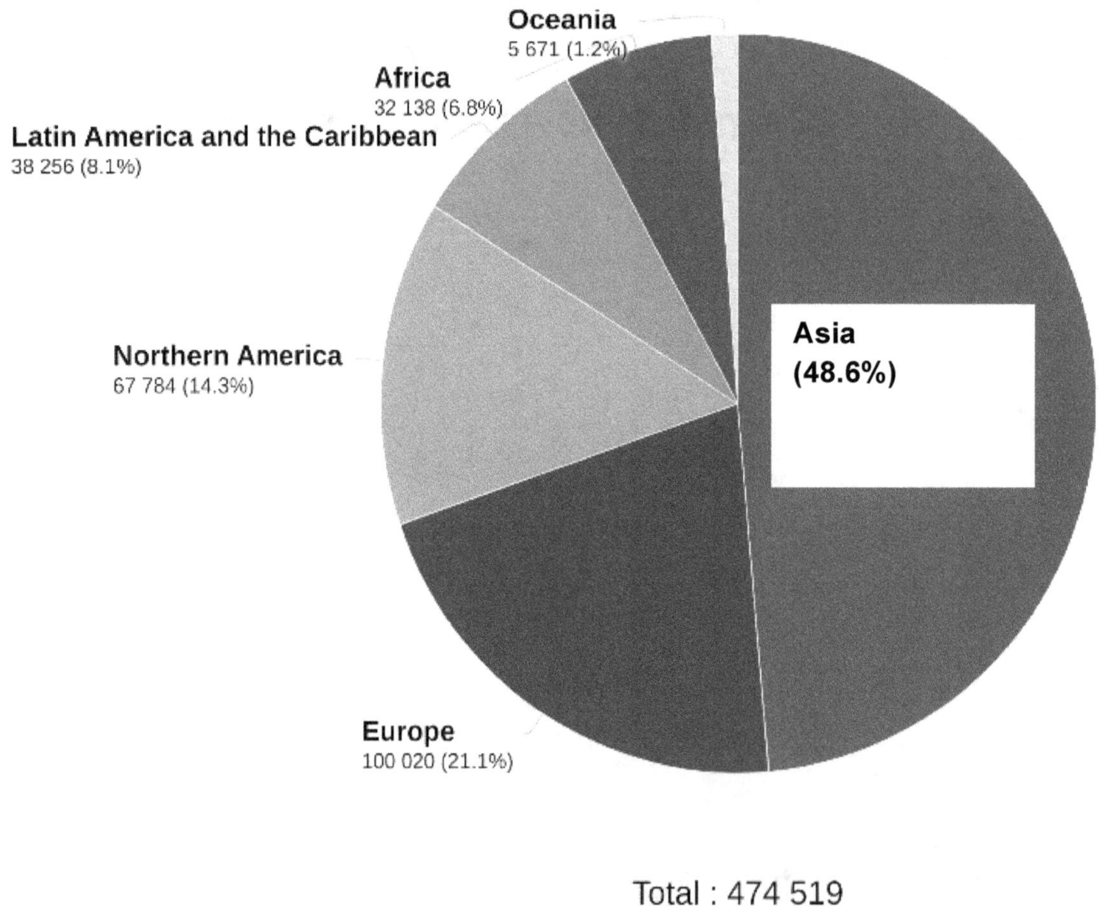

B

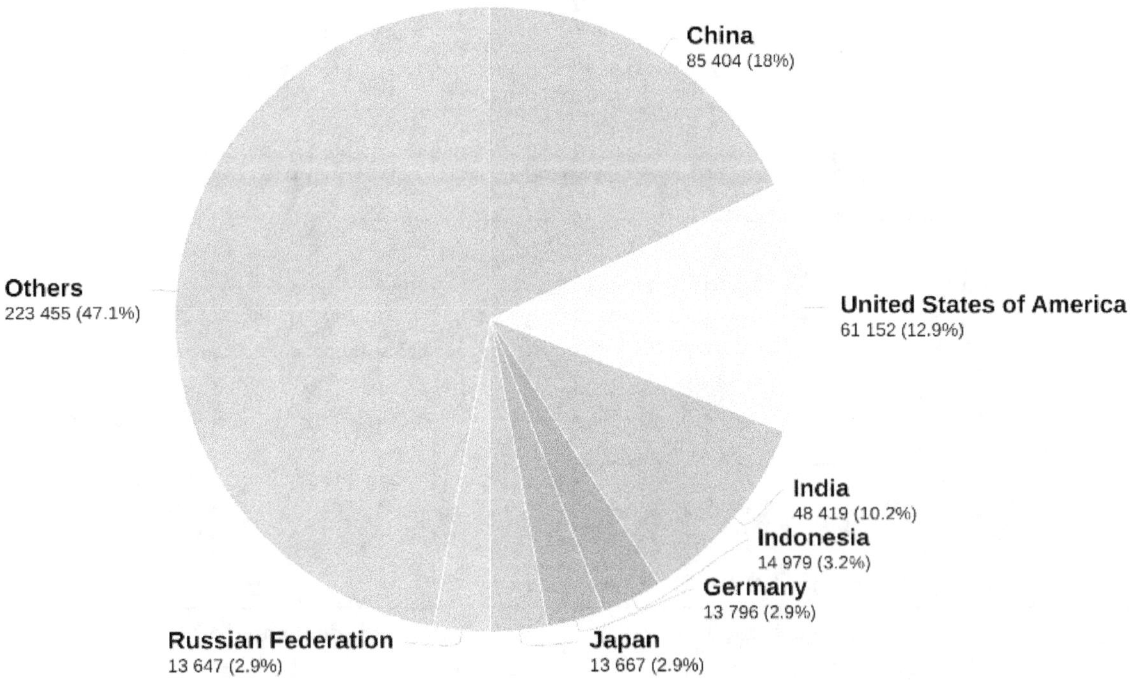

Figure 1.1: Estimated number of new cases across A) various continents and B) different countries as presented by GLOBOCAN 2020 statistics

To differentiate between the normal vs abnormal states in the formation of blood cells, we study the process of generation of blood cells from the hematopoietic stem cells called Hematopoiesis

1.2. Hematopoiesis

The blood cells are formed primarily in bone marrow in adults. Apart from bone marrow, the spleen and lungs are the sites of Hematopoiesis [6,7]. Mature blood cells differentiate from a shared pool of cells called Hematopoietic stem cells, which have the self-renewal capacity, differentiation of HSCs leads to the formation of multipotent progenitor cell (MPP), which further differentiates to form the common myeloid progenitor (CMP/EMP), lymphoid- primed multipotent progenitors (LMPP), and Common Lymphoid progenitors (CLP), which further differentiate to form the granulocytes such as neutrophils, eosinophils, basophils and B and T lymphocytes[8] (**Figure 1.2**).

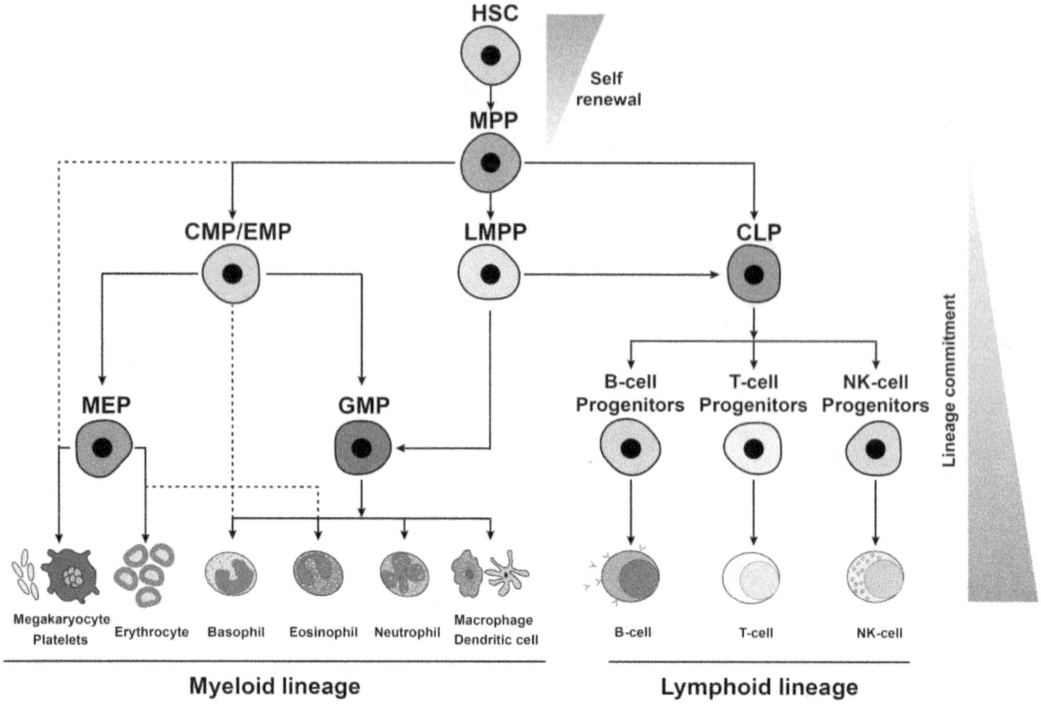

Figure 1.2: Haematopoetic Stem Cell differentiation into Myeloid and Lymphoid cells

Recent advances in RNA sequencing at the single-cell level have led to identifying the

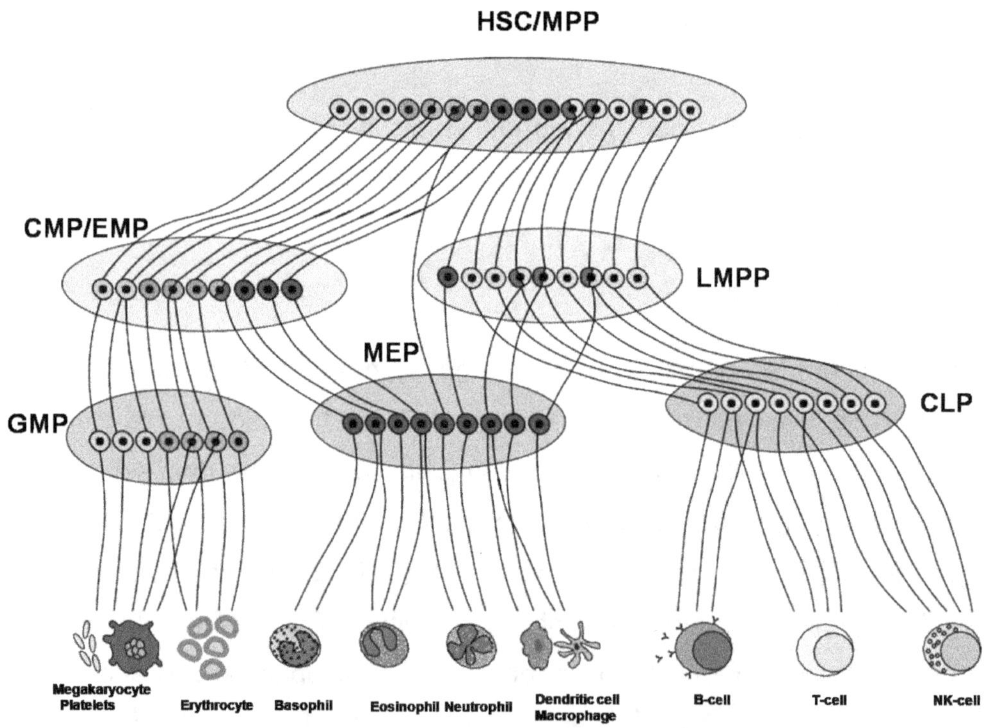

Figure 1.3: An MPP cell differentiating into 18 different states

differentiation of HSC/MPP into three lineages lymphoid, erythroid, and granulocytic/monocytic lineages [9].The MPP is not one cell but exhibits 18 different differentiation states, indicating the early differentiation signals [9]. Also, the idea is that multiple mature cells can arise from more than one lineage of progenitor cells [8,10]. The heterogeneity and the early lineage selectivity and differentiation routes can be appreciated during Hematopoiesis(**Figure 1.2**). Hematopoiesis is a highly regulated process controlled by external stimuli such as cytokines, chemokines, cell-matrix interactions in the bone microenvironment, and intrinsic factors, such as transcription factors, epigenetic modifiers, and cell cycle regulators [11,12]. Loss of regulation of Hematopoiesis leads to uncontrolled proliferation of myeloid or lymphoid lineage cells and is classified into two major types; myeloid Leukemia and lymphoid Leukemia (**Figure 1.3**) [8,13]. They are classified as chronic and acute Leukemia based on the disease progression.

1.3. Classification of Haematological Malignancies

To better understand the subtypes of Leukemia, understanding the bone marrow cell lineage is very important. The entire population of peripheral blood cells and certain cells in every tissue of the body is derived from hematopoietic stem cells present in the bone marrow.

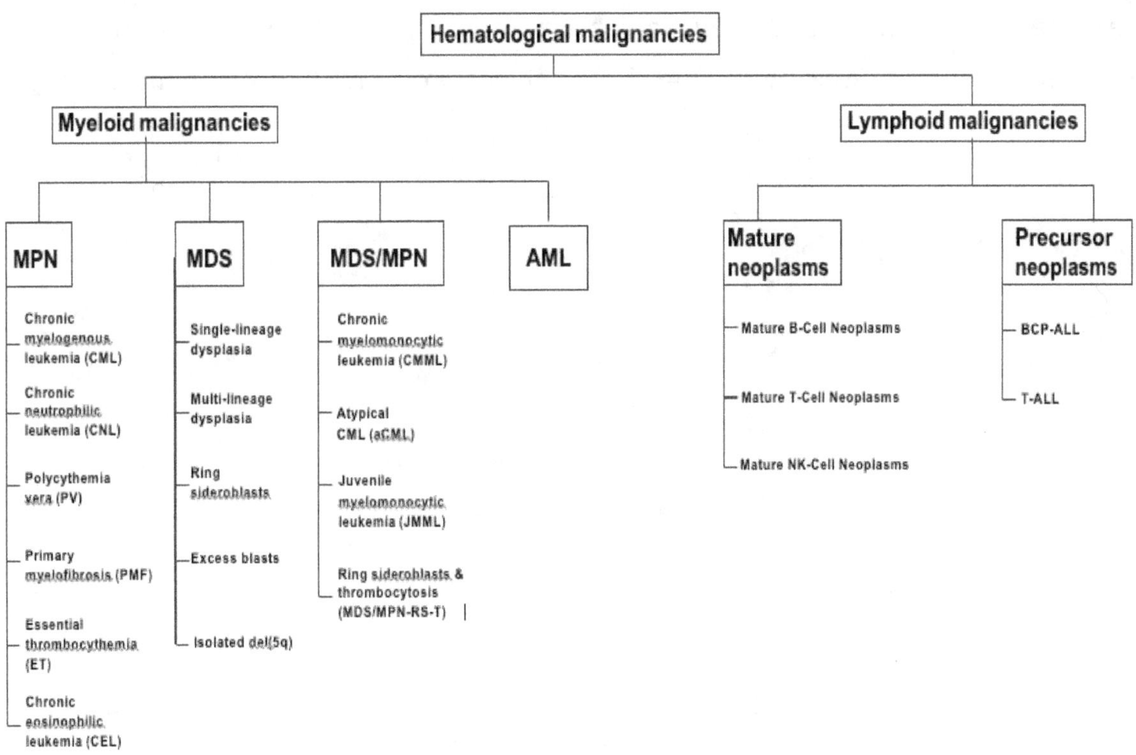

Figure 1.4: Types of Haematological malignancies

In the regular scenario, these stem cells have two major functions, either they undergo self-renewal or differentiate towards a specific lineage. The self-renewal process assures that a stem cell population can be sustained over time[14](**Figure 1.2**). They can differentiate into two lineages, i.e. myeloid lineage or lymphoid lineage. The myeloid lineage differentiates further, leading to leukocytes and erythrocytes, while the lymphoid lineage makes lymphocytes, i.e. B and T cells (**Figure 1.2**). The uncontrolled proliferation of these cells leads to Leukemia, either myeloid or lymphoid (**Figure 1.4**). AML can be classified based on multiple factors; two major ones are cellular morphology (FAB) and cytogenetic profiling (WHO).

1.3.1 Acute Myeloid Leukemia

AML is further classified based on cellular morphology (FAB) and cytogenetic profiling (WHO).

1.3.1.1 French-American-British classification.

French-American-British (FAB) classification system categorizes AML into subtypes based on the stage of the myeloid cell at which the disease occurred and the cellular morphology of the cell. AML diagnosis requires that the blast population contains 20-30% of WBCs. Promyelocytes, monoblasts, and megakaryoblasts are a part of this population, and their presence delineates the FAB subtypes[14]. The subtypes are as follows; Acute myeloblastic

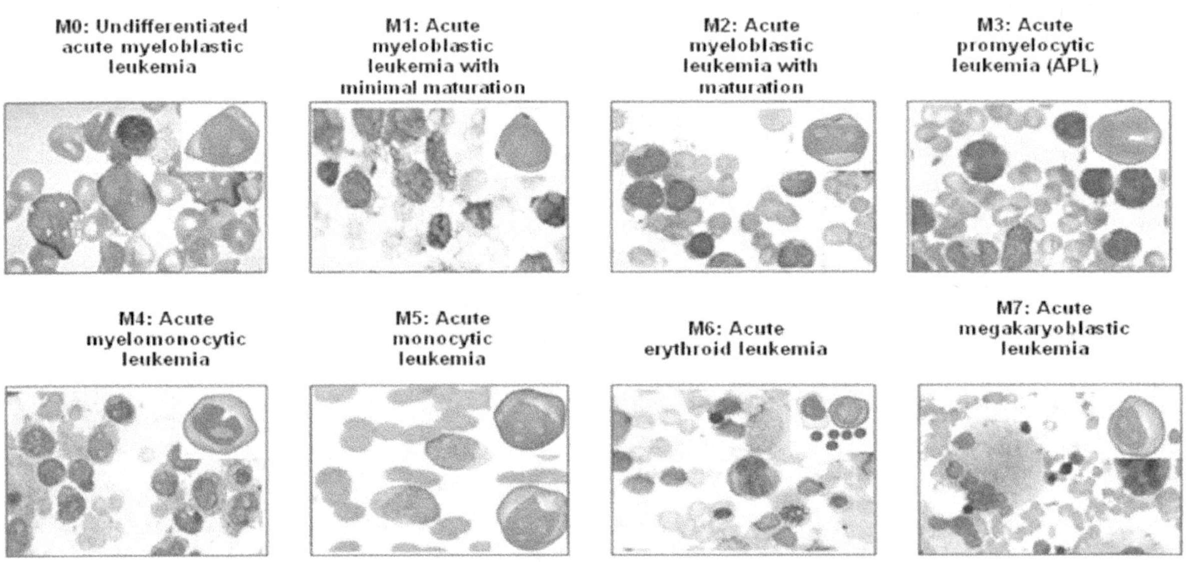

Figure 1.5: Microscopic images of subtypes of Acute Myeloid Leukemia by the FAB classification system

AML Subtype	MPO status	Immunophenotype	Translocation
M0	-	CD13+, CD33+, CD11b+, CD14+	
M1	+	CD13+, CD33+, CD34+/-	t(9;11): KMT2A;MLLT3
M2	+	CD13+, CD34 +/-	t(8;21): RUNX1;RUNX1T1
M3	+	CD13+, CD33+, CD34-	t(15;17): PML;RARA
M4	+	CD13+, CD33+, CD11b+, CD14+	Inversion 16
M5	-	CD14+	t(9;11): KMT2A;MLLT3
M6	-	C13+, CD33+	Trisomy 8
M7	-	CD13+, CD33+, CD34+	Trisomy 21

Table 1.1: AML subtypes with MPO status, Immunophenotype markers, and translocations attached to each FAB subtype

leukemia-M0 (with minimal differentiation), M1 (without maturation), and M2 (with maturation); Promyelocytic leukemia - M3, Acute myelomonocytic Leukemia - M4 (Myelomonocytic with Eosinophilia - M4E0), Acute monocytic leukemia - M5, Acute erythroid leukemia - M6, and finally Acute megakaryocytic Leukemia - M7 (Table 1.1 and **Figure 1.5**). On average, M0-M2 has a good prognosis, and M3 has the best prognosis, while M4-M7 correlates with a poor prognosis. Along with a morphological distinction, these subtypes also have a component of unique cell surface markers where antibodies against CD11b, CD13, CD14, CD33, CD34, C65, etc., are most commonly used for classification and diagnosis (Table 1.1)[14,15]. The presence of CD33 and CD13, specific myeloid lineage markers, in the absence of lymphoid-lineage markers, would help confirm AML. Expression of CD11b can be used as a positive test for granulocyte maturity, while CD34, on the other hand, marks stemness on leukemic blasts.

Various combinations of these markers (present or absent) can be used for identifying leukemic blasts and AML subtypes (Table 1.1)[15,16].

1.3.1.2 World Health Organization classification

FAB classification is useful, but there are important genetic factors that it does not consider. The second classification system, a more reliable and updated system, is given out by the World Health Organisation (WHO), which categorizes Leukemia into subtypes based on recurrent genetic abnormalities, which are different interchromosomal translocations(Table 1.1 and **Figure 1.6**)[17][18][19]. The subtypes are as follows;

1. AML with t(8:21);RUNX1-RUNXT1
2. AML with an inversion in chromosome 16 (t(16;16) or inv(16)),
3. APL with t(15;17);PML-RARA fusion gene,
4. AML with t(9;11);MLLT3-MLL,
5. AML with t(6;9);DEK-NUP214,
6. AML with inversion in chromosome 3 (t(3;3) or inv(3)),
7. AML (megakryoblastic) with t(1;22); RBM15-MKL1
8. AML with BCR-ABL1 *(Provisional entity)*
9. AML with mutated NPM1
10. AML with biallelic mutations in CEBPA
11. AML with mutated RUNX1 *(Provisional entity)*
12. AML with myelodysplasia related changes
13. AML: Not otherwise specified (NOS)

It is understood that although more robust, the WHO classification system still has its pitfalls because of the heterogeneity of the disease. The 13th subtype that says AML: NOS is where the categorization links to FAB classification when an AML case does not fall into any of the above categories and is similar to one of the FAB subtypes[39–42]. The FAB subtypes themselves can be linked to one of the above translocations, as seen in Table 1.1. Many a time, when an AML is of an unknown lineage or classification; it so happens that BCR-ABL1 ends up being the characteristic genetic abnormality, which could mean that it was a case of CML before it turned aggressive[41]. A considerable percentage of Acute leukemia cases still evade both the classification systems, which indicates that this field can benefit from advanced approaches for diagnosis and therapeutic interventions.

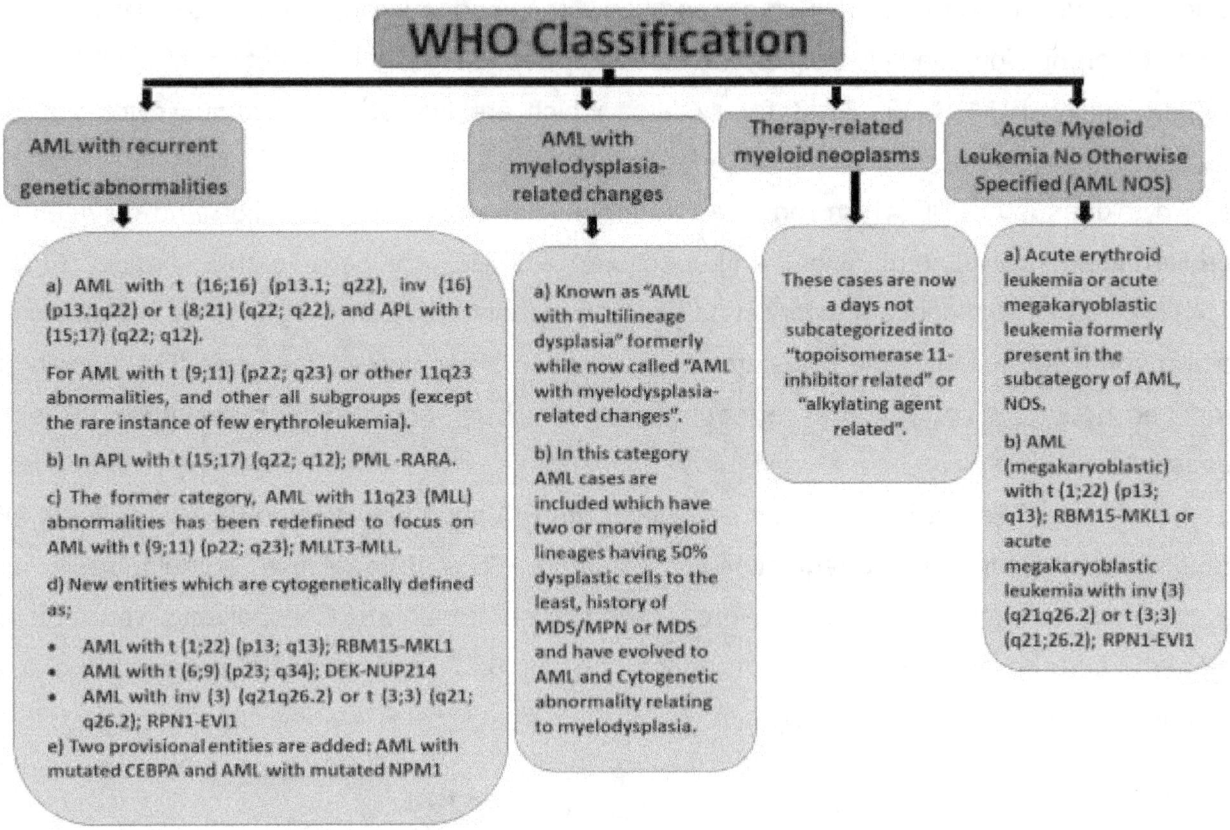

Figure 1.6: WHO classification of AML

AML can be studied at the cellular level as a differentiation block (defective granulopoiesis), the cytogenetic level (chromosomal translocations), and the molecular level mutations in the gene governing the disease progression.

1.3.2 Acute Myeloid Leukemia: a disease of defective granulopoiesis

Granulopoeiesis is when primitive blood cell precursors differentiate into mature and functionally active granulocytes, like neutrophils, eosinophils, and other myeloid cells (**Figure 1.7**) [20]. AML is a clonal disorder characterized by the accumulation of immature, poorly differentiated myeloid

blast cells, and based on differentiation; there are different types of AML. One of the differentiators of AML from ALL is the enzyme myeloperoxidase (MPO), which is predominantly present in neutrophils. MPO is an essential enzyme for the host's defense against infection and is used to diagnose acute leukemias as a myeloid marker[21]. (**Figure 1.7**, Table 1.1). MPO presence and the expression of CD33 and CD13 allow a confirmatory identification of AML[16,22]. Expression of MPO is induced by granulocyte
colony-stimulating factor (G-CSF) in cooperation with exogenous C/EBPα and SPI1(PU.1) as an early differentiation marker of granulopoiesis[23][21]. Several transcription factors like the C/EBP family, PU.1, CBF, STAT family, etc., which are activated by various cytokines, are essential regulators of granulopoiesis. A key player in this entire network of transcription factors and cytokines is G-CSF which regulates neutrophilic granulocyte production and elevates the proliferation, survival, maturation, and functional activation of cells in this lineage (**Figure 1.7**)[23]. In an infected/inflammatory state, the hematopoietic system responds by increasing the activity of these proteins, and this state is known as emergency granulopoiesis (EG), leading to reduced neutrophil count known as neutropenia, which is known to be prevalent in leukemia patients.

Some of these TFs are involved in modulating both EG and Leukemia development[20,24,25]. Studies have indicated dysregulation of common TFs in defective granulopoiesis and aggravated leukemic state. Also, severe congenital neutropenia (SCN) patients who required higher G-CSF doses show a higher incidence of AML[26,27], indicating that common TFs drive leukemogenesis and granulopoiesis.

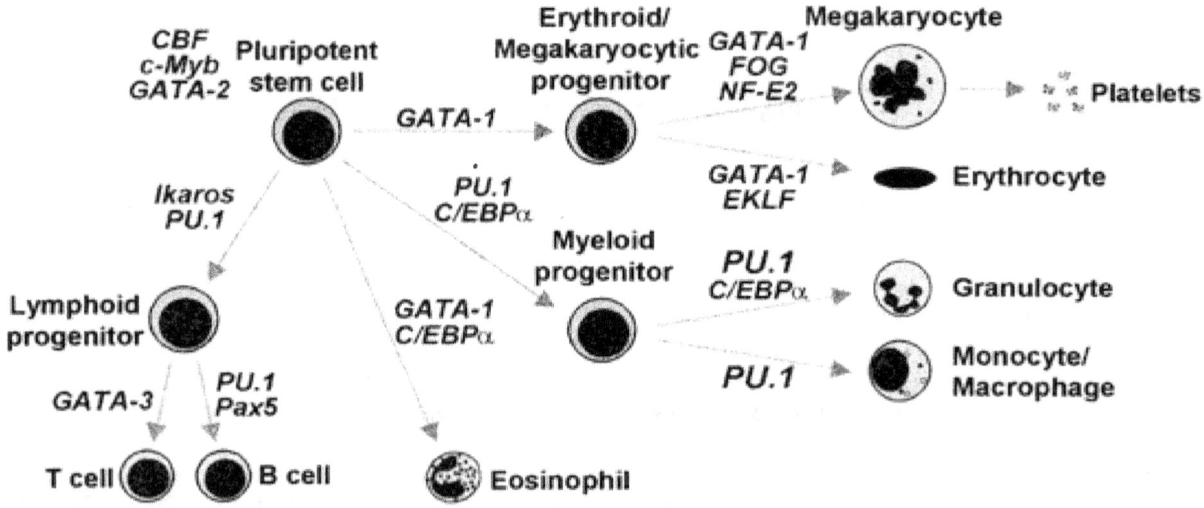

Figure 1.7: Network of transcription factors regulating granulopoiesis

The study of granulopoiesis in myeloid disorders goes back almost 5 decades. The early understanding of granulocytic proliferation and differentiation was through AML patients in a clinical setting. Colony-forming and colon stimulating capacities of leukemic and pre-leukemic cells were tapped into to understand the Lack of normal granulocytic differentiation, with white blood cells acting as the target population[28]. It is a well-established fact that AML inherently develops in different stages of granulopoiesis governed via the interaction of myeloid stem cells and GM-CSF units[29–31]. Myeloid progenitors in M1 and M3 FAB subtypes co-occur with azurophil granulocytes, and lineage-committed populations like neutrophils, eosinophils, and basophils develop at the myelocyte stages of AML, M4, and M5[29,32].

Faulty regulation of many TFs (also described in the previous section) leads to defective granulopoiesis in an aggravated leukemic [20]. HOXA10, a homeodomain-containing TF, is known to be a regulator of hematopoietic development[33]. As a part of the HOX family of genes, its overexpression has been linked to the development of AML in an MLL1 translocation-dependent manner[34,35]. Due to its regulatory role in EG by elevating TRIAD1 expression, it is suspected to partake in neutropenia in leukemic patients[20,36]. A well-known oncogene, C/EBP-β, which has a regulatory role in immune responses, is conversely correlated with BCR-ABL levels in CML patients[37]. A potential anti-cancer role of CEBPB is via its induction by ATRA in the presence of PML-RARA fusion, which leads to enhanced

Transcription Factor	Function
HOXA10	• Postnatal hematopoietic development and HSC self-renewal[33] • Development of lymphoid cells[44] • AML development[45] • EG response termination by TRIAD1 activation[36]
CEBP-β	• Granulocyte proliferation and differentiation during EG[46]
IRF8	• Expression of proinflammatory cytokines[47] • Macrophage differentiation[39] • Tumor suppression[48]
STAT3	• G-CSF signaling [49] • IRE activation in AML[50]

Table 1.2: Transcription factors with intersecting roles in EG and leukemia

proliferation in APL cases [38]. Another immune response-related transcription factor, IRF8, plays a critical role in myeloid cell development and drives them to macrophage development[39]. It is shown to have a tumor suppressor role through elevated BCR-ABL patients in CML patients. STAT3, a critical TF, is activated by IL-6 and G-CSF in hematopoietic precursor cells and neutrophils and eventually interacts with c-JUN and c-FOS, leading to IL-6 response element (IRE) activation[40–42]. Upregulated c-JUN blocks CEBPA[43]. These interactions are critical in AML proliferation. STAT3 and c-JUN probably act together towards accelerated leukemia progression and dysregulated EG response[20]. Functions of all the transcription factors have been described in Table 1.2

1.4. Chromosomal Translocations in Leukemia

Chromosomes are said to have translocated when there is a switch between either two loci of the same chromosome or two different chromosomes. However, half of the random exchanges produce unbalanced translocations leading to chimeric fusion transcripts disrupting gene expression and mechanism. Translocations are either reciprocal, i.e. arms from different chromosomes exchange places, or nonreciprocal, where only one arm migrates to the broken end of another chromosome[51]. Such translocations play key roles in tumorigenesis (as described above) (**Figure 1.8**). Among different abnormalities associated with lymphoid cancers, chromosomal translocations are considered a hallmark of hematopoietic neoplasms[52][53]. A classic example is the Philadelphia chromosome, t(9;22): BCR-ABL1 in

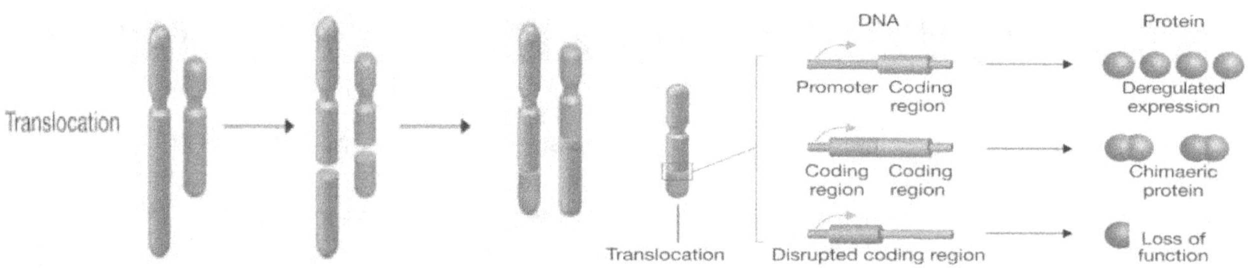

Figure 1.8: (A) chromosomal translocation. (B) Different fates of proteins as a result of translocation

CML, the first-ever correlation between a chromosomal abnormality and an oncological disease identified in 1960, an unbalanced reciprocal translocation in CML cases. To date, CML patients get diagnosed with t(9;22) and also some uncertain cases of Acute Leukemia, and it is known to result in the worst prognosis in children and adults[54][55]. Another example is the t(8;14): IGH/MYC translocation found in Burkitt's lymphoma[56]. As discussed in the previous sections, signature translocations have indeed been identified for various leukemias, and their subtypes (e.g., RUNX1-RUNX1T1 for AML, ETV6-RUNX1 for ALL), but the underlying mechanisms are not yet completely understood[53][57].

A prerequisite for chromosomal translocations is double-strand breaks, sealed by DNA repair mechanisms such as HR, NHEJ, Alt-NHEJ, and MMEJ. Defective DNA damage repair is the hallmark of cancer, and in Leukemia, several defective DNA repair mechanisms have been reported, some of which are described below:

1.5. DNA damage and repair pathways

A substantial understanding of how chromosomal translocations occur has recently been in place. Many double-strand breaks (DSBs) occur during a regular cell cycle progression[57]. However, physiological DSBs are also generated in the cell during V(D)J recombination and class switch recombination (CSR) in the developing B and T lymphocytes[58][59]. Translocations require at least two concurrent double-strand breaks (DSBs) in separate chromosomes; the failure to repair these breaks is what causes a translocation[57]. The two major pathways for repairing DSBs are Homologous recombination (HR), where sequence integrity is preserved, and nonhomologous end-joining (NHEJ), which is considered to be error-prone[60][61].

1.5.1 Homologous Recombination

After the recognition of the DSB, the HR pathway comprises two more processes; i) synthesis-dependent strand annealing (SDSA) and break-induced repair (BIR)[62–64]. The MRN (MRE11-RAD50-NBS1) complex recognizes the DSB and recruits ATM [65]. H2AX gets phosphorylated by ATM, serving as an anchor for MDC1, which also, in turn, gets phosphorylated by ATM, and scaffolds in the E3 ligases that ubiquitinate H2AX, which subsequently recruit 53BP1 and BRCA1[62,66,67]. BRCA1 ubiquitinates CtIP (which helps the MRN complex with its endonuclease activity for initial DSB resection[68,69]), while counteracting 53BP1[62–64,70]. Following this, the cells are committed to the HR pathway with a generation of 3' overhangs by 5'-to-3' nucleolytic degradation. Here, RPA, RAD51, BRCA1/2, and PALB2 have made their way to the repair site. RPA bound to the single-stranded DNA at the 3' overhang is replaced by RAD51, generating a nucleoprotein filament[62,63,68]. PALB2 promotes BRCA1-BRCA2 interactions at the filament, and the nucleoprotein filament occupies a neighboring template strand forming a D-loop, better known as a double Holliday junction[63,69]. The Holliday junctions are processed by the BLM complex, GEN1 endonuclease, the MUS81-EME1 complex, and the SLX1-SLX4 complex[62,71–74] (**Figure 1.9 A**).

1.5.2 Non-Homologous End Joining

The second and the most common DSB repair pathway in humans is NHEJ. It begins with a synapsis of the two ends by 53BP1, which subsequently recruits all the proteins of the

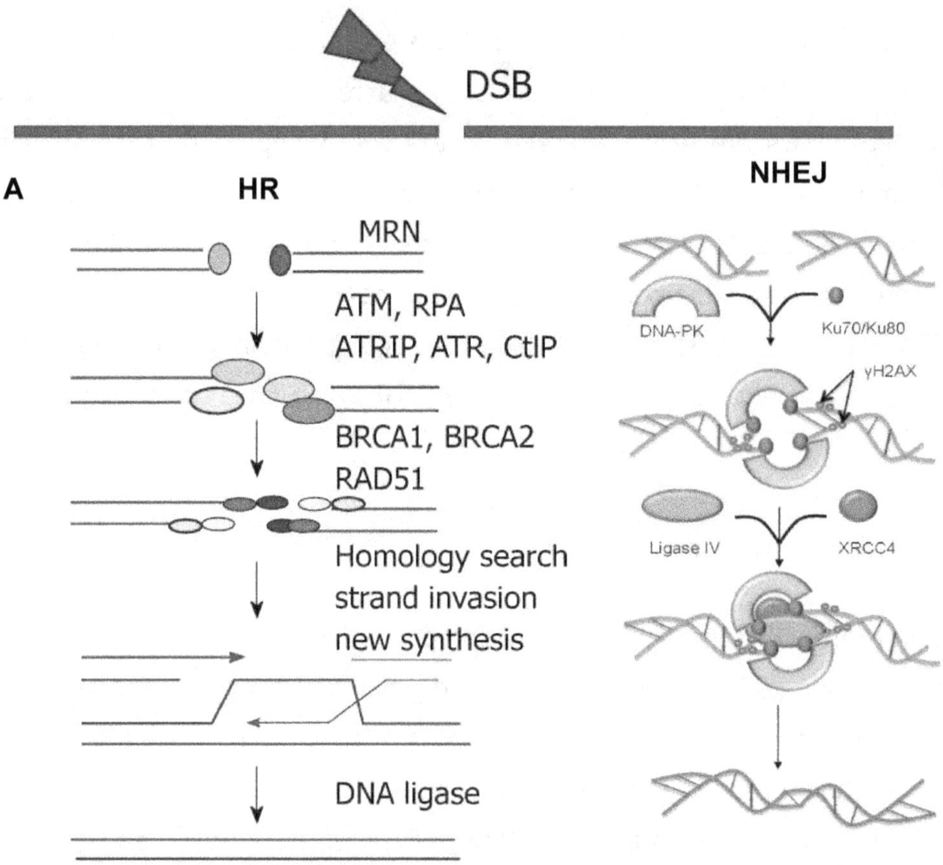

Figure 1.9: DNA repair pathways for double-stranded breaks, A) HR and B) NHEJ

pathway[62,64,75]. DSBs get recognized and bound by the Ku heterodimer (Ku70 and Ku80) to prevent further degradation[64,76,77]. Next in line are DNA-PKcs, which push Ku inwards on the DNA and can pull the two broken DNA ends closer and gets phosphorylated[78–80]. DNA-PKCs then recruit a bunch of proteins that work in conjunction. They are the DNA end processing enzymes ARTEMIS, PNKP, APE1, APLF, and WRN which replace the proteins blocking the ends and resect the hanging strands[62,81–83]. Ku dimer then recruits XRCC4, stabilizing the NHEJ complex by tethering the ends. XLF and LIG4 arrive, and form the XLF-

XRCC4-LIG4 bridge that fills the gaps using polymerases (POLμ or POLλ)[64,80,84]. Finally, LIG4 joins the ends to completion[62,85] (**Figure 1.9 B**).

HR and NHEJ are the repair mechanisms for DSBs and bulky lesions. There are repair mechanisms in place for such lesions as well. However, there are many other issues that the DNA faces during replication, transcription, and the regular cell cycle that occur during various processes which do not necessarily affect the DNA double helix in a major way. Damages arising from oxidation, deamination, alkylation, torsional stress during winding/unwinding, UV radiation, chemotherapeutic agents, incorporation of a wrong base during replication, etc.

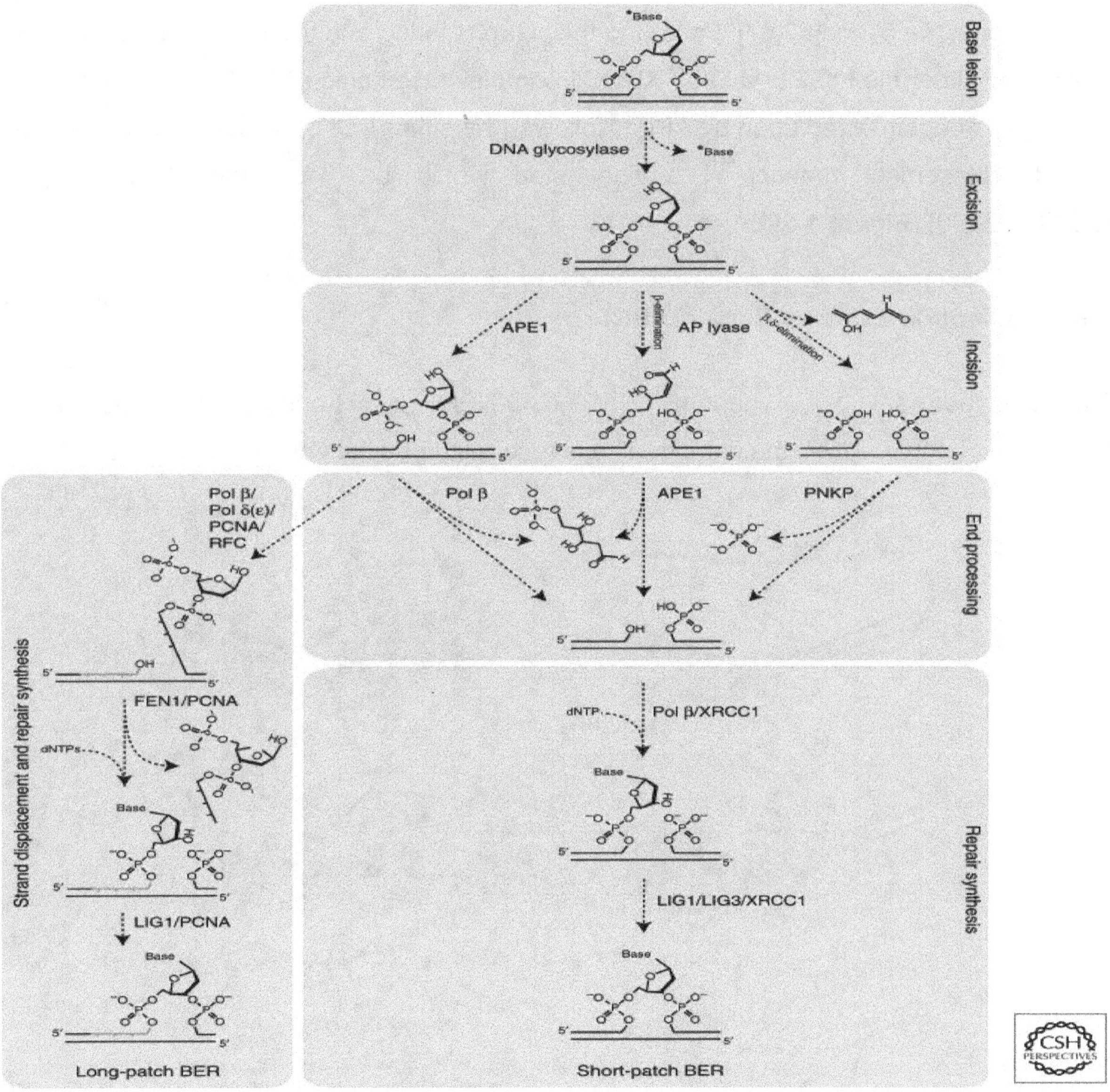

Figure 1.10 Base Excision Repair Pathway

1.5.3 Base Excision Repair (BER)

BER corrects the oxidative, alkylation, deamination, and abasic single base damages, which are not recognized as significant distortions to the DNA structure[62,86,87]. Chromatin remodeling at the damage site followed by damage recognition and correction by DNA glycosylase are the two major steps[63,87]. It can take either short patch repair or long patch repair, based on either an abasic site created from the monofunctional glycosylases or the repair gap left by the bifunctional glycosylase, respectively[62,87]. Short patch repair starts with recognition of the abasic site by APE1 endonuclease that generates a 3'-OH residue with a nascent deoxyribose phosphate at the 5'-end[62,87]. Following this, Gap tailoring and filling by POLβ and subsequent ligation by either the LIG1 or a LIG3-XRCC1 complex takes place[88]. For long patch repair, the repair gap is again acted upon by APE1, followed by either POLβ or POLδ tailoring the gap in a strand-displacement manner. The final step would be flap removal and ligation by LIG1[87,89,90] (**Figure 1.10**).

1.5.4 Nucleotide Excision Repair (NER)

Two subtypes are global genome NER (GG-NER) and transcription-coupled NER (TC-NER)[63,91]. In GG-NER, the damage site is recognized by the XPC-RAD23B-CETN2 complex,

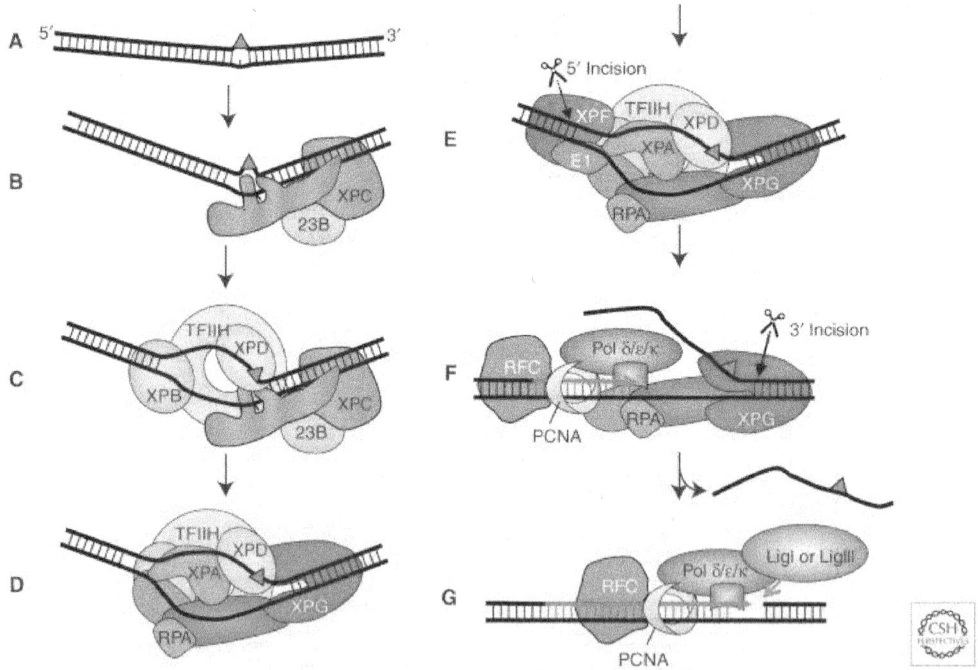

Figure 1.11: Nucleotide Excision Repair

while in TC-NER, the same happens with a lesion-stalled RNA Pol II in conjunction with the CSA-CSB complex with the XAB2-UVSSA anchor[92,93]. Post recognition, TFIIH is recruited to the lesion in both the pathways; by XPC in GG-NER and CSA-CSB complex by reverse translocation of RNA-POL-II in TC-NER for base excision and replacement[62,92,94,95]. The difference is that GG-NER recruits the endonucleases XPF-ERCC1 and XPG, which chews off a few bases in the flanking region of the lesion site[63,91]. In both, the final step is LIG3-XRCC1 mediated ligation[96] (**Figure 1.11**).

1.5.5 Mismatch Repair (MMR)

MMR is the mechanism that takes care of replication fidelity post occurrence. As is the case in other pathways, it starts with recognizing the mismatch by the MSH2-MSH6 homodimer, which binds to the DNA and forms a sliding clamp[97,98]. Once the error is recognized, the mismatched base is excised by the exonuclease EXO1 in a PCNA-dependent manner[99,100]. RPA stabilizes the gap at this point, and finally, RFC, HMGB1, and LIG1 come together to fill the gap with the correct base and ligate it to completion[101–103] (**Figure 1.12**).

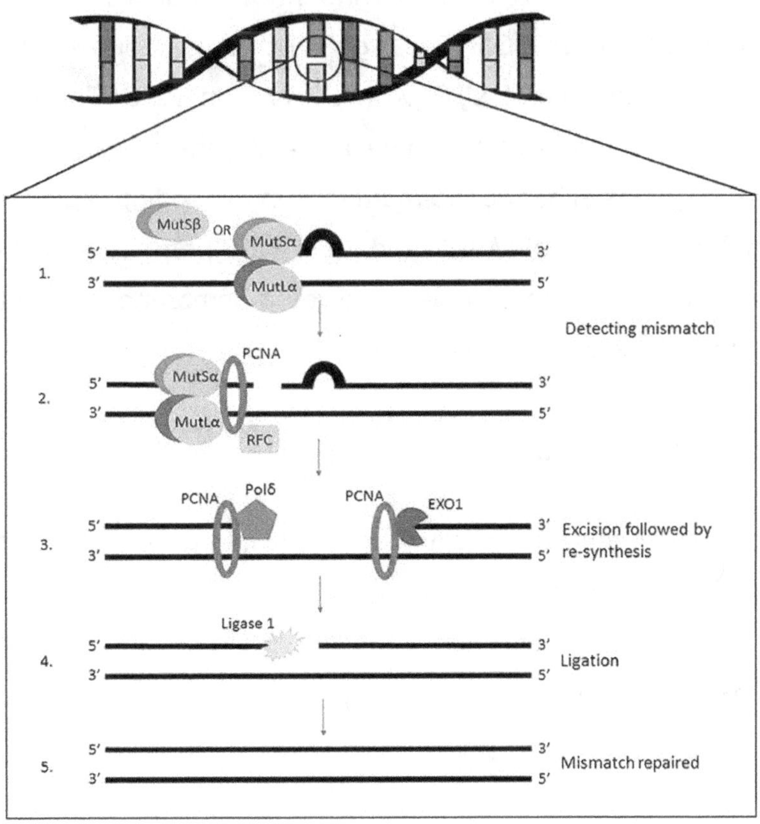

Figure 1.12: Mismatch Repair

1.5.6 Defective DNA repair in Leukemia

Abnormal response to DNA damage has been linked to AML for quite some time now[104,105]. Proteins of the NHEJ pathway are widely affected in all types of Leukemia. The majorly altered ones are Ku70/80 complex and DNA-PKC. Increased NHEJ activity via over-expressed Ku70/80 has been observed in myeloid luekemias[106]. Low Ku70 and Ku80 have been noted in AML cells with FLT3-ITD and in FLT3-ITD knock-in mice [107]. Lig3, a key enzyme involved in alternative end joining, is upregulated in AML cells with FLT3-ITD[107]. Increased levels of DNA-PK have been associated with B cell lymphocytic leukemia in that it enables the tumor cells to escape irradiation-induced apoptosis[108]. Altered LIG4 levels have been associated with ALL and BCR-ABL1 associated CML[109]. In HR, the focus has been on alterations in RAD51, BRCA1/2, and XRCC3 associated with Leukaemia risk [110,111]. BCR-ABL1 associated CML patients have shown a characteristic downregulation in BRCA1 expression and increased expression of RAD51 due to inhibition of caspase-3[112,113]. MRE11A and ATM, key players in the initial stages of DNA repair mechanisms, have been affected in t-AML patients[104]. In this regard, a variant RAD51-G135C correlates with an increased risk of t-AML. In denovo AML, RAD51-G135C and XRCC3-Thr241Met variants have been reported [114]. Components of BER, XRCC1 Arg399Gln and Arg194Trp have been associated with low repair capacity in AML [115]. Components of NER, XPD Lys751Gln, XPC Ala499Val, and XPA-4A>G variants have correlated with overall survival and chemoresistance in AML [115]. Downregulation of MMR genes either due to mutations in the coding region of MSH2 and MLH1 [116], methylation of the promoter of MSH2 and MLH1[116], or mutations in the 3′-UTR of the MLH1 gene [117] have been reported. Table XX gives a comprehensive set of examples, with alterations in genes associated with leukemias[105].

1.6. Signaling Pathways in Leukemia

The process of myeloid differentiation is regulated by the interplay of cytokines in hematopoietic cells through their corresponding receptors on progenitor cells. Once the cytokines interact with the target cell, a cascade of intracellular signaling proteins gets activated that drive the maturation and differentiation process.

1.6.1 Receptor tyrosine Kinases (RTKs)

RTKs are activated by ligands specific to certain receptors. Ligands bind to extracellular domains, the receptor dimerizes and/or oligomerizes, and the tyrosine kinase gets autophosphorylated[118]. These Autophospohrylated RTKs recruit and activate many downstream signaling proteins that further propagate important cell signaling pathways[119]. Mutations in RTKs are known to impact AML prognosis and are part of the WHO AML classification[120]. Translocations are a characteristic feature of leukemic malignancies, and the first fusion protein identified in CML was BCR-ABL from the t(9;22) translocation, the "Philadelphia Chromosome", where the partner ABL1 is a tyrosine kinase protein[121]. Two of the well-known RTKs, c-KIT and FLT3, have characteristic mutations that are used to classify and diagnose AML[122]. However, the mutation frequencies for c-KIT range from 20%-40% in AML patients, and those with a mutation present in this gene are considered at intermediate risk of developing AML[123]. FLT3 mutations are commonly found in pediatric and adult AML cases and are linked to poor survival rates in relapsed patients[122]. Many other RTKs, like the growth factor proteins, VEGFR and PDGFR, have important implications for AML prognosis[124,125].

1.6.2 Phosphatidyl-inositol-3-kinases(PI3K)/Akt/mechanistic target of rapamycin (mTOR) pathway

PI3K family of genes can be activated by RTKs, by G-protein coupled receptors (GPCRs), or by RAS family proteins, which further activate the serine/threonine kinase AKT and pyruvate dehydrogenase kinase (PDK)[126–128]. PDK phosphorylates AKT, which then activates mTOR[128]. Primary AML blasts show a highly active PI3K/AKT/mTOR signalling[128,129]. Phosphatase and tensin homolog (PTEN) inhibit PI3K[128]. Dysregulated activity of PI3K/AKT has been reported in 50-80% of AML cases[128,130]. Mutations in PTEN have been linked to the expansion of the blast population leading to AML[131].

1.6.3 TGFβ/SMAD signaling pathway

A family of multiple ligands/ isoforms (TGFβ1-TGFβ5) and 3 receptors (I, II, and III)[132–134], all of which signal through Serine/Threonine kinases (Type I and II) and activate a family of downstream Receptor-mediated Smad transcription factors, Common-partner Smads (Co-Smads) and Inhibitory Smads, which in turn mediate the TGFβ signaling [135–137]. These Smads eventually activate transcription of target genes that participate in cell proliferation, differentiation, and apoptosis[138]. TGFB isoforms are known to play critical suppressive roles in AML. TGFB is a known inhibitor of Hematopoiesis and myeloid differentiation[139].

1.6.4 Wnt/β-catenin Signalling pathway

The WNT signaling pathway gets activated the Wnt ligands bind to the Frizzled-LRP5/6 receptor complex, which leads to phosphorylation of LRP6. Further, the multi-protein complex GSK-3B, AXINs, and APC are inhibited, leading to the accumulation of B-catenin, which transcribes the T-cell factor/lymphocyte enhancer-binding factor and is important for the stimulation of hematopoietic lineage and self-renewal [126,140, 141]. Characteristic leukemic translocations like PML-RARA have been linked to the activation of WnT signaling. It is shown that B-catenin is involved in the differentiation of leukemic stem cells[142,143].

1.6.5 Janus kinase (JAK)/signal transducer and activator of transcription (STAT) pathway

In humans, there is four JAK (1,2,3 and tyrosine kinase 2 [TYK2]) and seven STAT (1-4, 5A. 5B, and 6) proteins which get activated by several cytokines[144,145]. JAK gets phosphorylated upon cytokine activation, which acts as a binding site for STATs that JAKs phosphorylate. STATs form homo/heterodimers and eventually regulate transcription via downstream signaling pathways like PI3K/AKT signaling[144]. JAK proteins form fusion proteins in hematological malignancies, e.g., TEL-JAK2, which activates STAT1 and 5, and the PI3K/AKT and NF-KB pathways[146,147]. Recent studies have found JAK mutations in non-BCR-ABL malignancies[148]. STAT proteins are already known to function in Leukemia through the granulopoiesis pathway, but very few mutations have been described.

1.7. The Advent of Next Generation Sequencing

Understanding how cancers are driven and discoveries related to that has always been a major challenge. The sheer complexity and heterogeneity arising from DNA mutations' accumulation and functional impact pose an obstacle[149,150]. The foundations of genetic and molecular studies of cancer have been a success but in a low-throughput fashion[149]. Right after Sanger sequencing was introduced to the world over three decades ago, sequencing technologies have evolved exponentially to attain the availability of high-throughput sequencing, better known as Next-generation sequencing (NGS), at our disposal[149,150]. Right after the success of the

Human Genome Project, the integration of sequencing data in clinical practices has helped in identifying novel mutations and biomarkers in a variety of cancers, which is also the case for Leukemia [150,151]. There have been several noteworthy milestones in acute Leukemia with the aid of NGS technologies, be it whole-genome sequencing, whole-exome sequencing, transcriptome sequencing, etc. [152–154]. The first application of gene expression studies in 1999 was on acute leukemias (**Figure 1.13**). This landscape of genome-wide studies needs to be tapped into towards a greater extent of therapeutic suggestions.

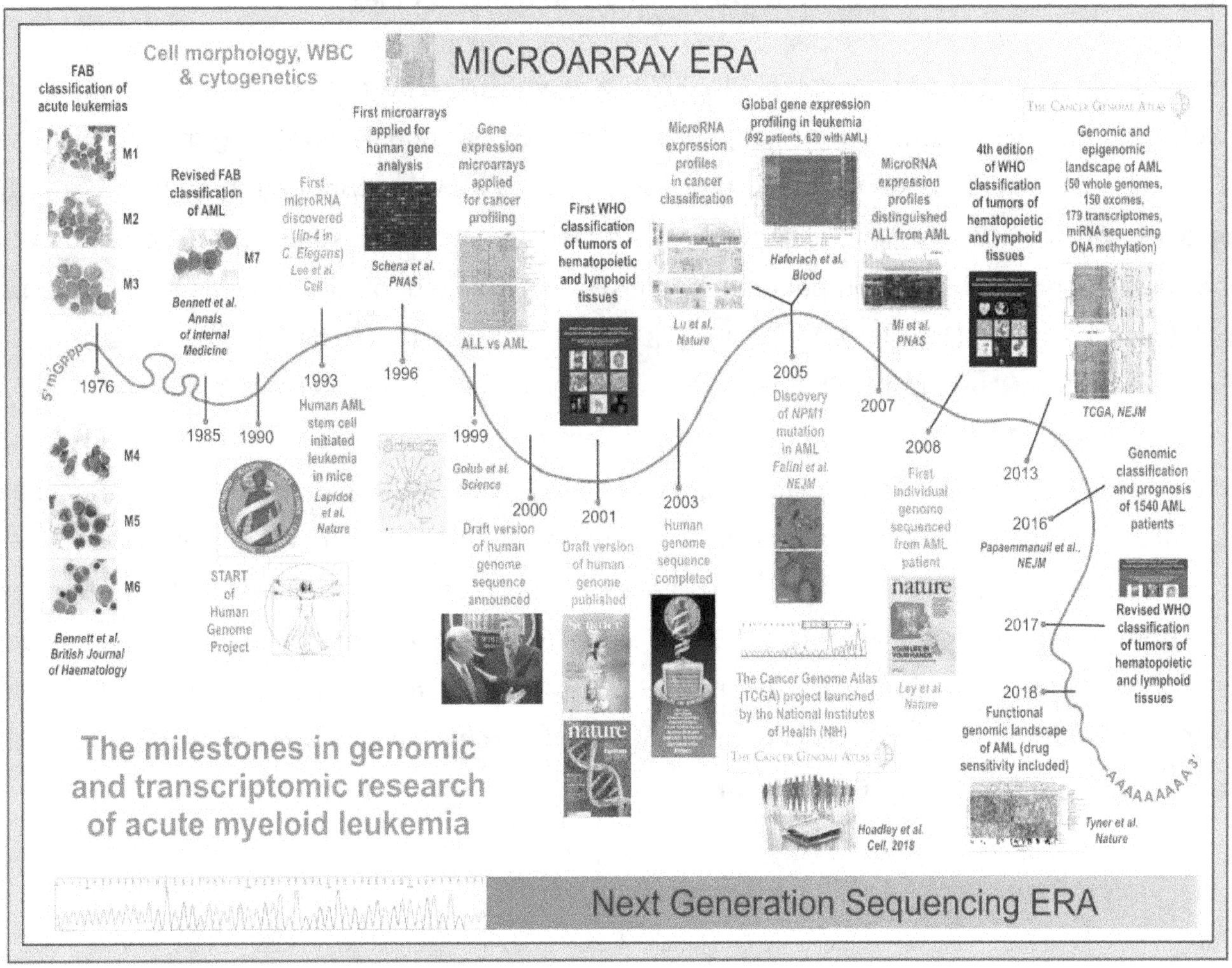

Figure 1.13: The milestones in genomic and transcriptomic research of AML

1.8. Importance of the noncoding region of the genome

One of the most striking outcomes of the Human Genome Project was the revelation that more than 98% of the human genome does not code for proteins[151,155]. These noncoding stretches of the genome were termed "junk". Most of them were repeat regions or regions between the exons of protein-coding genes, which allowed the propagation of the notion that variations in these regions would be of minimal significance[156,157]. Our capability to make any sense out of these variations is restricted because the functional impact of these regions is majorly unknown[158]. Regulatory mechanisms of gene expression, which largely stem from regions of the noncoding genome, are recently gaining importance in therapeutic studies.

1.8.1 Long noncoding RNAs (LncRNAs) in Myeloid malignancies

LnRNAs are a subset of noncoding RNA with a length of >200 nucleotides and are majorly involved in regulating gene expression[159,160]. In the first report highlighting the significance of lncRNAs in AML pathogenesis and prognosis, the study was performed through microarray analysis, where 148 CN-AML patients were studied for lncRNA expression associated with known AML genes. Expression patterns for lncRNA were linked to AML patients with signature mutations like FLT3-ITD, NPM1, CEBPA, IDH1/2, ASXL1, and RUNX1[161]. Several well-characterized lncRNAs, like MEG3, H19, NEAT1, TUG1, HOTAIR, HOTAIRM1, LUNAR1, etc., are known to play regulatory roles in Leukemia and have also been suggested as biomarkers[162–168]. At the cellular level, these lncRNAs are known to display critical functions in apoptosis, cancer cell proliferation, regulation of metabolism, drug resistance, cell differentiation, etc. [169]. Additionally, in the regulatory scenario, they also act as sponges formiRNAs in signaling pathways like PI3/AKT signaling, JAK/STAT signaling, c-KIT expression, regulation of MYC activation, etc. [170–172]. Building lncRNA-mRNA interaction networks using WGCNA has helped gain new insights into prognostic prediction and recurrence signatures in several leukemias[173,174] (**Figure 1.14**).

1.9. microRNAs (miRNAs) in Leukemia

Another important regulatory mechanism is via the function of miRNAs known to play physiological roles in cancer progression, including hematologic malignancies[175]. Like any other malignancy, in leukemias, miRNA are known to function as either oncomiRs or tumor suppressors, affecting multiple aspects of leukemic progression, like differentiation, proliferation, epigenetic regulation, and chemotherapy resistance[176]. For example, miR-9, miR-22, miR-29b, miR-125b, miR-126, etc., are known to be activated by translocations in leukemic conditions (Table 1.3) and act as tumor suppressors or oncogenes through various targets[177].

A classic example would be the widely studied miR-17-92 cluster, which is known to play a disruptive role in MLL-rearranged AML[178,179]. Apart from being involved in Leukemia in general, miRs are also known to distinguish karyotypes in AML[180].

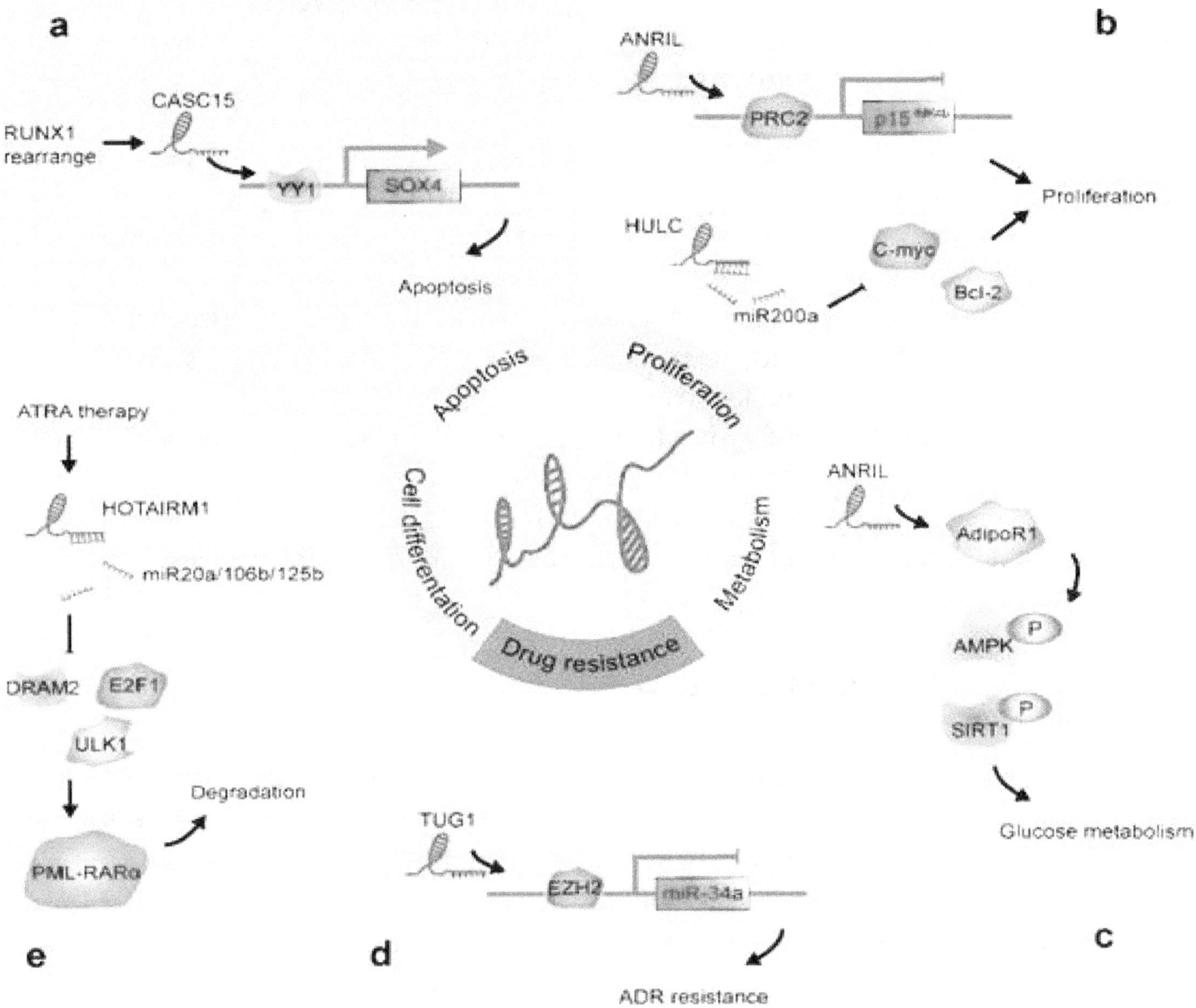

Figure 1.14: Roles of various lncRNAs in Leukemia; a) Apoptosis, b) Proliferation, c) Metabolism, d) Drug resistance, e) Cell differentiation

They can also act as prognostic biomarkers, where miRNA expression at the time of diagnosis can aid in predicting survival in certain AML cases or predict the progression of myelodysplastic syndrome (MDS) to AML[181–184].

miRNA	Target genes	OncomiR	Tumor Suppressor	Reference
miR-9	**RHOH, RYBO, HMGA2, FOXO1, FOXO3**	**Yes**	**Yes**	**[172]**
miR-17-92 cluster	**P21**	**Yes**	**No**	**[165]**
miR-22	**TET2, CRTC1, FLT3, MYCBP**	**Yes**	**No**	**[173,174]**
miR-125b	**LIN28A, IRF4**	**Yes**	**No**	**[175–177]**
mir-126	**PLK2, ADM9, ILK, CDK3, TOM1,**	**Yes**	**No**	**[178–181]**
miR-29b	**CDK6, AKT2, CCND2, SP1, DNMT3A, DNMT3B, MCL-1**	**No**	**Yes**	**[182–185]**

Table 1.3: Oncogenic and Tumor suppressor miRNA and their targets

1.10. Impact of UTR variants in cancer

A significant region in the gene is the untranslated regions (3' and 5' UTRs)[158,199]. Due to advances in whole-genome and transcriptome sequencing technologies, studies have explored the post-transcriptional function of UTRs in gene regulation[199]. Regulatory mechanisms in the 5'UTR, such as alteration of the upstream open reading frames and 3'UTR shortening, is due to variants in the 5' and 3'UTRs. miRNA mediated degradation of transcripts, Alternative Poly(A) signals, modification of UTRs (m^6A), etc., have been studied in correlation with oncogenic gene expression and cancer pathogenesis (**Figure 1.15**). The majority of m^6A residues are in the last exons, allowing the potential for 3' UTR regulation [200–204]. It is understood that comparatively, 3'UTR seems to be playing a more prominent role in cancer progression. Somatic variants in the 3'UTR regions have recently been correlated with disease progression in various cancers in a miRNA-dependent manner[199]. An early study showed that a polymorphism in the 3'UTR region was functionally involved in colorectal cancer susceptibility[205].

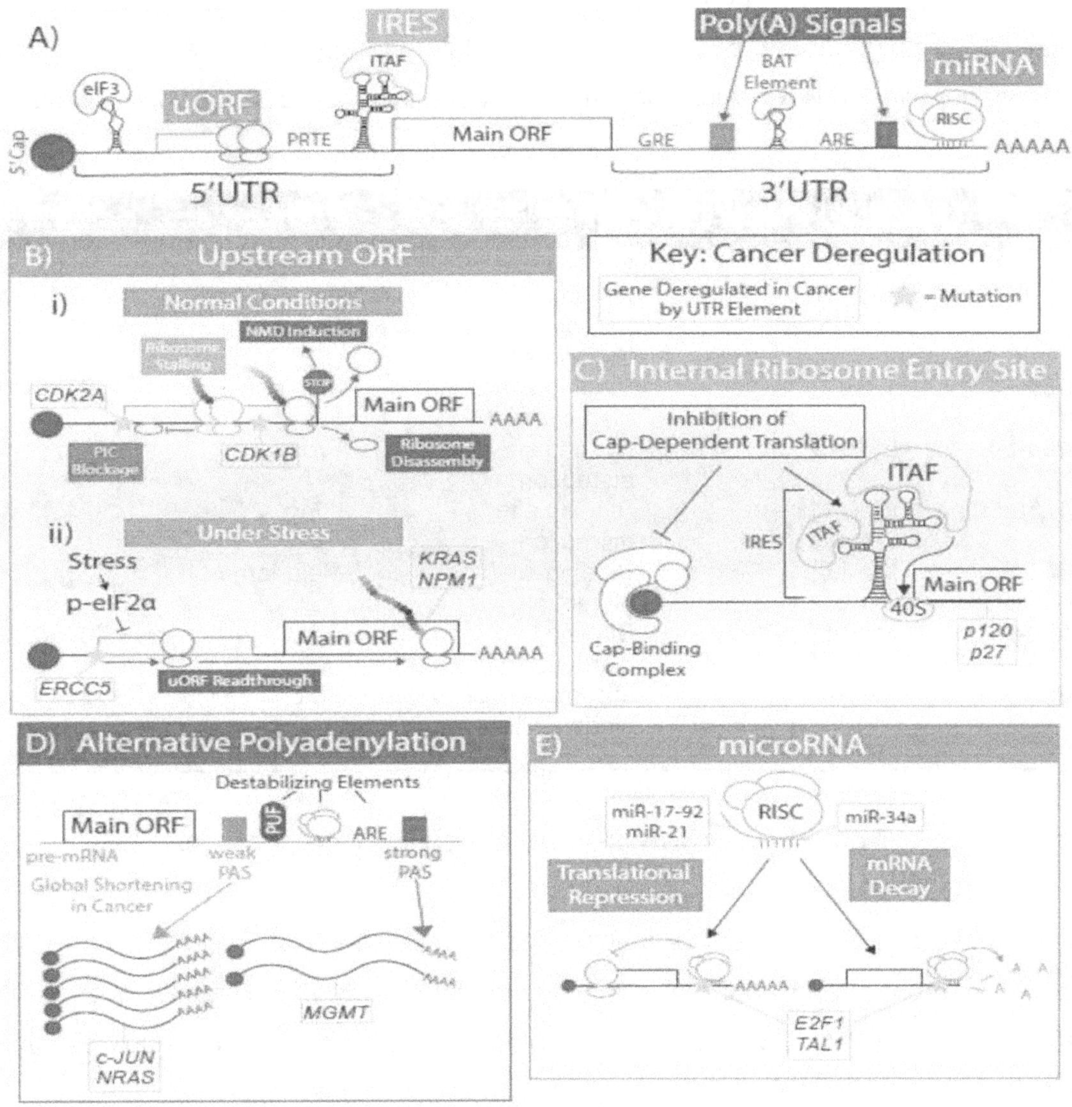

Figure 1.15: Regulation by 5' and 3'UTR elements in cancer; A) Regulatory elements in the UTRs, B) Upstream ORFs, C) Ribosome entry site, D) Alternative polyadenylation, E) miRNA binding

A novel mutation in the 3'UTR region of the oncogene E2F1 was associated with a 4-fold increase in its expression via disruption of the miR-136-5p binding site[199,206]. This increase in expression was validated using reporter assays. Whole-genome analysis of 4 cancers, melanoma, SCLC, lung and prostate, revealed multiple somatic mutations in known oncogenes like TAL1, BMPR1B, KDM5A, ELAVL2, and EPHA3, which impacted miRNA binding sites[207]

(Table 1.4) . While these studies show 3'UTR variants disrupting miRNA binding, on the flip side, there have also been cases like in ovarian cancer, where a somatic mutation in the 3'UTR of GAPDH aided miR-125b sponging onto the UTR, which led to overexpression of STAT3, eventually promoting cancer cell growth and proliferation[201,207]. Apart from influencing phenotypes, germline 3'UTR polymorphisms in breast cancer have also been associated with

miRNA	Target gene (UTR)	Mechanism	Cancer	Reference
miR-136-5p	E2F1	Binding site disruption	Colorectal	[206]
miR-125b	GAPDH	Introduction of Binding site	Ovarian cancer	[201]
miR-185-3p	TAL1	Binding site disruption	Melanoma	[211]
miR-18a-5p	EPHA3	Binding site disruption	Prostate	[212]
miR-125a-5miR-	BMPR1B	Binding site disruption	Lung	[213]
miR-505-5p	KDM5A	Binding site disruption	Melanoma	[214]
miR-532-3p	ELAVL2	Binding site disruption	SCLC	[215]
miR-337-5p	NPM1	Introduction of binding site	AML	[210]

Table 1.4: miRNA and their targets in different cancers

clinical parameters and risk factors like reduced overall survival, disease-free survival, bad prognosis, recurrence, and poor treatment outcomes[208]. 3'UTR variants in essential genes like NOTCH1 and NPM1 have been associated with CLL and AML, respectively[209][210] (Table 1.4).

Even though Acute Leukaemia's genetic and molecular characterization has been done extensively and therapies developed, acute Leukemia is associated with poor survival. It has become clear that the heterogeneous nature of the disease requires better markers for predicting disease outcomes and identifying new and more effective therapies. To achieve the goal, further analysis integrating variants and expression from the coding and noncoding region of the genome, the following objectives have been framed: 1) Exome 2) Transcriptome 3) Sequencing and Analysis of Indian AML Cohort

1.11. Key papers and their results

Topic	Title	Key highlight	References
Hematopoiesis	Self-Renewal Versus Differentiation in Hematopoietic Stem and Progenitor Cells	CLP further differentiates to form the granulocytes	(Giebel and Bruns, 2008)
	Single-cell RNA sequencing to track novel perspectives in HSC heterogeneity	The MPP exhibits 18 different differentiation states	(Zhang et al., 2022)
Leukemia classification	Morphologic Classification and Clinical and Laboratory Correlates	FAB classification based on blast population and myeloid cell stage	(Website)
	Morphology of leukaemias	Celll surface markers used for classification of leukemia	(Ladines-Castro et al., 2016)
	The 2016 revision to the World Health Organization classification of myeloid neoplasms and acute leukemia	WHO classification of Acute Leukemia	(Arber DA, Orazi A, Hasserjian R, et al. The 2016 revision to the World Health Organization classification of myeloid neoplasms and acute leukemia. Blood. 2016;127(20):2391-2405, 2016)
Granulopoiesis	Regulation of granulopoiesis by transcription factors and cytokine signals	Network of transcription factors regulating neutrophilic granulocyte production in hematopoietic lineage	(Ward et al., 2000)
Chromosomal transclocations in leukemia	The biogenesis of chromosome translocations	Chromosomes are said to have transclocated when there is a switch between either two	(Roukos and Misteli, 2014)

		loci of the same chromosomes or two different chromosomes	
	The Philadelphia chromosome in leukemogenesis	Philadelphia chromosome. t(9;22): BCR-ABL1 in CML, first correlation between a translocation and an oncological disease	(Kang et al., 2016)
Importance of DNA Damage and Repair in leukemia	The Mechanism of Human Nonhomologous DNA End Joining	Two major pathways for repairing DSBs are HR, where sequence integrity is preserved and NHEJ, which is error-prone	(Haber, 2006; Lieber, 2008)
	Transpositions and translocations induced by site-specific double-strand breaks in budding yeast		
	Taking a Bad Turn: Compromised DNA Damage Response in Leukemia	Abnormal response to DNA damage has been linked to AML	(Nilles and Fahrenkrog, 2017)
Importance of NGS technologies in cancer therapy	Next-generation sequencing to guide cancer therapy	Evolution sequencing tehcnologies from Sanger sequencing to high-throughput NGS	(Nilles and Fahrenkrog, 2017)
	Application of next-generation sequencing in clinical oncology to advance personalized treatment of cancer	Evolving NGS technologies being applied to cancer genomics	(Gagan and Van Allen, 2015)
Functional importance of non coding regions of the genome	Beyond the Exome: The Non-coding Genome and Enhancers in Neurodevelopmental Disorders and Malformations of Cortical Development	Highlighting the regulatory role of the non coding region of the genome and non-coding alterations causing genetic diseases	(Perenthaler et al., 2019)

	Expression profile analysis of prognostic long non-coding RNA in adult acute myeloid leukemia by weighted gene co-expression network analysis (WGCNA)	Usage of WGCNA to analyse correlation patterns among genes and associated lncRNA	(Chen et al., 2019)
	MicroRNAs and acute myeloid leukemia: therapeutic implications and emerging concepts	Translational importance of miRNA in AML	(Wallace and O'Connell, 2017)
	The Untranslated Regions of mRNAs in Cancer	Exploring the regulatory functions of UTRs in cancer	(Schuster and Hsieh, 2019)
	A frequent somatic mutation in the 3′UTR of GAPDH facilitates the development of ovarian cancer by creating a miR-125b binding site	Functional effect of somatic alterations in 3'UTR regions on tumorigenesis	(Liu et al., 2020)

1.12. References

1. Davis AS, Viera AJ, Mead MD. Leukemia: an overview for primary care. Am Fam Physician. 2014;89: 731–738.

2. Website. Available: Blumenreich MS. The White Blood Cell and Differential Count. In: Walker HK, Hall WD, Hurst JW, editors. Clinical Methods: The History, Physical, and Laboratory Examinations. 3rd edition. Boston: Butterworths; 1990. Chapter 153. Available from: https://www.ncbi.nlm.nih.gov/books/NBK261/

3. Sung H, Ferlay J, Siegel RL, Laversanne M, Soerjomataram I, Jemal A, et al. Global Cancer Statistics 2020: GLOBOCAN Estimates of Incidence and Mortality Worldwide for 36 Cancers in 185 Countries. CA Cancer J Clin. 2021;71: 209–249.

4. Ahirwar DR, Ahirwar R, Professor A, Department of Pathology, RKDF Medical College, Bhopal, et al. A study of leukemias Profile in central India. Tropical Journal of Pathology and Microbiology. 2018. pp. 181–187. doi:10.17511/jopm.2018.i02.12

5. Arora RS, Arora B. Acute leukemia in children: A review of the current Indian data. South Asian J Cancer. 2016;5: 155–160.

6. O'Neill HC, Griffiths KL, Periasamy P, Hinton RA, Hey Y-Y, Petvises S, et al. Spleen as a site for Hematopoiesis of a distinct antigen presenting cell type. Stem Cells Int. 2011;2011: 954275.

7. Borges I, Sena I, Azevedo P, Andreotti J, Almeida V, Paiva A, et al. Lung as a Niche for Hematopoietic Progenitors. Stem Cell Rev Rep. 2017;13: 567–574.

8. Giebel B, Bruns I. Self-Renewal Versus Differentiation in Hematopoietic Stem and Progenitor Cells: A Focus on Asymmetric Cell Divisions. Current Stem Cell Research & Therapy. 2008. pp. 9–16. doi:10.2174/157488808783489444

9. Zhang P, Li X, Pan C, Zheng X, Hu B, Xie R, et al. Single-cell RNA sequencing to track novel perspectives in HSC heterogeneity. Stem Cell Res Ther. 2022;13: 39.

10. Spitzer N, Sammons GS, Butts HM, Grover LM, Price EM. Multipotent progenitor cells derived from adult peripheral blood of swine have high neurogenic potential in vitro. J Cell Physiol. 2011;226: 3156–3168.

11. Aggarwal R, Lu J, Pompili VJ, Das H. Hematopoietic stem cells: transcriptional regulation, ex vivo expansion and clinical application. Curr Mol Med. 2012;12: 34–49.

12. Haladyna JN, Yamauchi T, Neff T, Bernt KM. Epigenetic modifiers in normal and malignant Hematopoiesis. Epigenomics. 2015;7: 301–320.

13. Seita J, Weissman IL. Hematopoietic stem cell: self-renewal versus differentiation. Wiley Interdiscip Rev Syst Biol Med. 2010;2: 640–653.

14. Schiffer CA, Stone RM. Morphologic Classification and Clinical and Laboratory Correlates. Holland-Frei Cancer Medicine 6th edition. BC Decker; 2003.

15. Morphology of leukaemias. Rev Med Hosp Gen . 2016;79: 107–113.

16. Béné MC, Nebe T, Bettelheim P, Buldini B, Bumbea H, Kern W, et al. Immunophenotyping of acute Leukemia and lymphoproliferative disorders: a consensus proposal of the European LeukemiaNet Work Package 10. Leukemia. 2011;25: 567–574.

17. Arber DA, Orazi A, Hasserjian R, Thiele J, Borowitz MJ, Le Beau MM, et al. The 2016 revision to the World Health Organization classification of myeloid neoplasms and acute leukemia. Blood. 2016;127: 2391–2405.

18. Falini B, Tiacci E, Martelli MP, Ascani S, Pileri SA. New classification of acute myeloid Leukemia and precursor-related neoplasms: changes and unsolved issues. Discov Med. 2010;10: 281–292.

19. Campo E, Harris NL, Pileri SA, Jaffe ES, Stein H, Thiele J. WHO Classification of Tumours of Haematopoietic and Lymphoid Tissues. IARC Who Classification of Tum; 2017.

20. Hasan S, Naqvi AR, Rizvi A. Transcriptional Regulation of Emergency Granulopoiesis in Leukemia. Front Immunol. 2018;9: 481.

21. Austin GE, Chan WC, Zhao W, Racine M. Myeloperoxidase Gene Expression in Normal Granulopoiesis and Acute Leukemias. Leukemia & Lymphoma. 1994. pp. 209–226. doi:10.3109/10428199409049717

22. [No title]. [cited 21 Apr 2022]. Available: https://main.icmr.nic.in/sites/default/files/guidelines/Acute_Myeloid_Leukemia.pdf

23. Ward AC, Loeb DM, Soede-Bobok AA, Touw IP, Friedman AD. Regulation of granulopoiesis by transcription factors and cytokine signals. Leukemia. 2000;14: 973–990.

24. Petersen K. Mandell, Douglas, and Bennett's Principles and Practice of Infectious Diseases, 7th Edition Mandell, Douglas, and Bennett's Principles and Practice of Infectious Diseases, 7th Edition Edited by Gerald L. Mandell , John E. Bennett , and Raphael Dolin Philadelphia, PA: Churchill Livingstone Elsevier, 2009. 4320 pp, illustrated. $415.00 (hardcover). Clinical Infectious Diseases. 2010. pp. 636–637. doi:10.1086/655696

25. DeLeo FR, Nauseef WM. Granulocytic Phagocytes. Mandell, Douglas, and Bennett's Principles and Practice of Infectious Diseases. 2015. pp. 78–92.e6. doi:10.1016/b978-1-4557-4801-3.00008-4

26. Severe congenital neutropenia. SpringerReference. doi:10.1007/springerreference_39698

27. Beekman R, Valkhof MG, Sanders MA, van Strien PMH, Haanstra JR, Broeders L, et al. Sequential gain of mutations in severe congenital neutropenia progressing to acute myeloid leukemia. Blood. 2012;119: 5071–5077.

28. Greenberg PL, Nichols WC, Schrier SL. Granulopoiesis in acute myeloid Leukemia and preleukemia. N Engl J Med. 1971;284: 1225–1232.

29. Bain BJ. What is a promonocyte? American Journal of Hematology. 2013. pp. 919–919. doi:10.1002/ajh.23548

30. Park D, Sykes DB, Scadden DT. The hematopoietic stem cell niche. Front Biosci . 2012;17: 30–39.

31. Zimta A-A, Tomuleasa C, Sahnoune I, Calin GA, Berindan-Neagoe I. Long Noncoding RNAs in Myeloid Malignancies. Frontiers in Oncology. 2019. doi:10.3389/fonc.2019.01048

32. Abdulsalam AH, Sabeeh N, Bain BJ. Myeloblasts with unusual morphology. Am J Hematol. 2011;86: 499.

33. Magnusson M, Brun ACM, Miyake N, Larsson J, Ehinger M, Bjornsson JM, et al. HOXA10 is a critical regulator for hematopoietic stem cells and erythroid/megakaryocyte development. Blood. 2007;109: 3687–3696.

34. Bei L, Shah C, Wang H, Huang W, Platanias LC, Eklund EA. Regulation of CDX4 gene

transcription by HoxA9, HoxA10, the Mll-Ell oncogene and Shp2 during leukemogenesis. Oncogenesis. 2014;3: e135.

35. Thorsteinsdottir U, Sauvageau G, Hough MR, Dragowska W, Lansdorp PM, Lawrence HJ, et al. Overexpression of HOXA10 in murine hematopoietic cells perturbs both myeloid and lymphoid differentiation and leads to acute myeloid Leukemia. Mol Cell Biol. 1997;17: 495–505.

36. Wang H, Bei L, Shah CA, Hu L, Eklund EA. HoxA10 Terminates Emergency Granulopoiesis by Increasing Expression of Triad1. J Immunol. 2015;194: 5375–5387.

37. Guerzoni C, Bardini M, Mariani SA, Ferrari-Amorotti G, Neviani P, Panno ML, et al. Inducible activation of CEBPB, a gene negatively regulated by BCR/ABL, inhibits proliferation and promotes differentiation of BCR/ABL-expressing cells. Blood. 2006;107: 4080–4089.

38. Duprez E. C/EBP : a major PML-RARA-responsive gene in retinoic acid-induced differentiation of APL cells. The EMBO Journal. 2003. pp. 5806–5816. doi:10.1093/emboj/cdg556

39. Tsujimura H, Nagamura-Inoue T, Tamura T, Ozato K. IFN consensus sequence binding protein/IFN regulatory factor-8 guides bone marrow progenitor cells toward the macrophage lineage. J Immunol. 2002;169: 1261–1269.

40. Tian SS, Lamb P, Seidel HM, Stein RB, Rosen J. Rapid activation of the STAT3 transcription factor by granulocyte colony-stimulating factor. Blood. 1994;84: 1760–1764.

41. Zhong Z, Wen Z, Darnell JE Jr. Stat3: a STAT family member activated by tyrosine phosphorylation in response to epidermal growth factor and interleukin-6. Science. 1994;264: 95–98.

42. Schuringa JJ, Timmer H, Luttickhuizen D, Vellenga E, Kruijer W. c-Jun and c-Fos cooperate with STAT3 in IL-6-induced transactivation of the IL-6 respone element (IRE). Cytokine. 2001;14: 78–87.

43. Rangatia J, Vangala RK, Singh SM, Peer Zada AA, Elsässer A, Kohlmann A, et al. Elevated c-Jun expression in acute myeloid leukemias inhibits C/EBPalpha DNA binding via leucine zipper domain interaction. Oncogene. 2003;22: 4760–4764.

44. Konieczna IM, DeLuca TA, Eklund EA, Miller WM. Hoxa10 null animals exhibit reduced platelet biogenesis. Br J Haematol. 2016;173: 303–313.

45. Wang H, Lindsey S, Konieczna I, Bei L, Horvath E, Huang W, et al. Constitutively active SHP2 cooperates with HoxA10 overexpression to induce acute myeloid Leukemia. J Biol Chem. 2009;284: 2549–2567.

46. Hirai H, Zhang P, Dayaram T, Hetherington CJ, Mizuno S-I, Imanishi J, et al. C/EBPbeta is required for "emergency" granulopoiesis. Nat Immunol. 2006;7: 732–739.

47. Masumi A, Tamaoki S, Wang IM, Ozato K, Komuro K. IRF-8/ICSBP and IRF-1 cooperatively stimulate mouse IL-12 promoter activity in macrophages. FEBS Lett. 2002;531: 348–353.

48. Schmidt M, Nagel S, Proba J, Thiede C, Ritter M, Waring JF, et al. Lack of interferon consensus sequence binding protein (ICSBP) transcripts in human myeloid leukemias. Blood. 1998;91: 22–29.

49. Akbarzadeh S, Ward AC, McPhee DOM, Alexander WS, Lieschke GJ, Layton JE. Tyrosine residues of the granulocyte colony-stimulating factor receptor transmit proliferation and differentiation signals in murine bone marrow cells. Blood. 2002;99: 879–887.

50. Spiekermann K, Biethahn S, Wilde S, Hiddemann W, Alves F. Constitutive activation of STAT transcription factors in acute myelogenous Leukemia. European Journal of Haematology. 2001. pp. 63–71. doi:10.1034/j.1600-0609.2001.t01-1-00385.x

51. Roukos V, Misteli T. The biogenesis of chromosome translocations. Nat Cell Biol. 2014;16: 293–300.

52. Küppers R, Dalla-Favera R. Mechanisms of chromosomal translocations in B cell lymphomas. Oncogene. 2001;20: 5580–5594.

53. Nambiar M, Kari V, Raghavan SC. Chromosomal translocations in cancer. BiochimBiophys Acta. 2008;1786: 139–152.

54. Kang Z-J, Liu Y-F, Xu L-Z, Long Z-J, Huang D, Yang Y, et al. The Philadelphia chromosome in leukemogenesis. Chin J Cancer. 2016;35: 48.

55. Sampaio MM, Santos MLC, Marques HS, Gonçalves VL de S, Araújo GRL, Lopes LW, et

al. Chronic myeloid leukemia-from the Philadelphia chromosome to specific target drugs: A literature review. World J Clin Oncol. 2021;12: 69–94.

56. Gauwerky CE, Croce CM. Chromosomal translocations in leukaemia. Semin Cancer Biol. 1993;4: 333–340.

57. Nickoloff JA, De Haro LP, Wray J, Hromas R. Mechanisms of leukemia translocations. CurrOpinHematol. 2008;15: 338–345.

58. Chaudhuri J, Basu U, Zarrin A, Yan C, Franco S, Perlot T, et al. Evolution of the immunoglobulin heavy chain class switch recombination mechanism. Adv Immunol. 2007;94: 157–214.

59. Dudley DD, Chaudhuri J, Bassing CH, Alt FW. Mechanism and Control of V(D)J Recombination versus Class Switch Recombination: Similarities and Differences. Advances in Immunology. 2005. pp. 43–112. doi:10.1016/s0065-2776(04)86002-4

60. Lieber MR. The Mechanism of Human Nonhomologous DNA End Joining. Journal of Biological Chemistry. 2008. pp. 1–5. doi:10.1074/jbc.r700039200

61. Haber JE. Transpositions and translocations induced by site-specific double-strand breaks in budding yeast. DNA Repair . 2006;5: 998–1009.

62. Chatterjee N, Walker GC. Mechanisms of DNA damage, repair, and mutagenesis. Environ Mol Mutagen. 2017;58: 235–263.

63. Huang R, Zhou P-K. DNA damage repair: historical perspectives, mechanistic pathways and clinical translation for targeted cancer therapy. Signal Transduct Target Ther. 2021;6: 254.

64. Chapman JR, Taylor MRG, Boulton SJ. Playing the end game: DNA double-strand break repair pathway choice. Mol Cell. 2012;47: 497–510.

65. Stracker TH, Petrini JHJ. The MRE11 complex: starting from the ends. Nat Rev Mol Cell Biol. 2011;12: 90–103.

66. Bhatti S, Kozlov S, Farooqi AA, Naqi A, Lavin M, Khanna KK. ATM protein kinase: the linchpin of cellular defenses to stress. Cell Mol Life Sci. 2011;68: 2977–3006.

67. Altmeyer M, Lukas J. To spread or not to spread—chromatin modifications in response to DNA damage. Current Opinion in Genetics & Development. 2013. pp. 156–165. doi:10.1016/j.gde.2012.11.001

68. Nimonkar AV, Genschel J, Kinoshita E, Polaczek P, Campbell JL, Wyman C, et al. BLM-DNA2-RPA-MRN and EXO1-BLM-RPA-MRN constitute two DNA end resection machineries for human DNA break repair. Genes Dev. 2011;25: 350–362.

69. Zhang F, Fan Q, Ren K, Andreassen PR. PALB2 functionally connects the breast cancer susceptibility proteins BRCA1 and BRCA2. Mol Cancer Res. 2009;7: 1110–1118.

70. Yu X, Fu S, Lai M, Baer R, Chen J. BRCA1 ubiquitinates its phosphorylation-dependent binding partner CtIP. Genes Dev. 2006;20: 1721–1726.

71. Ciccia A, McDonald N, West SC. Structural and functional relationships of the XPF/MUS81 family of proteins. Annu Rev Biochem. 2008;77: 259–287.

72. Xu D, Guo R, Sobeck A, Bachrati CZ, Yang J, Enomoto T, et al. RMI, a new OB-fold complex essential for Bloom syndrome protein to maintain genome stability. Genes Dev. 2008;22: 2843–2855.

73. Rass U, Compton SA, Matos J, Singleton MR, Ip SCY, Blanco MG, et al. Mechanism of Holliday junction resolution by the human GEN1 protein. Genes Dev. 2010;24: 1559–1569.

74. Fekairi S, Scaglione S, Chahwan C, Taylor ER, Tissier A, Coulon S, et al. Human SLX4 is a Holliday junction resolvase subunit that binds multiple DNA repair/recombination endonucleases. Cell. 2009;138: 78–89.

75. Panier S, Boulton SJ. Double-strand break repair: 53BP1 comes into focus. Nat Rev Mol Cell Biol. 2014;15: 7–18.

76. Mari P-O, Florea BI, Persengiev SP, Verkaik NS, Brüggenwirth HT, Modesti M, et al. Dynamic assembly of end-joining complexes requires interaction between Ku70/80 and XRCC4. Proc Natl Acad Sci U S A. 2006;103: 18597–18602.

77. Soutoglou E, Dorn JF, Sengupta K, Jasin M, Nussenzweig A, Ried T, et al. Positional stability of single double-strand breaks in mammalian cells. Nat Cell Biol. 2007;9: 675–682.

78. Yoo S. Geometry of a complex formed by double strand break repair proteins at a single

DNA end: recruitment of DNA-PKcs induces inward translocation of Ku protein. Nucleic Acids Research. 1999. pp. 4679–4686. doi:10.1093/nar/27.24.4679

79. Gottlieb TM, Jackson SP. The DNA-dependent protein kinase: requirement for DNA ends and association with Ku antigen. Cell. 1993;72: 131–142.

80. Nick McElhinny SA, Snowden CM, McCarville J, Ramsden DA. Ku recruits the XRCC4-ligase IV complex to DNA ends. Mol Cell Biol. 2000;20: 2996–3003.

81. Ma Y, Pannicke U, Schwarz K, Lieber MR. Hairpin Opening and Overhang Processing by an Artemis/DNA-Dependent Protein Kinase Complex in Nonhomologous End Joining and V(D)J Recombination. Cell. 2002. pp. 781–794. doi:10.1016/s0092-8674(02)00671-2

82. Davis AJ, Chen DJ. DNA double strand break repair via nonhomologous end-joining. Transl Cancer Res. 2013;2: 130–143.

83. Lieber MR. The mechanism of double-strand DNA break repair by the nonhomologous DNA end-joining pathway. Annu Rev Biochem. 2010;79: 181–211.

84. Yano K-I, Morotomi-Yano K, Wang S-Y, Uematsu N, Lee K-J, Asaithamby A, et al. Ku recruits XLF to DNA double-strand breaks. EMBO Rep. 2008;9: 91–96.

85. Grawunder U, Wilm M, Wu X, Kulesza P, Wilson TE, Mann M, et al. Activity of DNA ligase IV stimulated by complex formation with XRCC4 protein in mammalian cells. Nature. 1997;388: 492–495.

86. Dianov GL, Hübscher U. Mammalian base excision repair: the forgotten archangel. Nucleic Acids Res. 2013;41: 3483–3490.

87. Krokan HE, Bjørås M. Base excision repair. Cold Spring HarbPerspect Biol. 2013;5: a012583.

88. Almeida KH, Sobol RW. A unified view of base excision repair: lesion-dependent protein complexes regulated by post-translational modification. DNA Repair . 2007;6: 695–711.

89. Akbari M, Peña-Diaz J, Andersen S, Liabakk N-B, Otterlei M, Krokan HE. Extracts of proliferating and non-proliferating human cells display different base excision pathways and repair fidelity. DNA Repair . 2009;8: 834–843.

90. Svilar D, Goellner EM, Almeida KH, Sobol RW. Base excision repair and lesion-dependent subpathways for repair of oxidative DNA damage. Antioxid Redox Signal. 2011;14: 2491–2507.

91. Fagbemi AF, Orelli B, Schärer OD. Regulation of endonuclease activity in human nucleotide excision repair. DNA Repair. 2011. pp. 722–729. doi:10.1016/j.dnarep.2011.04.022

92. Schärer OD. Nucleotide excision repair in eukaryotes. Cold Spring HarbPerspect Biol. 2013;5: a012609.

93. Nishi R, Okuda Y, Watanabe E, Mori T, Iwai S, Masutani C, et al. Centrin 2 Stimulates Nucleotide Excision Repair by Interacting with Xeroderma Pigmentosum Group C Protein. Molecular and Cellular Biology. 2005. pp. 5664–5674. doi:10.1128/mcb.25.13.5664-5674.2005

94. Compe E, Egly J-M. TFIIH: when transcription met DNA repair. Nat Rev Mol Cell Biol. 2012;13: 343–354.

95. Yokoi M, Masutani C, Maekawa T, Sugasawa K, Ohkuma Y, Hanaoka F. The Xeroderma Pigmentosum Group C Protein Complex XPC-HR23B Plays an Important Role in the Recruitment of Transcription Factor IIH to Damaged DNA. Journal of Biological Chemistry. 2000. pp. 9870–9875. doi:10.1074/jbc.275.13.9870

96. Marteijn JA, Lans H, Vermeulen W, Hoeijmakers JHJ. Understanding nucleotide excision repair and its roles in cancer and ageing. Nature Reviews Molecular Cell Biology. 2014. pp. 465–481. doi:10.1038/nrm3822

97. Sachadyn P. Conservation and diversity of MutS proteins. Mutat Res. 2010;694: 20–30.

98. Kunkel TA, Erie DA. DNA MISMATCH REPAIR. Annual Review of Biochemistry. 2005. pp. 681–710. doi:10.1146/annurev.biochem.74.082803.133243

99. Zhang Y, Yuan F, Presnell SR, Tian K, Gao Y, Tomkinson AE, et al. Reconstitution of 5′-Directed Human Mismatch Repair in a Purified System. Cell. 2005. pp. 693–705. doi:10.1016/j.cell.2005.06.027

100. Umar A, Buermeyer AB, Simon JA, Thomas DC, Clark AB, Michael Liskay R, et al.

Requirement for PCNA in DNA Mismatch Repair at a Step Preceding DNA Resynthesis. Cell. 1996. pp. 65–73. doi:10.1016/s0092-8674(00)81323-9

101. Genschel J, Modrich P. Mechanism of 5′-Directed Excision in Human Mismatch Repair. Molecular Cell. 2003. pp. 1077–1086. doi:10.1016/s1097-2765(03)00428-3

102. Guo S, Zhang Y, Yuan F, Gao Y, Gu L, Wong I, et al. Regulation of replication protein A functions in DNA mismatch repair by phosphorylation. J Biol Chem. 2006;281: 21607–21616.

103. Pećina-Šlaus N, Kafka A, Salamon I, Bukovac A. Mismatch Repair Pathway, Genome Stability and Cancer. Frontiers in Molecular Biosciences. 2020. doi:10.3389/fmolb.2020.00122

104. Jacoby MA, De Jesus Pizarro RE, Shao J, Koboldt DC, Fulton RS, Zhou G, et al. The DNA double-strand break response is abnormal in myeloblasts from patients with therapy-related acute myeloid Leukemia. Leukemia. 2014;28: 1242–1251.

105. Nilles N, Fahrenkrog B. Taking a Bad Turn: Compromised DNA Damage Response in Leukemia. Cells. 2017;6. doi:10.3390/cells6020011

106. Gaymes TJ, Mufti GJ, Rassool FV. Myeloid leukemias have increased activity of the nonhomologous end-joining pathway and concomitant DNA misrepair that is dependent on the Ku70/86 heterodimer. Cancer Res. 2002;62: 2791–2797.

107. Fan J, Li L, Small D, Rassool F. Cells expressing FLT3/ITD mutations exhibit elevated repair errors generated through alternative NHEJ pathways: implications for genomic instability and therapy. Blood. 2010. pp. 5298–5305. doi:10.1182/blood-2010-03-272591

108. Deriano L, Guipaud O, Merle-Béral H, Binet J-L, Ricoul M, Potocki-Veronese G, et al. Human chronic lymphocytic leukemia B cells can escape DNA damage-induced apoptosis through the nonhomologous end-joining DNA repair pathway. Blood. 2005;105: 4776–4783.

109. Riballo E, Critchlow SE, Teo S-H, Doherty AJ, Priestley A, Broughton B, et al. identification of a defect in DNA ligase IV in a radiosensitive leukaemia patient. Current Biology. 1999. pp. 699–S2. doi:10.1016/s0960-9822(99)80311-x

110. Rollinson S, Smith AG, Allan JM, Adamson PJ, Scott K, Skibola CF, et al. RAD51

homologous recombination repair gene haplotypes and risk of acute myeloid leukaemia. Leuk Res. 2007;31: 169–174.

111. Seedhouse C, Faulkner R, Ashraf N, Das-Gupta E, Russell N. Polymorphisms in genes involved in homologous recombination repair interact to increase the risk of developing acute myeloid Leukemia. Clin Cancer Res. 2004;10: 2675–2680.

112. Deutsch E, Jarrousse S, Buet D, Dugray A, Bonnet M-L, Vozenin-Brotons M-C, et al. Down-regulation of BRCA1 in BCR-ABL-expressing hematopoietic cells. Blood. 2003;101: 4583–4588.

113. Slupianek A, Schmutte C, Tombline G, Nieborowska-Skorska M, Hoser G, Nowicki MO, et al. BCR/ABL regulates mammalian RecA homologs, resulting in drug resistance. Mol Cell. 2001;8: 795–806.

114. Bhatla D, Gerbing RB, Alonzo TA, Mehta PA, Deal K, Elliott J, et al. DNA repair polymorphisms and outcome of chemotherapy for acute myelogenous Leukemia: a report from the Children's Oncology Group. Leukemia. 2008. pp. 265–272. doi:10.1038/sj.leu.2405000

115. Bănescu C, Duicu C, Trifa AP, Dobreanu M. XRCC1 Arg194Trp and Arg399Gln polymorphisms are significantly associated with shorter survival in acute myeloid Leukemia. Leuk Lymphoma. 2014;55: 365–370.

116. Parine NR, Varsha RS, Alanazi MS. Microsatellite Instability in Colorectal Cancer. Microsatellite Markers. 2016. doi:10.5772/65429

117. Mao G, Pan X, Gu L. Evidence that a mutation in the MLH1 3'-untranslated region confers a mutator phenotype and mismatch repair deficiency in patients with relapsed Leukemia. J Biol Chem. 2008;283: 3211–3216.

118. Schlessinger J. Cell Signaling by Receptor Tyrosine Kinases. Cell. 2000. pp. 211–225. doi:10.1016/s0092-8674(00)00114-8

119. Du Z, Lovly CM. Mechanisms of receptor tyrosine kinase activation in cancer. Molecular Cancer. 2018. doi:10.1186/s12943-018-0782-4

120. Kühnl A, Grimwade D. Molecular markers in acute myeloid leukaemia. International

Journal of Hematology. 2012. pp. 153–163. doi:10.1007/s12185-012-1123-9

121. Nowell PC. Discovery of the Philadelphia chromosome: a personal perspective. Journal of Clinical Investigation. 2007. pp. 2033–2035. doi:10.1172/jci31771

122. Berenstein R. Class III Receptor Tyrosine Kinases in Acute Leukemia - Biological Functions and Modern Laboratory Analysis. Biomark Insights. 2015;10: 1–14.

123. Foran JM. New prognostic markers in acute myeloid Leukemia: perspective from the clinic. Hematology Am Soc Hematol Educ Program. 2010;2010: 47–55.

124. Ribatti D, Ranieri G, Basile A, Azzariti A, Paradiso A, Vacca A. Tumor endothelial markers as a target in cancer. Expert Opinion on Therapeutic Targets. 2012. pp. 1215–1225. doi:10.1517/14728222.2012.725047

125. Gialeli C, Nikitovic D, Kletsas D, Theocharis AD, Tzanakakis GN, Karamanos NK. PDGF/PDGFR signaling and targeting in cancer growth and progression: Focus on tumor microenvironment and cancer-associated fibroblasts. Curr Pharm Des. 2014;20: 2843–2848.

126. Gurska LM, Ames K, Gritsman K. Signaling Pathways in Leukemic Stem Cells. Adv Exp Med Biol. 2019;1143: 1–39.

127. Vanhaesebroeck B, Guillermet-Guibert J, Graupera M, Bilanges B. The emerging mechanisms of isoform-specific PI3K signalling. Nat Rev Mol Cell Biol. 2010;11: 329–341.

128. Alessi DR, Andjelkovic M, Caudwell B, Cron P, Morrice N, Cohen P, et al. mechanism of activation of protein kinase B by insulin and IGF-1. The EMBO Journal. 1996. pp. 6541–6551. doi:10.1002/j.1460-2075.1996.tb01045.x

129. Xu Q, Simpson S-E, Scialla TJ, Bagg A, Carroll M. Survival of acute myeloid leukemia cells requires PI3 kinase activation. Blood. 2003;102: 972–980.

130. Horne GA, Kinstrie R, Copland M. Novel drug therapies in myeloid Leukemia: a patent review. Pharmaceutical Patent Analyst. 2015. pp. 187–205. doi:10.4155/ppa.15.3

131. Zhang J, Grindley JC, Yin T, Jayasinghe S, He XC, Ross JT, et al. PTEN maintains haematopoietic stem cells and acts in lineage choice and leukaemia prevention. Nature. 2006;441: 518–522.

132. Assoian RK, Komoriya A, Meyers CA, Miller DM, Sporn MB. Transforming growth factor-beta in human platelets. Identification of a major storage site, purification, and characterization. Journal of Biological Chemistry. 1983. pp. 7155–7160. doi:10.1016/s0021-9258(18)32345-7

133. Franzén P, ten Dijke P, Ichijo H, Yamashita H, Schulz P, Heldin CH, et al. Cloning of a TGF beta type I receptor that forms a heteromeric complex with the TGF beta type II receptor. Cell. 1993;75: 681–692.

134. Lin HY, Wang X-F, Ng-Eaton E, Weinberg RA, Lodish HF. Expression cloning of the TGF-β type II receptor, a functional transmembrane serine/threonine kinase. Cell. 1992. pp. 775–785. doi:10.1016/0092-8674(92)90152-3

135. Vaidya A, Kale VP. TGF-β signaling and its role in the regulation of hematopoietic stem cells. Systems and Synthetic Biology. 2015. pp. 1–10. doi:10.1007/s11693-015-9161-2

136. Wrana JL, Attisano L. MAD-related proteins in TGF-β signalling. Trends in Genetics. 1996. pp. 493–496. doi:10.1016/s0168-9525(96)30109-1

137. Dennler S, ten Dijke P. Smad Proteins in TGF-Beta Signaling. Encyclopedia of Cancer. 2014. pp. 4257–4260. doi:10.1007/978-3-662-46875-3_5364

138. Farooqi AA, de la Roche M, Djamgoz MBA, Siddik ZH. Overview of the oncogenic signaling pathways in colorectal cancer: Mechanistic insights. Semin Cancer Biol. 2019;58: 65–79.

139. Fortunel NO, Hatzfeld A, Hatzfeld JA. Transforming growth factor-beta: pleiotropic role in the regulation of Hematopoiesis. Blood. 2000;96: 2022–2036.

140. Staal F, Famili F, Perez LG, Pike-Overzet K. Aberrant Wnt Signaling in Leukemia. Cancers. 2016. p. 78. doi:10.3390/cancers8090078

141. Reya T, Duncan AW, Ailles L, Domen J, Scherer DC, Willert K, et al. A role for Wntsignalling in self-renewal of haematopoietic stem cells. Nature. 2003;423: 409–414.

142. Ghosh N, Hossain U, Mandal A, Sil PC. The Wnt signaling pathway: a potential therapeutic target against cancer. Annals of the New York Academy of Sciences. 2019. pp. 54–74. doi:10.1111/nyas.14027

143. Wang Y, Krivtsov AV, Sinha AU, North TE, Goessling W, Feng Z, et al. The Wnt/beta-catenin pathway is required for the development of leukemia stem cells in AML. Science. 2010;327: 1650–1653.

144. Watowich SS, Wu H, Socolovsky M, Klingmuller U, Constantinescu SN, Lodish HF. CYTOKINE RECEPTOR SIGNAL TRANSDUCTION AND THE CONTROL OF HEMATOPOIETIC CELL DEVELOPMENT. Annual Review of Cell and Developmental Biology. 1996. pp. 91–128. doi:10.1146/annurev.cellbio.12.1.91

145. Vainchenker W, Constantinescu SN. JAK/STAT signaling in hematological malignancies. Oncogene. 2013. pp. 2601–2613. doi:10.1038/onc.2012.347

146. Velazquez L, Fellous M, Stark GR, Pellegrini S. A protein tyrosine kinase in the interferon alpha/beta signaling pathway. Cell. 1992;70: 313–322.

147. Nguyen MH, Ho JM, Beattie BK, Barber DL. TEL-JAK2 mediates constitutive activation of the phosphatidylinositol 3'-kinase/protein kinase B signaling pathway. J Biol Chem. 2001;276: 32704–32713.

148. Tefferi A. Classification, diagnosis and management of myeloproliferative disorders in the JAK2V617F era. Hematology Am Soc Hematol Educ Program. 2006; 240–245.

149. Gagan J, Van Allen EM. Next-generation sequencing to guide cancer therapy. Genome Medicine. 2015. doi:10.1186/s13073-015-0203-x

150. Guan Y-F, Li G-R, Wang R-J, Yi Y-T, Yang L, Jiang D, et al. application of next-generation sequencing in clinical oncology to advance personalized treatment of cancer. Chin J Cancer. 2012;31: 463–470.

151. ENCODE Project Consortium. An integrated encyclopedia of DNA elements in the human genome. Nature. 2012;489: 57–74.

152. Golub TR, Slonim DK, Tamayo P, Huard C, Gaasenbeek M, Mesirov JP, et al. Molecular classification of cancer: class discovery and class prediction by gene expression monitoring. Science. 1999;286: 531–537.

153. Handschuh L. Not Only Mutations Matter: Molecular Picture of Acute Myeloid Leukemia Emerging from Transcriptome Studies. J Oncol. 2019;2019: 7239206.

154. Mardis ER, Ding L, Dooling DJ, Larson DE, McLellan MD, Chen K, et al. Recurring mutations found by sequencing an acute myeloid leukemia genome. N Engl J Med. 2009;361: 1058–1066.

155. Perenthaler E, Yousefi S, Niggl E, Barakat TS. Beyond the Exome: The Noncoding Genome and Enhancers in Neurodevelopmental Disorders and Malformations of Cortical Development. Front Cell Neurosci. 2019;13: 352.

156. Ohno S. So much "junk" DNA in our genome. Brookhaven Symp Biol. 1972;23: 366–370.

157. Kuska B. Should scientists scrap the notion of junk DNA? J Natl Cancer Inst. 1998;90: 1032–1033.

158. Vitsios D, Dhindsa RS, Middleton L, Gussow AB, Petrovski S. Prioritizing noncoding regions based on human genomic constraint and sequence context with deep learning. Nat Commun. 2021;12: 1504.

159. Ling H, Vincent K, Pichler M, Fodde R, Berindan-Neagoe I, Slack FJ, et al. Junk DNA and the long noncoding RNA twist in cancer genetics. Oncogene. 2015. pp. 5003–5011. doi:10.1038/onc.2014.456

160. Kurokawa R. Promoter-associated long noncoding RNAs repress transcription through a RNA binding protein TLS. Adv Exp Med Biol. 2011;722: 196–208.

161. Garzon R, Volinia S, Papaioannou D, Nicolet D, Kohlschmidt J, Yan PS, et al. expression and prognostic impact of lncRNAs in acute myeloid Leukemia. Proc Natl Acad Sci U S A. 2014;111: 18679–18684.

162. Lyu Y, Lou J, Yang Y, Feng J, Hao Y, Huang S, et al. Dysfunction of the WT1-MEG3 signaling promotes AML leukemogenesis via p53-dependent and -independent pathways. Leukemia. 2017;31: 2543–2551.

163. Zhang T-J, Zhou J-D, Zhang W, Lin J, Ma J-C, Wen X-M, et al. H19 overexpression promotes leukemogenesis and predicts unfavorable prognosis in acute myeloid Leukemia. Clinical Epigenetics. 2018. doi:10.1186/s13148-018-0486-z

164. Hao S, Shao Z. HOTAIR is upregulated in acute myeloid Leukemia and that indicates a

poor prognosis. Int J Clin Exp Pathol. 2015;8: 7223–7228.

165. Li Q, Song W, Wang J. TUG1 confers Adriamycin resistance in acute myeloid Leukemia by epigenetically suppressing miR-34a expression via EZH2. Biomed Pharmacother. 2019;109: 1793–1801.

166. Zhao C, Wang S, Zhao Y, Du F, Wang W, Lv P, et al. Long noncoding RNA NEAT1 modulates cell proliferation and apoptosis by regulating miR-23a-3p/SMC1A in acute myeloid Leukemia. J Cell Physiol. 2019;234: 6161–6172.

167. Trimarchi T, Bilal E, Ntziachristos P, Fabbri G, Dalla-Favera R, Tsirigos A, et al. Genome-wide mapping and characterization of Notch-regulated long noncoding RNAs in acute Leukemia. Cell. 2014;158: 593–606.

168. Chen Z-H, Wang W-T, Huang W, Fang K, Sun Y-M, Liu S-R, et al. The lncRNA HOTAIRM1 regulates the degradation of PML-RARA oncoprotein and myeloid cell differentiation by enhancing the autophagy pathway. Cell Death Differ. 2017;24: 212–224.

169. Gao J, Wang F, Wu P, Chen Y, Jia Y. Aberrant LncRNA Expression in Leukemia. J Cancer. 2020;11: 4284–4296.

170. Gao S, Zhou B, Li H, Huang X, Wu Y, Xing C, et al. Long noncoding RNA HOTAIR promotes the self-renewal of leukemia stem cells through epigenetic silencing of p15. Exp Hematol. 2018;67: 32–40.e3.

171. Zhang Y, Liu Y, Xu X. Knockdown of LncRNA-UCA1 suppresses chemoresistance of pediatric AML by inhibiting glycolysis through the microRNA-125a/hexokinase 2 pathway. J Cell Biochem. 2018;119: 6296–6308.

172. El-Khazragy N, Elayat W, Matbouly S, Seliman S, Sami A, Safwat G, et al. The prognostic significance of the long noncoding RNAs "CCAT1, PVT1" in t(8;21) associated Acute Myeloid Leukemia. Gene. 2019. pp. 172–177. doi:10.1016/j.gene.2019.03.055

173. Chen C-T, Wang P-P, Mo W-J, Zhang Y-P, Zhou W, Deng T-F, et al. Expression profile analysis of prognostic long noncoding RNA in adult acute myeloid leukemia by weighted gene co-expression network analysis (WGCNA). J Cancer. 2019;10: 4707–4718.

174. Qi H, Chi L, Wang X, Jin X, Wang W, Lan J. Identification of a Seven-lncRNA-mRNA

Signature for Recurrence and Prognostic Prediction in Relapsed Acute Lymphoblastic Leukemia Based on WGCNA and LASSO Analyses. Anal Cell Pathol . 2021;2021: 6692022.

175. Fabbri M, Garzon R, Andreeff M, Kantarjian HM, Garcia-Manero G, Calin GA. MicroRNAs and noncoding RNAs in hematological malignancies: molecular, clinical and therapeutic implications. Leukemia. 2008;22: 1095–1105.

176. Mardani R, Abadi MHJ, Motieian M, Taghizadeh-Boroujeni S, Bayat A, Farsinezhad A, et al. MicroRNA in Leukemia: Tumor suppressors and oncogenes with prognostic potential. Journal of Cellular Physiology. 2019. pp. 8465–8486. doi:10.1002/jcp.27776

177. Wallace JA, O'Connell RM. MicroRNAs and acute myeloid Leukemia: therapeutic implications and emerging concepts. Blood. 2017;130: 1290–1301.

178. Wong P, Iwasaki M, Somervaille TCP, Ficara F, Carico C, Arnold C, et al. The miR-17-92 microRNA polycistron regulates MLL leukemia stem cell potential by modulating p21 expression. Cancer Res. 2010;70: 3833–3842.

179. Mi S, Li Z, Chen P, He C, Cao D, Elkahloun A, et al. Aberrant overexpression and function of the miR-17-92 cluster in MLL-rearranged acute Leukemia. Proc Natl Acad Sci U S A. 2010;107: 3710–3715.

180. Dixon-McIver A, East P, Mein CA, Cazier J-B, Molloy G, Chaplin T, et al. Distinctive patterns of microRNA expression associated with karyotype in acute myeloid leukaemia. PLoS One. 2008;3: e2141.

181. Grasedieck S, Sorrentino A, Langer C, Buske C, Döhner H, Mertens D, et al. Circulating microRNAs in hematological diseases: principles, challenges, and perspectives. Blood. 2013;121: 4977–4984.

182. Díaz-Beyá M, Brunet S, Nomdedéu J, Tejero R, Díaz T, Pratcorona M, et al. MicroRNA expression at diagnosis adds relevant prognostic information to molecular categorization in patients with intermediate-risk cytogenetic acute myeloid Leukemia. Leukemia. 2014;28: 804–812.

183. Sun SM, Rockova V, Bullinger L, Dijkstra MK, Döhner H, Löwenberg B, et al. The prognostic relevance of miR-212 expression with survival in cytogenetically and molecularly

heterogeneous AML. Leukemia. 2013;27: 100–106.

184. Guo Y, Strickland SA, Mohan S, Li S, Bosompem A, Vickers KC, et al. MicroRNAs and tRNA-derived fragments predict the transformation of myelodysplastic syndromes to acute myeloid Leukemia. Leuk Lymphoma. 2017;58: 1–15.

185. Chen P, Price C, Li Z, Li Y, Cao D, Wiley A, et al. miR-9 is an essential oncogenic microRNA specifically overexpressed in mixed lineage leukemia-rearranged Leukemia. Proc Natl Acad Sci U S A. 2013;110: 11511–11516.

186. Jiang X, Hu C, Arnovitz S, Bugno J, Yu M, Zuo Z, et al. miR-22 has a potent anti-tumour role with therapeutic potential in acute myeloid leukaemia. Nature Communications. 2016. doi:10.1038/ncomms11452

187. Song SJ, Ito K, Ala U, Kats L, Webster K, Sun SM, et al. The oncogenic microRNA miR-22 targets the TET2 tumor suppressor to promote hematopoietic stem cell self-renewal and transformation. Cell Stem Cell. 2013;13: 87–101.

188. Bousquet M, Quelen C, Rosati R, Mas VM-D, Bastard C, Lippert E, et al. Myeloid Cell Differentiation Arrest by Mir-125b-1 in Myelodysplasic Syndrome and Acute Myeloid Leukemia with the T(2;11)(p21;q23) Translocation. Blood. 2008. pp. 4148–4148. doi:10.1182/blood.v112.11.4148.4148

189. Chaudhuri AA, So AY-L, Mehta A, Minisandram A, Sinha N, Jonsson VD, et al. Oncomir miR-125b regulates Hematopoiesis by targeting the gene Lin28A. Proc Natl Acad Sci U S A. 2012;109: 4233–4238.

190. So AY-L, Sookram R, Chaudhuri AA, Minisandram A, Cheng D, Xie C, et al. Dual mechanisms by which miR-125b represses IRF4 to induce myeloid and B-cell leukemias. Blood. 2014;124: 1502–1512.

191. Dorrance AM, Neviani P, Ferenchak GJ, Huang X, Nicolet D, Maharry KS, et al. Targeting leukemia stem cells in vivo with antagomiR-126 nanoparticles in acute myeloid Leukemia. Leukemia. 2015;29: 2143–2153.

192. Li Z, Chen P, Su R, Li Y, Hu C, Wang Y, et al. overexpression and knockout of miR-126 both promote leukemogenesis. Blood. 2015;126: 2005–2015.

193. Lechman ER, Gentner B, Ng SWK, Schoof EM, van Galen P, Kennedy JA, et al. miR-126 Regulates Distinct Self-Renewal Outcomes in Normal and Malignant Hematopoietic Stem Cells. Cancer Cell. 2016;29: 602–606.

194. de Leeuw DC, Denkers F, Olthof MC, Rutten AP, Pouwels W, Schuurhuis GJ, et al. Attenuation of microRNA-126 expression that drives CD34+38- stem/progenitor cells in acute myeloid leukemia leads to tumor eradication. Cancer Res. 2014;74: 2094–2105.

195. Gong J-N, Yu J, Lin H-S, Zhang X-H, Yin X-L, Xiao Z, et al. The role, mechanism and potentially therapeutic application of microRNA-29 family in acute myeloid Leukemia. Cell Death Differ. 2014;21: 100–112.

196. Garzon R, Heaphy CEA, Havelange V, Fabbri M, Volinia S, Tsao T, et al. MicroRNA 29b functions in acute myeloid Leukemia. Blood. 2009;114: 5331–5341.

197. Liu S, Wu L-C, Pang J, Santhanam R, Schwind S, Wu Y-Z, et al. Sp1/NFkappaB/HDAC/miR-29b regulatory network in KIT-driven myeloid leukemia. Cancer Cell. 2010;17: 333–347.

198. Garzon R, Liu S, Fabbri M, Liu Z, Heaphy CEA, Callegari E, et al. MicroRNA-29b induces global DNA hypomethylation and tumor suppressor gene reexpression in acute myeloid Leukemia by targeting directly DNMT3A and 3B and indirectly DNMT1. Blood. 2009;113: 6411–6418.

199. Schuster SL, Hsieh AC. The Untranslated Regions of mRNAs in cancer. Trends Cancer Res. 2019;5: 245–262.

200. Park HJ, Ji P, Kim S, Xia Z, Rodriguez B, Li L, et al. 3′ UTR shortening represses tumor-suppressor genes in trans by disrupting ceRNA crosstalk. Nature Genetics. 2018. pp. 783–789. doi:10.1038/s41588-018-0118-8

201. Liu P, Zhong Y, Cao T, Sheng X, Huang H. A frequent somatic mutation in the 3'UTR of GAPDH facilitates the development of ovarian cancer by creating a miR-125b binding site. Oncol Rep. 2020;44: 887–896.

202. Zhang Y, Liu L, Qiu Q, Zhou Q, Ding J, Lu Y, et al. Alternative polyadenylation: methods, mechanism, function, and role in cancer. J Exp Clin Cancer Res. 2021;40: 51.

203. Li Z, Tzeng C-M. Integrated Analysis of miRNA and mRNA Expression Profiles to Identify miRNA Targets. mRNA Decay. 2018. pp. 141–148. doi:10.1007/978-1-4939-7540-2_10

204. Ke S, Alemu EA, Mertens C, Gantman EC, Fak JJ, Mele A, et al. A majority of m6A residues are in the last exons, allowing the potential for 3' UTR regulation. Genes Dev. 2015;29: 2037–2053.

205. Bermano G, Pagmantidis V, Holloway N, Kadri S, Mowat NAG, Shiel RS, et al. Evidence that a polymorphism within the 3'UTR of glutathione peroxidase 4 is functional and is associated with susceptibility to colorectal cancer. Genes Nutr. 2007;2: 225–232.

206. Lopes-Ramos CM, Barros BP, Koyama FC, Carpinetti PA, Pezuk J, Doimo NTS, et al. E2F1 somatic mutation within miRNA target site impairs gene regulation in colorectal cancer. PLoS One. 2017;12: e0181153.

207. Ziebarth JD, Bhattacharya A, Cui Y. Integrative analysis of somatic mutations altering microRNA targeting in cancer genomes. PLoS One. 2012;7: e47137.

208. Pamuła-Piłat J, Tęcza K, Kalinowska-Herok M, Grzybowska E. Genetic 3′UTR variations and clinical factors significantly contribute to survival prediction and clinical response in breast cancer patients. Scientific Reports. 2020. doi:10.1038/s41598-020-62662-z

209. Abramenko IV, Bilous NI, Chumak AA, Dyagil IS, Martina ZV. ANALYSIS OF THE 3′UTR REGION OF THE NOTCH1 GENE IN CHRONIC LYMPHOCYTIC LEUKEMIA PATIENTS. Experimental Oncology. 2018. pp. 211–217. doi:10.31768/2312-8852.2018.40(3):211-217

210. Cheng CK, Kwan TK, Cheung CY, Ng K, Liang P, Cheng SH, et al. A polymorphism in the 3'-untranslated region of the NPM1 gene causes illegitimate regulation by microRNA-337-5p and correlates with adverse outcome in acute myeloid Leukemia. Haematologica. 2013;98: 913–917.

211. Zhang L, Huang J, Yang N, Greshock J, Megraw MS, Giannakakis A, et al. microRNAs exhibit high frequency genomic alterations in human cancer. Proc Natl Acad Sci U S A. 2006;103: 9136–9141.

212. Jukic DM, Rao UNM, Kelly L, Skaf JS, Drogowski LM, Kirkwood JM, et al. Microrna

profiling analysis of differences between the melanoma of young adults and older adults. J Transl Med. 2010;8: 27.

213. Jiang J, Lee EJ, Gusev Y, Schmittgen TD. Real-time expression profiling of microRNA precursors in human cancer cell lines. Nucleic Acids Res. 2005;33: 5394–5403.

214. Guo C, Sah JF, Beard L, Willson JKV, Markowitz SD, Guda K. The noncoding RNA, miR-126, suppresses the growth of neoplastic cells by targeting phosphatidylinositol 3-kinase signaling and is frequently lost in colon cancers. Genes Chromosomes Cancer. 2008;47: 939–946.

215. Chen X, Ba Y, Ma L, Cai X, Yin Y, Wang K, et al. characterization of microRNAs in serum: a novel class of biomarkers for diagnosis of cancer and other diseases. Cell Res. 2008;18: 997–1006.

Chapter 2: Material and Methods

2.1. Software and Databases

2.1.1. Programming languages

- Shell scripting
- AWK
- R
- Python

2.1.2. Aligners

- Bowtie2[1]
- BWA[2]
- Hisat2 (splice aware) [3]
- STAR (splice aware) [4]
- STAR-Fusion (splice aware)[5]

2.1.3. File Processing and Analysis

- SAMTools[6]
- BEDTools[7]
- BCFtools[8]
- Picard Tools
- Genome Analysis Toolkit (GATK)[9]
- Decision Tree classifier[10]
- Lasso-Cox regression[11]

2.1.4. CNV analysis

- exomeCopy (https://bioconductor.org/packages/release/bioc/html/exomeCopy.html)
- CNVkit[12]

2.1.5. Online Tools and Databases

- UCSC Browser[13,14]
- miRDB[15]
- miRBASE[16]
- TargetScan[17]
- STRINGdb
- REACTOME
- KEGG
- CIBERSORTx[18]
- ROC analysis
- ClustVis [19]

2.1.6. R packages for visualization and statistics

- GenVisR[20]
- WGCNA[21]
- DESeq2[22]
- Pheatmap
- ggplot2[23]

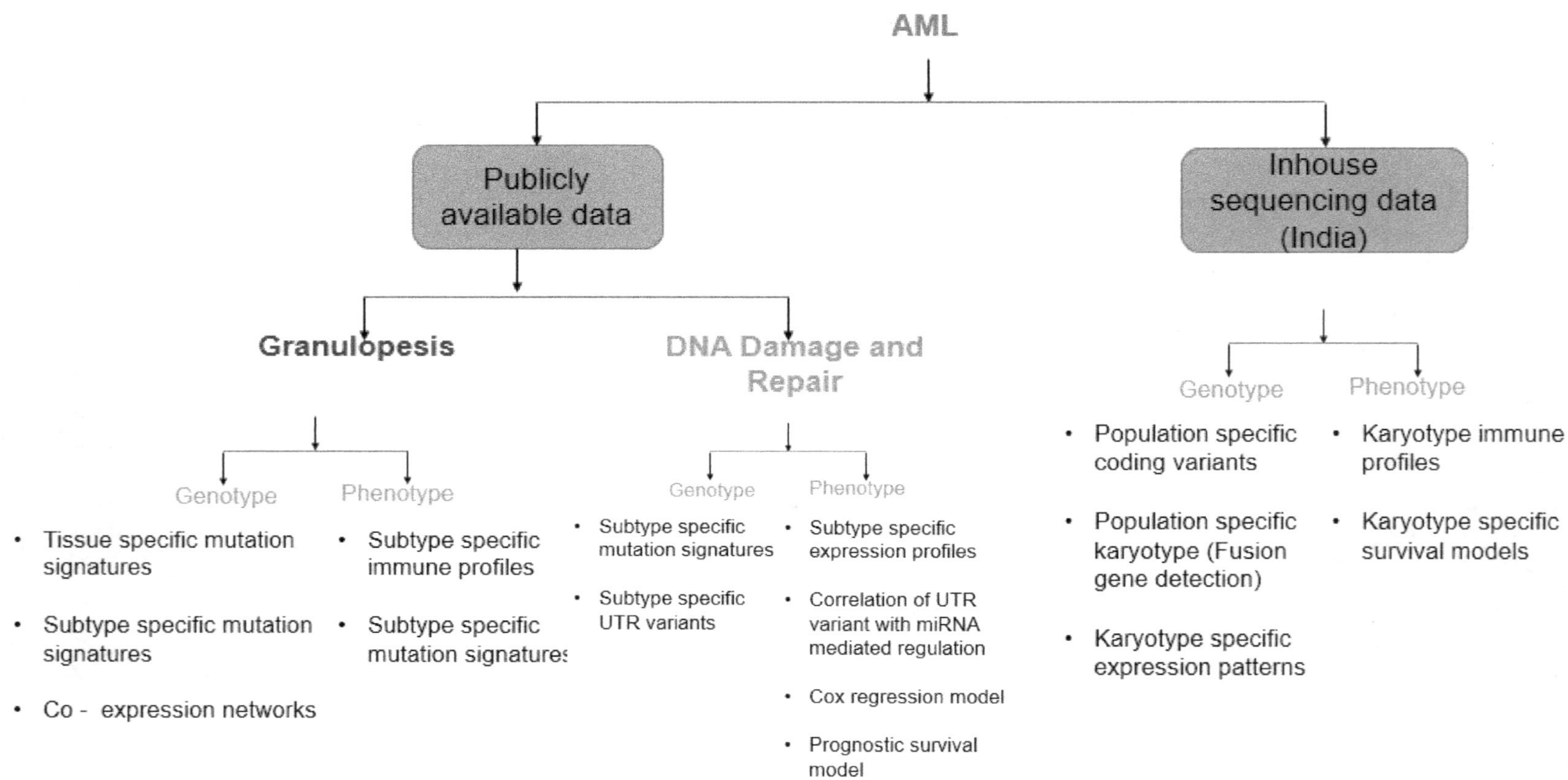

Figure 2.1: Overall flowchart for the study

2.2. Materials

Fine chemicals of molecular biology grade were obtained from Sigma Aldrich (St Louis, MO, USA), MP biomedicals (Santa Ana, California, USA), Invitrogen (San Diego, CA, USA), Thermo Fisher Scientific (Waltham, Massachusetts, United States), KAPA Biosystems (Wilmington, United States of America) and SRL (Mumbai, India). Fetal bovine serum (FBS) and PenStrep were from Gibco Invitrogen (San Diego, CA, USA). PCR reagents were obtained from KAPA Biosystems (Wilmington, United States of America). Next-Generation Sequencing (NGS) reagents were purchased from Illumina (San Diego, California, United States) and NEB (New England Biolabs, Ipswich, Massachusetts, United States). Analytical quality water collected from the MilliQ water purification system from Thermo Fisher Scientific (Waltham, Massachusetts, United States) was used throughout the study.

2.3. Methods

2.3.1 Sample collection and culture of PBMCs

We obtained 10 peripheral blood samples diagnosed with AML at the Healthcare Global Enterprises Ltd, Bengaluru, Karnataka, India. The study has been approved by the Institutional Ethics Committee of IBAB and HCG; Study no: **HIEC/48/21/08**. Informed consent was collected from all the patients participating in the study.

The Indian Acute Leukemia blood samples were collected in Anti-coagulant EDTA/HEPARIN (3-5ml each) vacutainers. PBS (equal to that of the sample) was added to the samples, followed by layering the blood on lymphocyte separation media (LSM) (1:2 LSM: Blood) along the walls of the tube and was centrifuged at 500 RCF for 30 mins. The buffy coat was collected and washed 3 times with PBS at 1000 rpm for 10 mins. The washed pellet (cells) were resuspended in 5-10 ml RPMI media and cultured inT-25 flasks at 37C with 5%CO2. After the cells reached 80% confluency, they were passaged. The cells were washed with PBS and stored at -80°C in 500 µl of Trizol Reagent.

2.3.2 DNA Extraction

Blood samples were subjected to RBC lysis using cold water treatment. Briefly, 10 times the vol of blood, ice-coldwater was added and incubated at 4°C for 5 minutes. 10x PBS was added to attain 1XPBS, and the cells were centrifuged at 6000 rpm for 10 mins. The supernatant was discarded, and the pellet containing cells (WBCs) was washed with 1x PBS at 6000 rpm (X2). DNA was isolated using DNA lysis buffer (For 100ml: NaCl 584.4 mg, 10% SDS 5 ml, Triton X-100 100µl, 0.5M EDTA 200µl, 1M Tris-HCl pH8 1ml, Proteinase K 20mg/ml) and incubated at 37C O/N. The lysed cells were then subjected to phenol-chloroform extraction, and then DNA was precipitated using absolute alcohol (2.5x volume of solution) and washed with 70% ethanol. DNA samples were then dissolved in the TE buffer.

2.3.3 Whole-genome library preparation

Whole-genome libraries were prepared using the NEBNext Ultra II FS DNA Library Prep Kit for Illumina sequencing. 500ng of genomic DNA was fragmented using Covaris, followed by end repair and adaptor ligation. The fragments were size-selected (350-500 bp) using the 0.7 volume of AMPure XP beads, then PCR enriched, followed by a final clean up. The library insert size and concentration were assessed using Agilent Tapestation and Qubit. The whole-genome library sequencing was outsourced to Medgenome, Bengaluru, Karnataka, India, to obtain 150-bp paired-end reads.

2.3.4 Total RNA Extraction

RNA extraction was carried out using Trizol Reagent (Ambion). 0.5x106 cells were resuspended in 500ul of Trizol, 1/10 vol of 2M sodium acetate(pH4) was added to the tube and mixed, followed by 100ul of chloroform. The tube was mixed vigorously and incubated on ice for 20 mins. RNA precipitation was done using an equal volume of isopropanol, and the pellet was washed with 75% ethanol. The pellet was dried and resuspended in DEPC-treated MilliQ water. RNA concentration and purity were checked using Qubit, and its integrity was examined by capillary electrophoresis (Tapestation 2200 Agilent) to ensure RNA integrity number >9 for RNA library preparation.

2.3.5 Illumina Truseq Total RNA library preparation and sequencing

For RNA-seq, libraries were prepared using Illumina TruSeq RNA Library Prep Kit v2. Briefly, the mRNA was isolated from total RNA using oligo-dT beads (NEB; New England Biolabs, Ipswich, Massachusetts, United States). The isolated mRNA was then fragmented to 200-250bp, followed by double-stranded cDNA synthesis. For adapter ligation, end repairing was done by 3' adenylation followed by ligation and PCR amplification. After constructing the libraries, their concentrations and insert sizes were detected using Qubit and Agilent Tapestation, respectively. Library sequencing was outsourced to Medgenome, Bengaluru, Karnataka, India, to obtain 150-bp paired-end reads on Illumina HiSeq X platform.

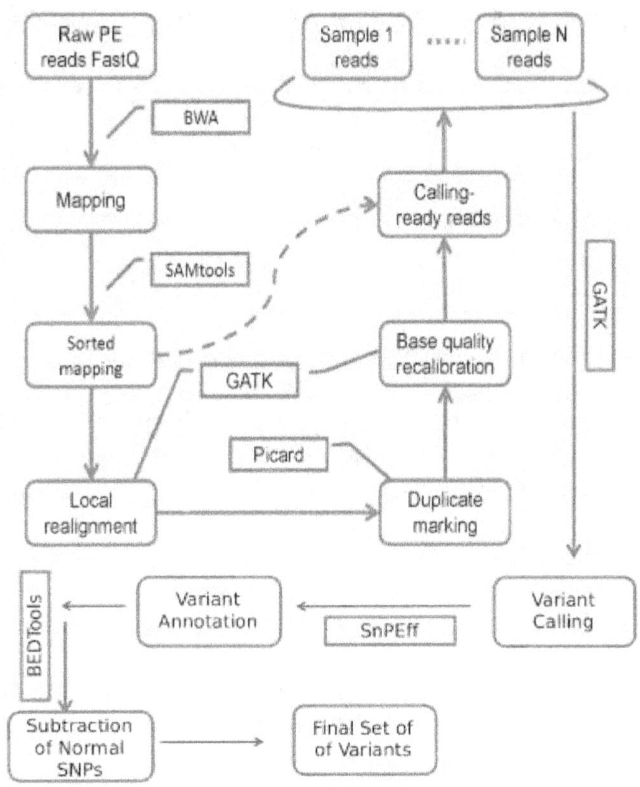

Figure 2.2: Standard GATK pipeline for Variant calling and analysis

2.3.6 Whole-exome sequencing variant analysis

Raw reads obtained from public datasets were quality checked using the FastQC (https://www.bioinformatics.babraham.ac.uk/projects/fastqc/) tool. The reads were aligned to the hg38 human genome using Bowtie2. The alignment files were processed to binary form using the SAMtools suite. PCR duplicates were removed using Picard tools (http://broadinstitute.github.io/picard/). Variant calling was performed using the best practices Mutect2 module of GATK (Genome Analysis Toolkit, Broad Institute), including local realignment around insertions/deletions and base-quality score recalibration (Figure 2.2). Variants spanned by more than 3 reads were annotated using the SnpEff and SnpSift tools[24][25]. Only the variants not present in the 1000G database were considered for further analysis[26]. Variants associated with the coding and 3'UTR regions of the genes of interest were identified for further analysis.

2.3.7 Whole-genome variant analysis

Raw reads obtained after sequencing were quality checked using the FastQC (https://www.bioinformatics.babraham.ac.uk/projects/fastqc/) tool. Illumina adapter contamination was removed using Trim Galore (https://www.bioinformatics.babraham.ac.uk/projects/trim_galore/) coupled with Cutadapt[27]. The reads were aligned to the hg38 human genome using BWA. The alignment files were processed to binary form using the SAMtools suite. PCR duplicates were removed using Picard tools (http://broadinstitute.github.io/picard/). Variant calling was performed using the best practices Mutect2 module of GATK (Genome Analysis Toolkit, Broad Institute), including local realignment around insertions/deletions and base-quality score recalibration (**Figure 2.2**). Variants spanned by more than 3 reads were annotated using the SnpEff and SnpSift tools. Only the variants not present in the 1000G database were considered for further analysis. Variants associated with the coding and 3'UTR regions of the genes of interest were identified for further analysis. All the files were merged using the BCFTools merge utility.

2.3.8 Obtaining mutation profiles

All the vcf files were primarily processed using custom shell scripts. The samples were grouped according to the tissue, blood vs bone marrow, and AML subtypes (**Table 2.1**). The vcf files of each category were merged using BCFTools. Tumor Mutational burden (Number of coding mutations /Mb) was obtained for samples across all the groups. The mutation frequency of genes implicated in AML and transcription factors involved in granulopoiesis was depicted using a waterfall plot from the R package GenVisR. CNV analysis was performed using exomeCopy in R and CNVkit. Mutation frequencies of DDR genes in coding and 3 prime UTR regions were obtained across all the subtypes and the two tissue groups. A preliminary statistic was obtained for the mutation per chromosome per subtype. The variant data was divided into i) Entire dataset and ii) DNA Repair - UTR variants. Only one variant occurrence per subtype was considered, eliminating the frequency bias of the number of samples present in each subtype. Their values were represented in a relative 100% stacked column chart.

2.3.9 Identification of 3'UTR variant signatures

Variant signatures specific and common to all the AML subtypes were obtained for genes of the DDR pathways. A holistic approach was taken to find different potential subtype signatures present in the UTR region of DNA Repair genes in leukaemia. The pipeline was designed using a three-step approach, obtaining variant frequency for better screening of variants in the samples, followed by a subtype normalization method for variants unique to variants, and cross-validate mutation signatures using Decision Tree. The data was separated into three categories:

Type	Name	Samples
M0	Undifferentiated acute myeloblastic leukemia	8
M1	Acute myeloblastic leukemia with minimal maturation	35
M2	Acute myeloblastic leukemia with maturation	6
M4	Acute myelomonocytic leukemia	9
M4 eos	Acute myelomonocytic leukemia with eosinophilia	7
M5*	Acute monocytic leukemia	1
M5A	Acute monoblastic leukemia	19
M5B	Acute promonocytic leukemia	8
NC*	Not Classified	16

Table 2.1: Subtypes with number of samples per subtype. *These were not included in the signature analysis

1. Mutations that were common to both blood and bone marrow samples
2. Mutations that were unique to either bone or blood samples
3. Unique mutations for each subtype to make waterfall plots to get a better visualization of the genes the mutations were present in each sample, classified further according to their subtypes

There was a definite subtype bias as the number of samples present in each subtype was not consistent. Hence, to eliminate this bias, the occurrences of mutations were normalized for each subtype. The normalization method used the total occurrences of these mutations across samples per subtype were counted and normalized as per c=n/s, where n=number of samples in which the mutation is found s=Total number of samples in that subtype. The machine learning algorithm, Decision Tree, was used to find potential signatures and cross-validate the most frequently mutated genes obtained from the subtype-specific signature identification. As the dataset, we dealt with varied concerning the mutation and the subtype classification, the feature selection and data optimization became essential aspects of obtaining a model with higher accuracy. The features included for this exercise were gene name, the chromosomal location of the variant, and the mutation itself (REF->ALT) as the independent variables and the subtype as the dependent variable. The three datasets to be used were

1. UTR variants (with specific cut-off to limit data points),
2. DNA Repair-UTR variants, and
3. Supervised top genes as obtained from subtype-specific waterfall plots.

The analysis was performed using python's sci-kit learn- Decision Tree Classifier (**Figure 2.3**). Since the features were all categorical, One Hot Encoding was performed; this creates a new column with the variable name and gives it a binary value (0 - Absent or 1 - Present) for the machine to understand. We identified genes as potential targets for miRNA binding in leukaemia for the genes we obtained from our signature analysis. To check whether the variants could interrupt or introduce miRNA binding sites in the 3' UTRs of target genes, we used the custom prediction utility of the miRDB database. The 3' UTR nucleotide sequences were obtained from the UCSC genome browser and submitted to the custom prediction tool of miRDB. The sequences were submitted before and after introducing the signature mutation corresponding to the gene. The results were compared for the predicted miRNA list binding to the UTRs in both cases.

2.3.10 Identification of Novel-Deleterious variants unique to the Indian Population

To check for the presence of novel variants in our data, from the merged vcf file of all the samples containing all the mutations, the first 5 columns, namely the chromosome, the position

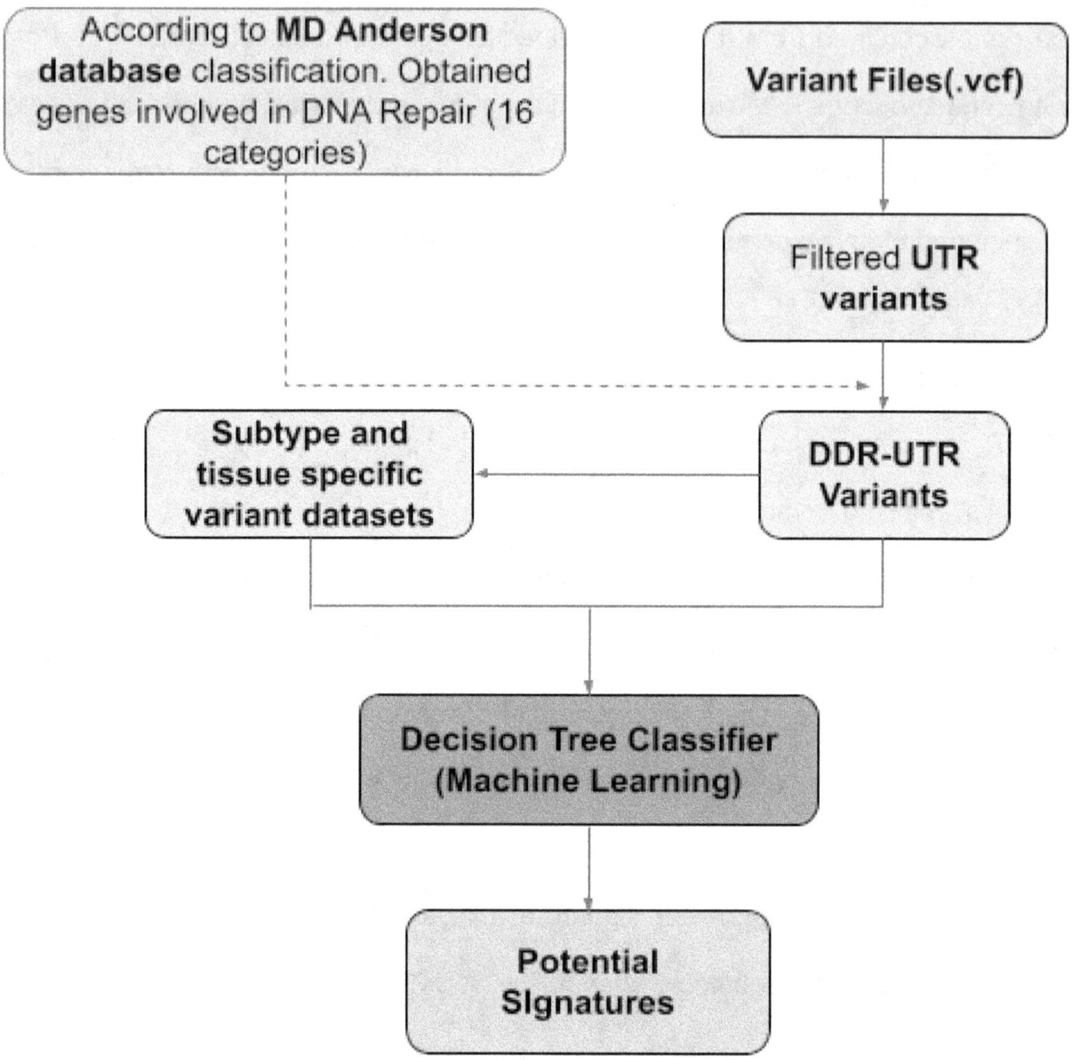

Figure 2.3: Variant Analysis for Obtaining Putative Signatures

of the mutation, reference allele, alternate allele, and the quality score were separated and uploaded onto the Ensembl Variant Effect Predictor (VEP). From the output file of VEP, the variants having neither a dbSNP -rs ID nor any COSMIC ID associated with it were filtered out and termed as novel variants. Further, the pathogenic variants were extracted based on the "deleterious" factor from Sift and the "probably_damaging" factor from the PolyPhen databases and obtained a list of genes associated with AML. These genes were uploaded onto the STRING database for pathway analysis[28].

2.3.11 Profiling of Indian Variants belonging to the DDR pathways

All the coding and non-coding variants specific to genes of the DDR pathways were extracted and profiled. From the 3' UTR mutations, those which interrupted miRNA binding sites were isolated based on the method described above.

2.3.12 Obtaining Expression profiles using transcriptome analysis

According to their isolate ids, exome-matched transcriptome samples were collected for further analysis. Two random, normal bone marrow RNA-seq samples were also considered as control. The mapping of quality-checked samples to the hg38 reference genome was performed using the splice-aware HISAT2 aligner. The alignment files are compressed to bam files, further sorted and indexed. The read counts per gene per sample were generated using the multiBamCov utility of the BEDTools suite. These counts were normalized using in-house python scripts by the TPM (Transcripts Per Million) method (**Figure 2.4**).

2.3.13 Immune cell fractions across tissues and subtypes

To determine the average immune cell fractions in all the samples using their transcriptome profiles, the samples were first grouped into bone marrow vs blood samples and various subtypes. The immune cell fractions were subsequently compared between groups using the online tool CYBERSORTx. CYBERSORTx has a predetermined set of signature genes defined for every immune cell type and their standard expression values known as the Lm22 matrix. On uploading your transcriptome data into the software, it is compared to the Lm22 matrix, and the percentage of immune cell fraction in every sample is determined (**Figure 2.5**).

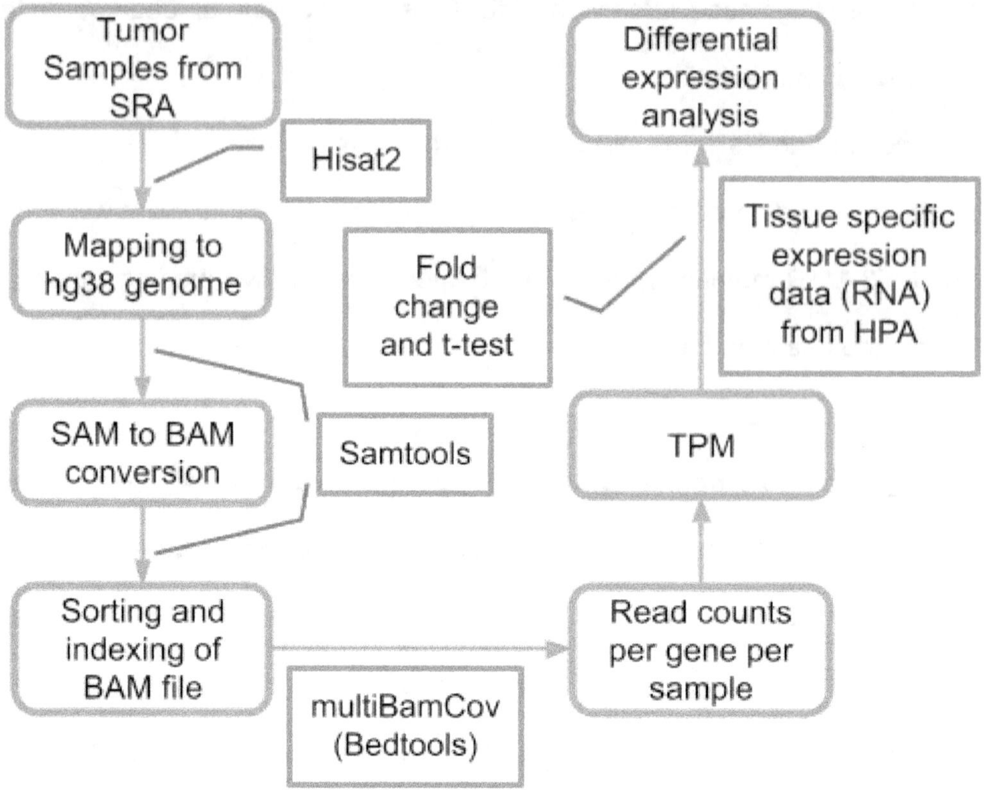

Figure 2.4: Transcriptome analysis pipeline for public dataset

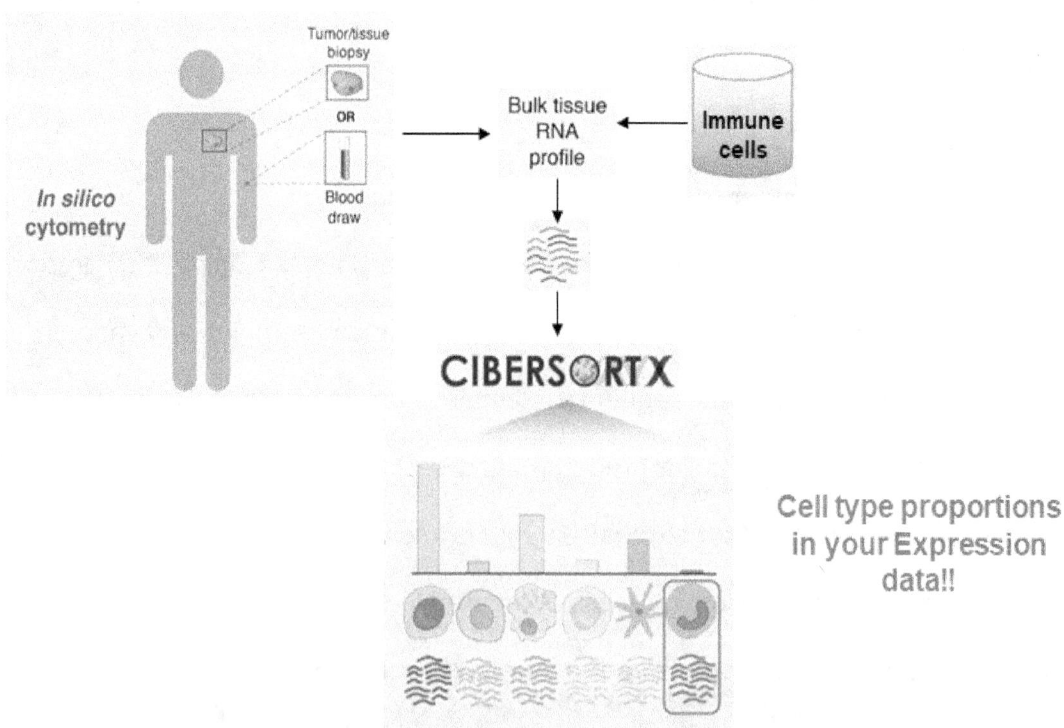

Fig 2.5: Working of CIBERSORTx with user's expression data

2.3.14 Correlate expression patterns in tissue groups to Immune cell fraction

To correlate gene expression data of samples from blood and bone marrow groups with their respective immune cell fractions, we used the R package WGCNA. It starts by constructing a gene co-expression network followed by identifying gene modules based on hierarchical clustering. It correlates these modules to the clinical data/parameters provided by the user and provides correlations values along with the significance of the correlation. The user can then select the most significantly correlated parameter-module pair and proceed with pathway analysis or network analysis of the genes in the module (**Figure 2.6**).

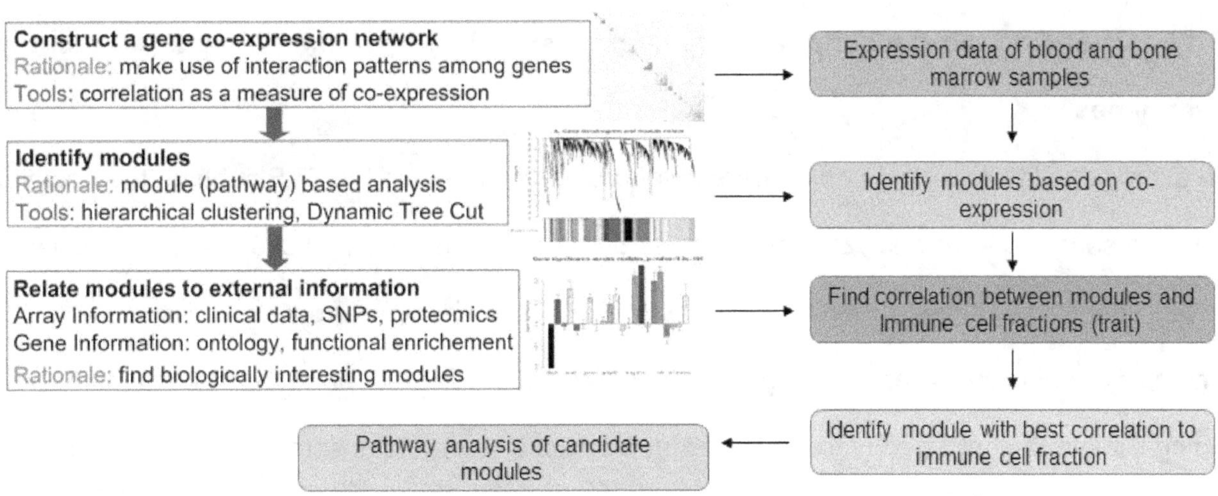

Figure 2.6: Working of WGCNA to correlate co-expression of genes with traits

2.3.15 Identifying lncRNA sponges against miRNA specific to target genes

The Gencode lncRNA gtf file [29] was downloaded and their readcounts were calculated using the bedtools suite. Subtype specific lncRNA were identified using differential expresion analysis. The potential binding sites of candidate miRNA seed sequences on to the lncRNA were identified using inhouse shell scripts and the binding was checked in-silico using the online IntaRNA tool [30].

2.3.16 Transcriptome analysis of Indian Acute Leukemia Samples

Raw reads obtained after sequencing were quality checked using FastQC and trimmed off sequencing adapters using Trim Galore. Quality checked reads were aligned with the standard paired-end alignment options to the human hg38 genome using the STAR aligner. The sorted alignment files were indexed using SAMTools, and the read counts were generated using the multiBamCov utility of the BEDTools suite. Normalized TPM values were calculated from the read counts using in-house python scripts. Fusion genes were identified in the samples using the STAR-Fusion aligner.

2.3.17 Correlating the transcriptome (gene expression) with exome (variants) to identify driver genes

The expression levels of all samples were categorized according to the FAB subtype they belong to. These samples were analyzed for all genes of interest. The log2-fold change was calculated between genes of interest expression values in the normal bone marrow and all samples. The samples were also classified according to the mutations and filtered for mutations only at miRNA binding sites in the genes of interest. The expression changes across samples with mutation and without mutations were tested for significance (p-value) using a t-test to obtain significant mutations in genes of interest.

2.3.18 Lasso-cox regression and ROC analysis

We obtained matched data of survival and mRNA expression from the TARGET database, which was fed to lasso-cox regression analysis and for correlational analysis of gene expression with survival to get a powerful combination of genes that could help us predict the survivability of patients. "LASSO" is a linear form of regularization technique (to minimize the error because of overfitting data while constructing a model). As the name suggests, it uses a "shrinkage/penalty term(lambda)" in its regression equation to be able to predict with accuracy and precision. This is a good method to reduce the variables/features present in the dataset and choose significant features (ex: genes). The usage of Lasso regression on cox survival analysis is a good way to predict the possible features in a condition or event (like death, recurrence, etc.) for any disease; therefore, we applied this analysis to our survival data, which gave us significant genes that were involved with survival. This was achieved by using the "sksurv" or "scikit-survival" module of python, present as a part of "scikit-learn". The accuracy of a prognostic model combining the survival data of the signature genes of interest was predicted using Receiver Operating Curve (ROC) Analysis. The genes were also checked for differences in their survival probabilities based expression patterns using Damage-Net tool [31].

2.3.19 Creating a database of RAG regulators during B, T cell development and leukaemia

Publicly available Total RNA and small RNA Transcriptome Sequencing data from Human and mouse B and T cell developmental stages and T-ALL and CLL Leukemia and AML.

2.3.20 Computation of Transcript Expression

Raw reads from the small RNA sequencing datasets were checked for their quality using the FastQC. Based on the Phred score quality cut-off, low-quality reads were trimmed from both the ends keeping a minimum of 18 nucleotides from an initial read length of 26-36 nucleotides. Post trimming, the reads were mapped to the mouse reference (mm10) and human reference (hg38) genome, respectively, using the Bowtie2 aligner. The SAM files were converted to compressed BAM format using the SAMtools package. The read counts per miRNA transcript were obtained using the BEDtools suite to quantify the expression. The read counts were normalized using the RPM method, i.e., RPM = number of reads mapped per transcript/(total number of mapped reads/106). The rpm values were extracted and analyzed for differences in expression. The miRNA known to regulate RAG1 and RAG2 were obtained from miRDB and TargetScan. The miRNAs targeting RAGs were obtained based on a custom prediction available in the databases based on the presence of seed sequences that bind to the 3'UTR of RAG1 and RAG2. The shortlisted miRNA was then checked for their expression in the small-RNA datasets. For the T-ALL and CLL patients' datasets, Normalized Read count files for miRNA transcripts and mRNA transcripts from 15 CLL patients were downloaded from the GEO datasets (Table). The GEO database downloaded raw read count files for miRNA and mRNA transcripts for 48 T-ALL patients. RPM values for miRNA and RPKM values for mRNA were calculated for both the datasets using the following formulae, RPM = read count/(total number of reads mapped/106) and RPKM = read count/(transcript length/1000) ∗(total number of reads mapped/106). The normalized values for RAG1, its interacting partners, and the miRNA known to regulate RAG1 were plotted in a heatmap using the pheatmap package in R.

2.3.21 Database Framework

The database has been structured and constructed using the Shiny package from RStudio (https://shiny.rstudio.com/). The application works on static TSV/CSV files resulting from the expression data analysis. The application is written in 3 separate R files, namely ui.R, server.R, and global.R. The ui.R renders the user interface, whereas server.R does data processing per user input and global.R reads all CSV files required for the database (**Figure 2.7**).

2.3.22 Statistical Analysis

All statistical tests were performed using R. Pearson correlation was performed to correlate eigen modules with clinical parameters in WGCNA analysis. Student's t-test was performed to compare Tmbs between blood and bone marrow groups, to compare the difference in target gene expression between patients with and without 3'UTR mutations. The log-rank and Wilcoxon tests are performed to compare the differences between survival groups. DESeq2

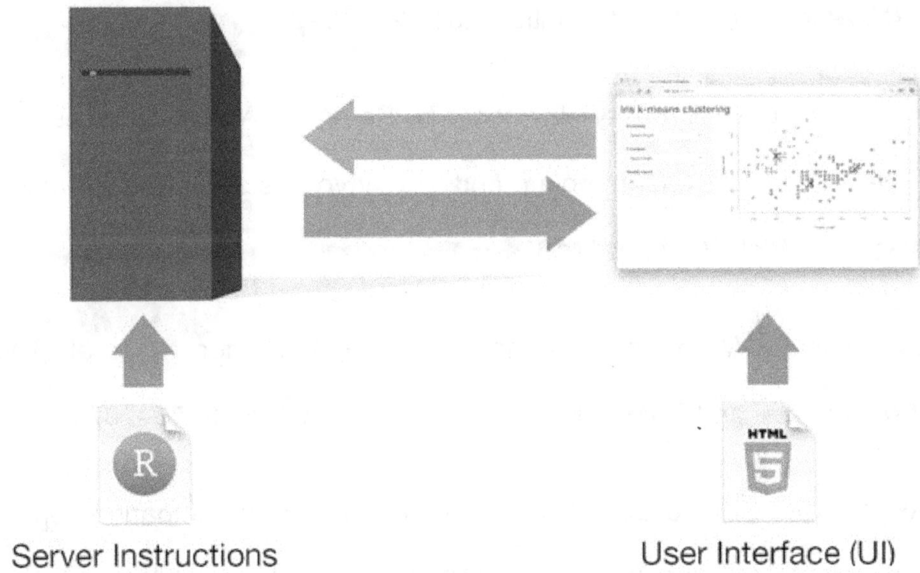

Figure 2.7: Working on Shiny R application

internally uses student's t-test and negative binomial distribution to obtain significantly differentially expressed genes. Values with a p-value less than 0.05 are considered to be significant.

2.4. References

1. Langmead B, Salzberg SL. Fast gapped-read alignment with Bowtie 2. Nature Methods. 2012. pp. 357–359. doi:10.1038/nmeth.1923

2. Li H, Durbin R. Fast and accurate short read alignment with Burrows-Wheeler transform. Bioinformatics. 2009;25: 1754–1760.

3. Kim D, Paggi JM, Park C, Bennett C, Salzberg SL. Graph-based genome alignment and genotyping with HISAT2 and HISAT-genotype. Nature Biotechnology. 2019. pp. 907–915. doi:10.1038/s41587-019-0201-4

4. Dobin A, Davis CA, Schlesinger F, Drenkow J, Zaleski C, Jha S, et al. STAR: ultrafast

universal RNA-seq aligner. Bioinformatics. 2013;29: 15–21.

5. Haas BJ, Dobin A, Li B, Stransky N, Pochet N, Regev A. Accuracy assessment of fusion transcript detection via read-mapping and de novo fusion transcript assembly-based methods. Genome Biol. 2019;20: 1–16.

6. Li H, Handsaker B, Wysoker A, Fennell T, Ruan J, Homer N, et al. The Sequence Alignment/Map format and SAMtools. Bioinformatics. 2009;25: 2078–2079.

7. Quinlan AR, Hall IM. BEDTools: a flexible suite of utilities for comparing genomic features. Bioinformatics. 2010. pp. 841–842. doi:10.1093/bioinformatics/btq033

8. Danecek P, Bonfield JK, Liddle J, Marshall J, Ohan V, Pollard MO, et al. Twelve years of SAMtools and BCFtools. Gigascience. 2021;10. doi:10.1093/gigascience/giab008

9. DePristo MA, Banks E, Poplin R, Garimella KV, Maguire JR, Hartl C, et al. A framework for variation discovery and genotyping using next-generation DNA sequencing data. Nature Genetics. 2011. pp. 491–498. doi:10.1038/ng.806

10. Website. Available: Lee, K., Jeong, Ho., Lee, S. et al. CPEM: Accurate cancer type classification based on somatic alterations using an ensemble of a random forest and a deep neural network. Sci Rep 9, 16927 (2019). https://doi.org/10.1038/s41598-019-53034-3

11. Tibshirani R. THE LASSO METHOD FOR VARIABLE SELECTION IN THE COX MODEL. Statistics in Medicine. 1997. pp. 385–395. doi:10.1002/(sici)1097-0258(19970228)16:4<385::aid-sim380>3.0.co;2-3

12. Talevich E, Hunter Shain A, Botton T, Bastian BC. CNVkit: Genome-Wide Copy Number Detection and Visualization from Targeted DNA Sequencing. PLOS Computational Biology. 2016. p. e1004873. doi:10.1371/journal.pcbi.1004873

13. Kent WJ, Sugnet CW, Furey TS, Roskin KM, Pringle TH, Zahler AM, et al. The human genome browser at UCSC. Genome Res. 2002;12: 996–1006.

14. Karolchik D, Hinrichs AS, Furey TS, Roskin KM, Sugnet CW, Haussler D, et al. The UCSC Table Browser data retrieval tool. Nucleic Acids Res. 2004;32: D493–6.

15. Wang X. miRDB: A microRNA target prediction and functional annotation database with a wiki interface. RNA. 2008. pp. 1012–1017. doi:10.1261/rna.965408

16. Griffiths-Jones S. The microRNA Registry. Nucleic Acids Research. 2004. p. 109D–111. doi:10.1093/nar/gkh023

17. Agarwal V, Bell GW, Nam J-W, Bartel DP. Predicting effective microRNA target sites in mammalian mRNAs. Elife. 2015;4. doi:10.7554/eLife.05005

18. Newman AM, Steen CB, Liu CL, Gentles AJ, Chaudhuri AA, Scherer F, et al. Determining cell type abundance and expression from bulk tissues with digital cytometry. Nat Biotechnol. 2019;37: 773–782.

19. Metsalu T, Vilo J. ClustVis: a web tool for visualizing clustering of multivariate data using Principal Component Analysis and heatmap. Nucleic Acids Res. 2015;43: W566–70.

20. Skidmore ZL, Wagner AH, Lesurf R, Campbell KM, Kunisaki J, Griffith OL, et al. GenVisR: Genomic Visualizations in R. Bioinformatics. 2016. pp. 3012–3014. doi:10.1093/bioinformatics/btw325

21. Langfelder P, Horvath S. WGCNA: an R package for weighted correlation network analysis. BMC Bioinformatics. 2008. doi:10.1186/1471-2105-9-559

22. Love MI, Huber W, Anders S. Moderated estimation of fold change and dispersion for RNA-seq data with DESeq2. Genome Biol. 2014;15: 550.

23. Wilkinson L. ggplot2: Elegant Graphics for Data Analysis by WICKHAM, H. Biometrics. 2011. pp. 678–679. doi:10.1111/j.1541-0420.2011.01616.x

24. Cingolani P, Platts A, Wang LL, Coon M, Nguyen T, Wang L, et al. A program for annotating and predicting the effects of single nucleotide polymorphisms, SnpEff. Fly. 2012. pp. 80–92. doi:10.4161/fly.19695

25. Cingolani P, Patel VM, Coon M, Nguyen T, Land SJ, Ruden DM, et al. Using Drosophila melanogaster as a Model for Genotoxic Chemical Mutational Studies with a New Program, SnpSift. Front Genet. 2012;3: 35.

26. Fairley S, Lowy-Gallego E, Perry E, Flicek P. The International Genome Sample Resource (IGSR) collection of open human genomic variation resources. Nucleic Acids Res. 2019;48: D941–D947.

27. Martin M. Cutadapt removes adapter sequences from high-throughput sequencing reads. EMBnet.journal. 2011. p. 10. doi:10.14806/ej.17.1.200

28. Szklarczyk D, Gable AL, Nastou KC, Lyon D, Kirsch R, Pyysalo S, et al. The STRING database in 2021: customizable protein-protein networks, and functional characterization of user-uploaded gene/measurement sets. Nucleic Acids Res. 2021;49: D605–D612.

29. Frankish A, Diekhans M, Jungreis I, Lagarde J, Loveland JE, Mudge JM, et al. GENCODE 2021. Nucleic Acids Res. 2021;49: D916–D923.

30. Mann M, Wright PR, Backofen R. IntaRNA 2.0: enhanced and customizable prediction of RNA-RNA interactions. Nucleic Acids Res. 2017;45: W435–W439.

31. Bader AS, Bushell M. Damage-Net: A program for DNA repair meta-analysis identifies a network of novel repair genes that facilitate cancer evolution. DNA Repair . 2021;105: 103158.

Chapter 3: Identify mutations in coding and non-coding regions of genes implicated in the DNA Damage and Repair Pathway from Acute Leukemia patient samples available from public databases.

3.1 INTRODUCTION

Acute myeloid leukemia is (AML) characterized by clonal proliferation of hematopoietic stem cells or progenitor cells and abnormal differentiation of myeloid progenitor cells [1,2]. Among four types of leukemia are CLL, CML, ALL, and AML[3,4]. AML is observed in older people (>60 years of age) and is prevalent in the Asian population[1]. AML develops rapidly and is associated with bone marrow failure and can be fatal if left untreated. AML is a highly heterogeneous disease [5], and subtypes of AML have mainly been based on 1) the maturation stage, morphology, and granulocytic stage of the myeloid cell population (FAB classification), and 2) recurring chromosomal abnormalities (WHO classification).

In many bone marrow failure syndromes, patients develop MDS (myelodysplasia) or (acute myeloid leukemia) AML[6]. Also, severe congenital neutropenia (SCN) patients, an inherited disorder of granulopoiesis, have an increased risk of developing MDS/AML[7]. The process of neutrophil/granulocyte regulation and maturation, known as emergency granulopoiesis (EG), going haywire is a known phenomenon in leukemic conditions[8,9]. The central mechanism of dysregulated granulopoiesis is not very well understood in leukemia patients, but there are several transcription factors, that function at the junction of granulopoiesis and leukemia progression[10]. One of the contributing factors observed in AML is damage to the DNA in the bone marrow. The damaged cells in bone marrow can transform into abnormal, cancerous cells, called blasts or myeloblasts. In AML, 50% of the patients present with chromosomal anomalies and exhibit genomic instability[11]. Mutations in ATM (ataxia telangiectasia mutated) gene have been observed in several cancers, including acute leukemia[12]. AML pathogenesis can be partly explained by defects in DNA repair, which could lead to defects in myeloid progenitors leading to neutropenia, which has been observed in preleukemic states or relapsed AML and reduced G-CSF production, leading to a decrease in proliferation of normal bone marrow cells and proliferation of myeloblasts[13,14]. The faulty DNA repair interplay leads to low levels of differentiated myeloblast/ granulopoiesis, which develops into AML or ALL, leading to neutropenia[13,14]. Mutations in several genes in the neutrophil development and differentiation and DNA repair genes have been studied in AML using Whole-exome sequencing[14,15]. Understanding variants in the regulatory region of the genome 5' and 3'UTR is crucial for understanding leukemogenesis. Several mutations in the 3'UTR regions affecting miRNA-binding sites have been reported in several cancers that correlate with clinical parameters like reduced overall and disease-free survival, poor prognosis, recurrence, etc.[16,17].

The disease burden or minimal residual disease after treatment in leukemic patients during follow-up is usually done using flow cytometry techniques but there are merging pieces of evidence that blood could be used for immunophenotyping. The presence of MRD in blood correlated with relapse within a year vs that in bone marrow [18]. There is initial evidence pointing toward better outcomes in pediatric AML where the assessment of risk is based on MRD and genetics in pediatric AML [19]. In an initial assessment of 50 patients' sequencing data, the presence of mutations in the patients under remission predicted a worse outcome [20].

This study aimed to identify a clonal population of cells in blood and bone marrow using mutations in the genes involved in granulopoiesis and DNA damage response. The focus of the study was to identify mutations in 3'UTR of the DDR genes and identify subtype-specific mutations. Further evaluation of subtype-specific signatures at the chromosomal level was performed to identify chromosomal signatures of AML subtypes. We have identified subtype-specific signatures in Neutropenia and DDR pathways genes in AML patients using public exome data. We have explored somatic mutations in 3'UTR regions of critical genes and identified subtype-specific DNA repair pathway mutations. Using sequential curation and machine learning algorithms, we have obtained two genes, MRE11A and UBE2A, with 3'UTR variants specific to the M1 subtype that could have potential regulatory implications. The signatures might help guide therapies and the identification of potential targets that can be developed as therapeutics.

3.2 RESULTS

3.2.1. Characterization of Tumor Mutation Burden, Signatures associated with Neutropenia, in blood and bone marrow across AML subtypes

Variant analysis was performed on 109 AML exome samples from the publicly available study PRJNA358716. The average number of reads, of length 100, was 90.5 million with an average alignment percentage per sample being 98.61%. To identify if there was a chromosome bias for mutations, we analyzed the mutations from all the samples. The density of mutations was highest in ChrX (average 3206) followed by Chr1 (average 2080), while Chr18 (average 367) and ChrY (average 160) had the least number of variants (Figure 3.1). We were interested in identifying signatures associated with different types of AML in terms of no. of mutations across the genome (Tumour mutation burden) and checking if blood and bone marrow represented differences in no. of mutations. The tumor mutational burden was higher in bone marrow samples as compared to blood samples, and between subtypes, the average Tmb was highest in M4 and lowest in M0 (Figure 3.2).

To obtain mutation profiles associated with genes affected in AML, a waterfall plot was generated of the genes with somatic mutations encompassing frameshift (high impact), missense mutations (moderate impact), and 5' and 3'UTR, etc (Figure 3.2). Genes involved in cell cycle proliferation, regulation, chromatin modification, etc., which are used to identify and classify AML, like DNMT3A, NPM1, FLT3, TET2, and IDH2 showed a mutation frequency of 20-40%, where mutations in these genes co-occurred in patients, whereas transcription factors and known oncogenes like KRAS, KIT, ASXL1, TP53, RUNX1, etc., had a frequency of 10-20%. Interestingly, a key classification gene, CEBPA, had the lowest frequency of ~3%. Analysis of subtypes' specific mutations led to the identification of the absence of TP53 mutations in the M1 subtype and ASXL1 in the M2 and M4 subtypes (Figure 3.3).

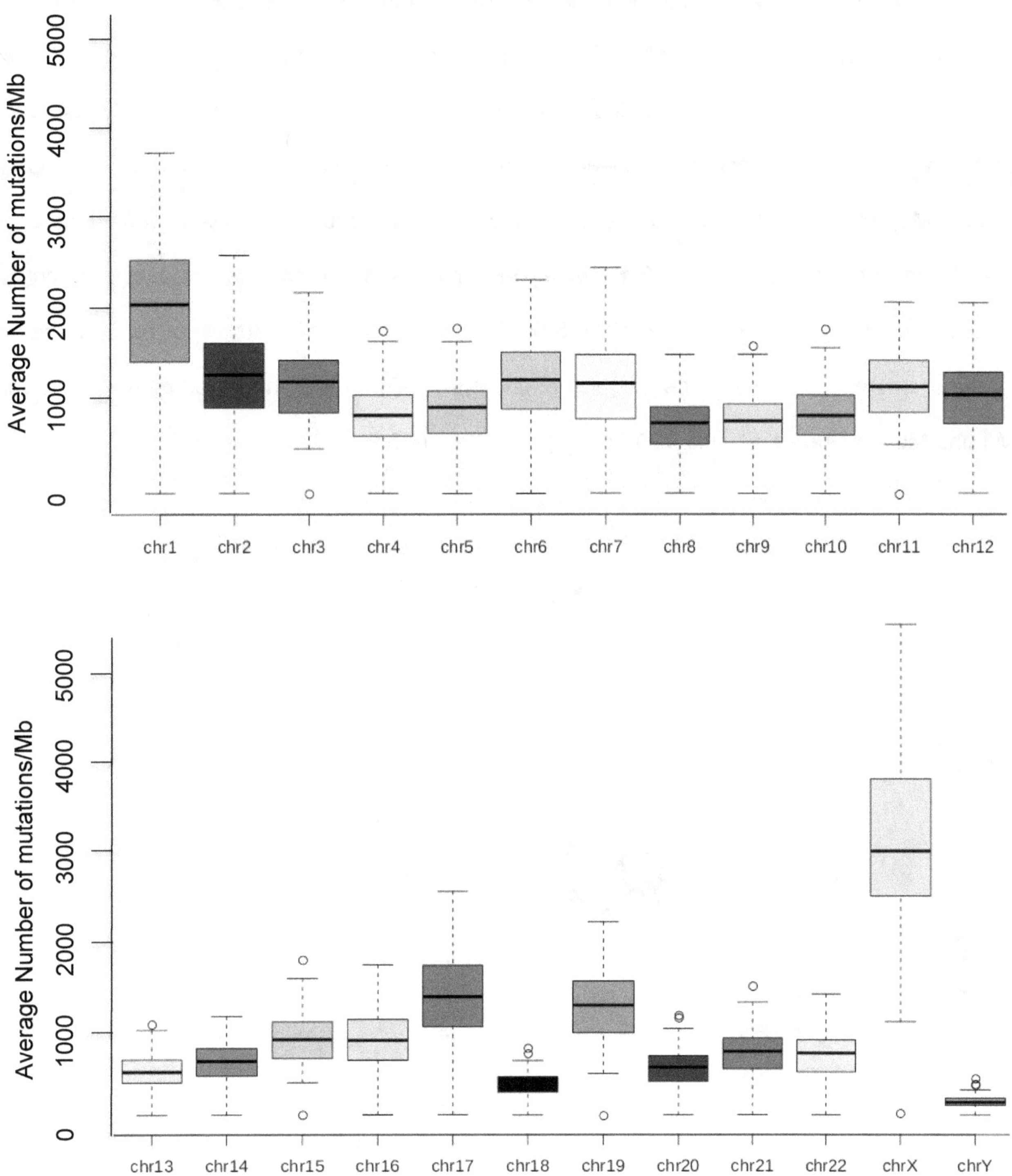

Figure 3.1: Aggregate number of mutations for all the AML samples per Mb in all the chromosomes chrX shows the highest number of mutations with the highest number of variations between samples, with the next highest being chr1.

To identify Neutropenia/Granulopoiesis signatures in AML, we first started by determining the mutation frequency of genes involved in neutropenia/granulopoiesis. AHNAK, HLA-DRB5, and ELANE genes were frequently mutated with a frequency of 50-60% across all subtypes. Clear tissue specificity was observed between blood and bone marrow samples, where XCR1, CEACAM1, and ITGAM mutations were specific to blood samples and HAX1 mutations were specific to bone marrow (Figure 3.4), while on comparison across different subtypes, critical transcription factors of granulopoiesis like STAT3 and RARA were mutated specifically in the M5 subtype. Interestingly, one of the diagnostic markers of AML, MPO, harbored mutations in only M0 and M5 subtypes, known to be MPO negative (Figure 3.5).

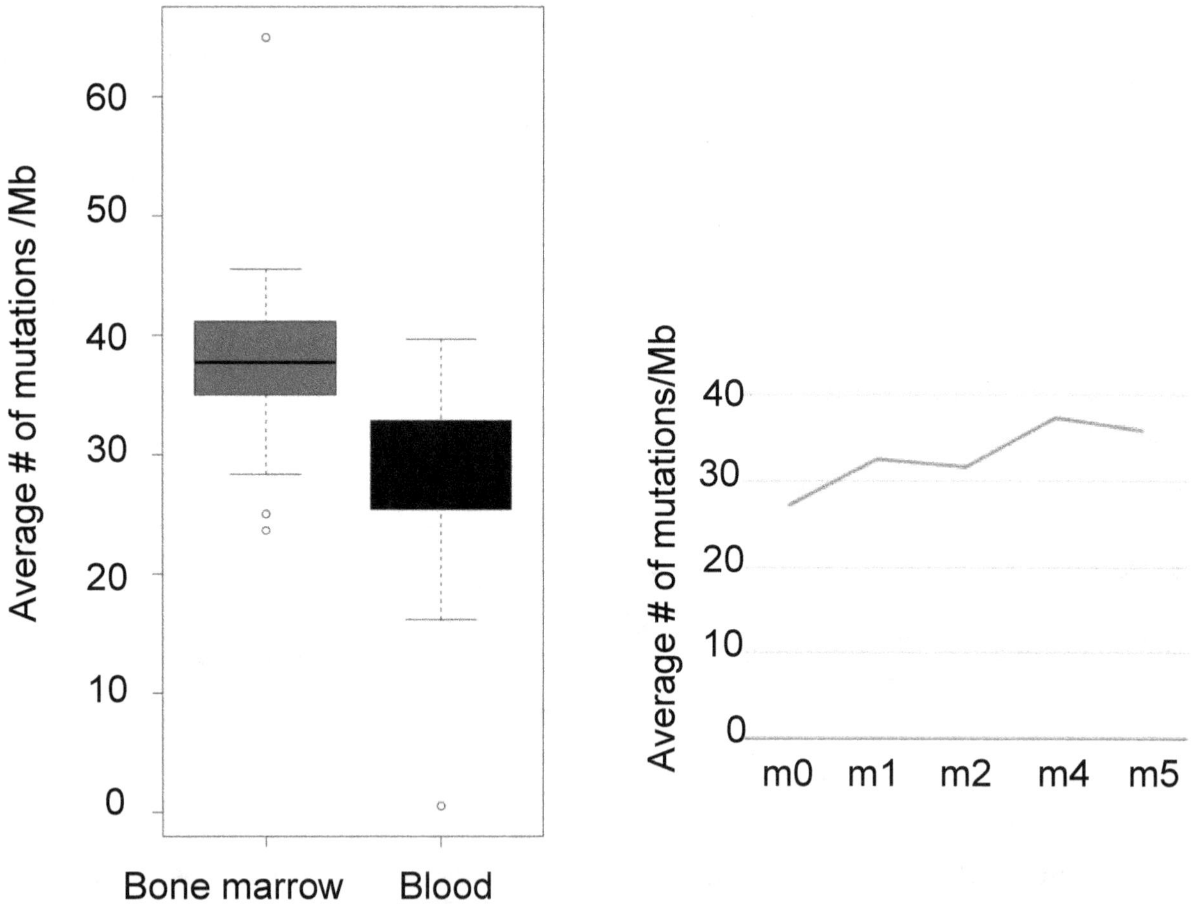

Figure 3.2: Comparison of the mutation load between Bone marrow and Blood and across AML subtypes

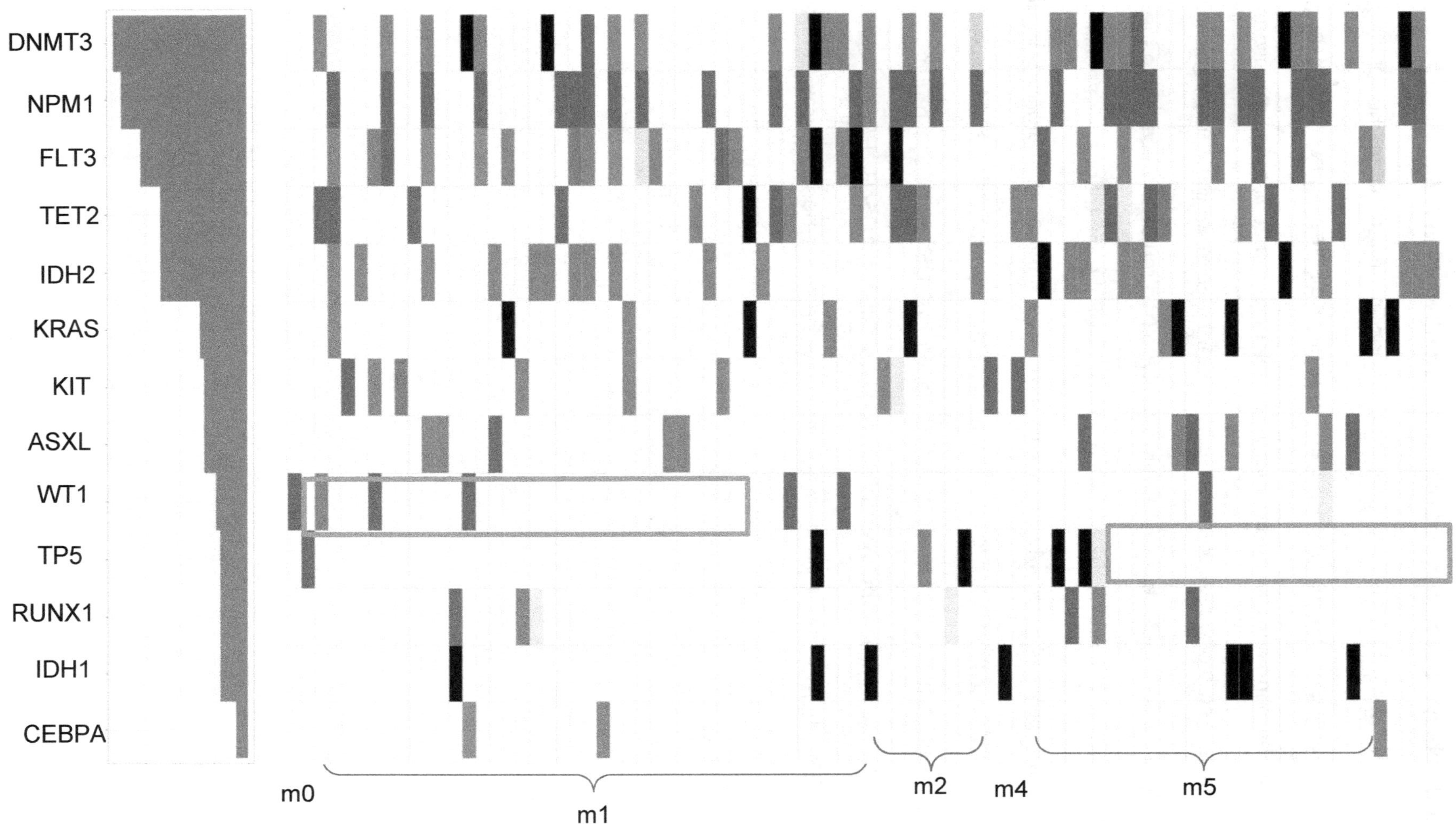

Figure 3.3: A waterfall plot showing mutation frequency of genes known to be implicated in AML, across different AML subtypes.

3.2.2. Tissue and subtype-specific mutations in DDR pathways in AML.

To understand if there were subtype and tissue type-specific mutations in the DDR genes, mutations in DDR pathway genes were cataloged and the analysis revealed that 63% of the genes were mutated both in the bone marrow and blood, whereas 11% and 26% of the mutations were unique to bone marrow and blood respectively (Figure 3.6). HR and BER pathway genes were mutated specifically in the M1 subtype, while the M5 subtype had mutations specific to the NER, HR, and MMEJ pathways (Figure 3.7). Mutation analysis of the mutations in specific DDR pathways revealed subtypes M1 and M5 carry the maximum number of mutations in all the pathways whereas the M4 subtype is the least mutated. The observation that the M4 subtype with the highest mutation burden had the least mutated genes in DDR pathways requires further investigation. Mutually exclusive mutations in the genes POLK, RAD54B, ERCC4 and ATR, PMS2, RPA3, PRKDC, PDS5B, and LIG4 were observed between bone marrow and blood, indicating clones of cells in the peripheral blood were not similar to ones in the bone marrow (Figure 3.8).

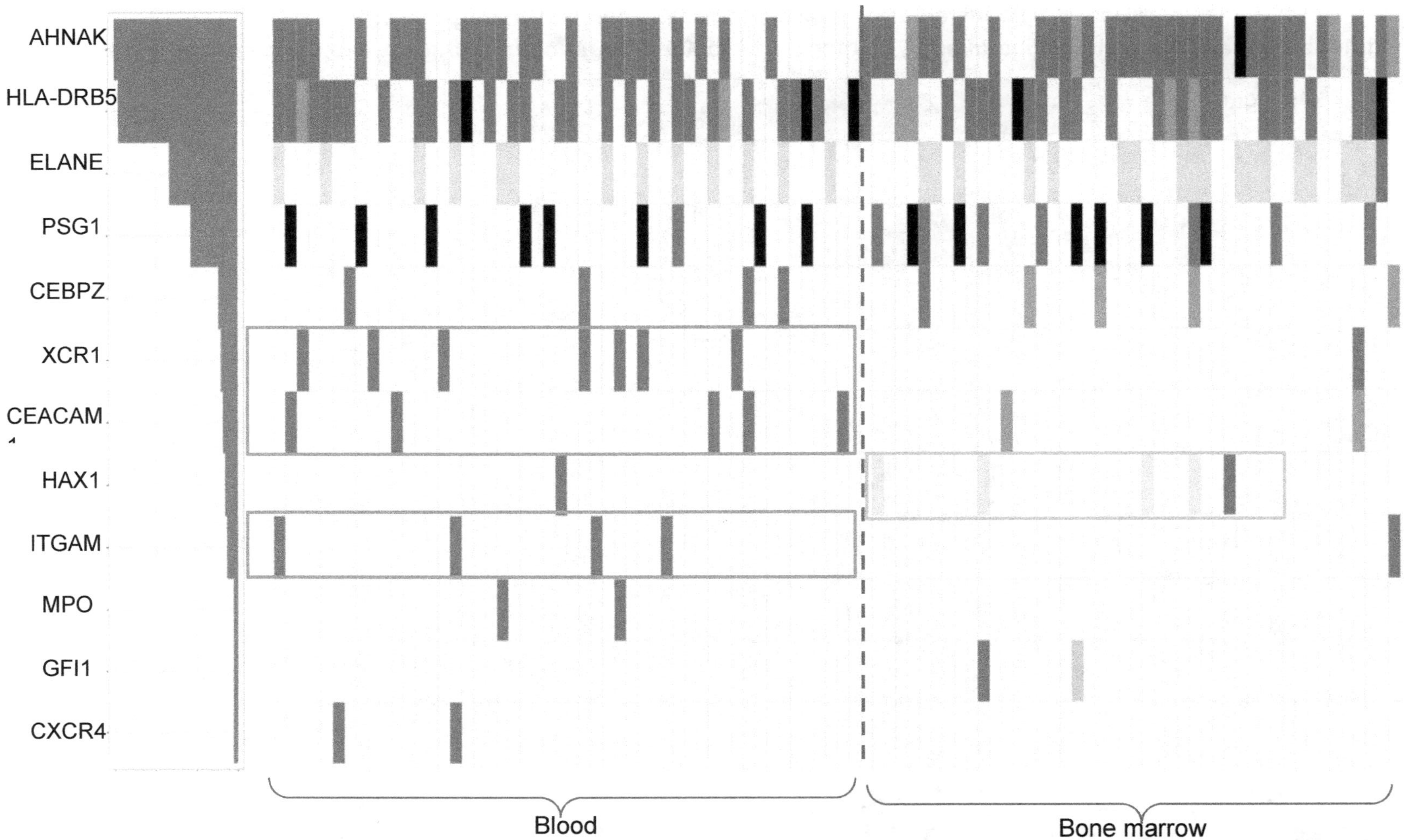

Figure 3.4: A waterfall plot showing mutation frequency of genes known to be implicated in neutropenia/granulopoiesis between blood and bone marrow samples

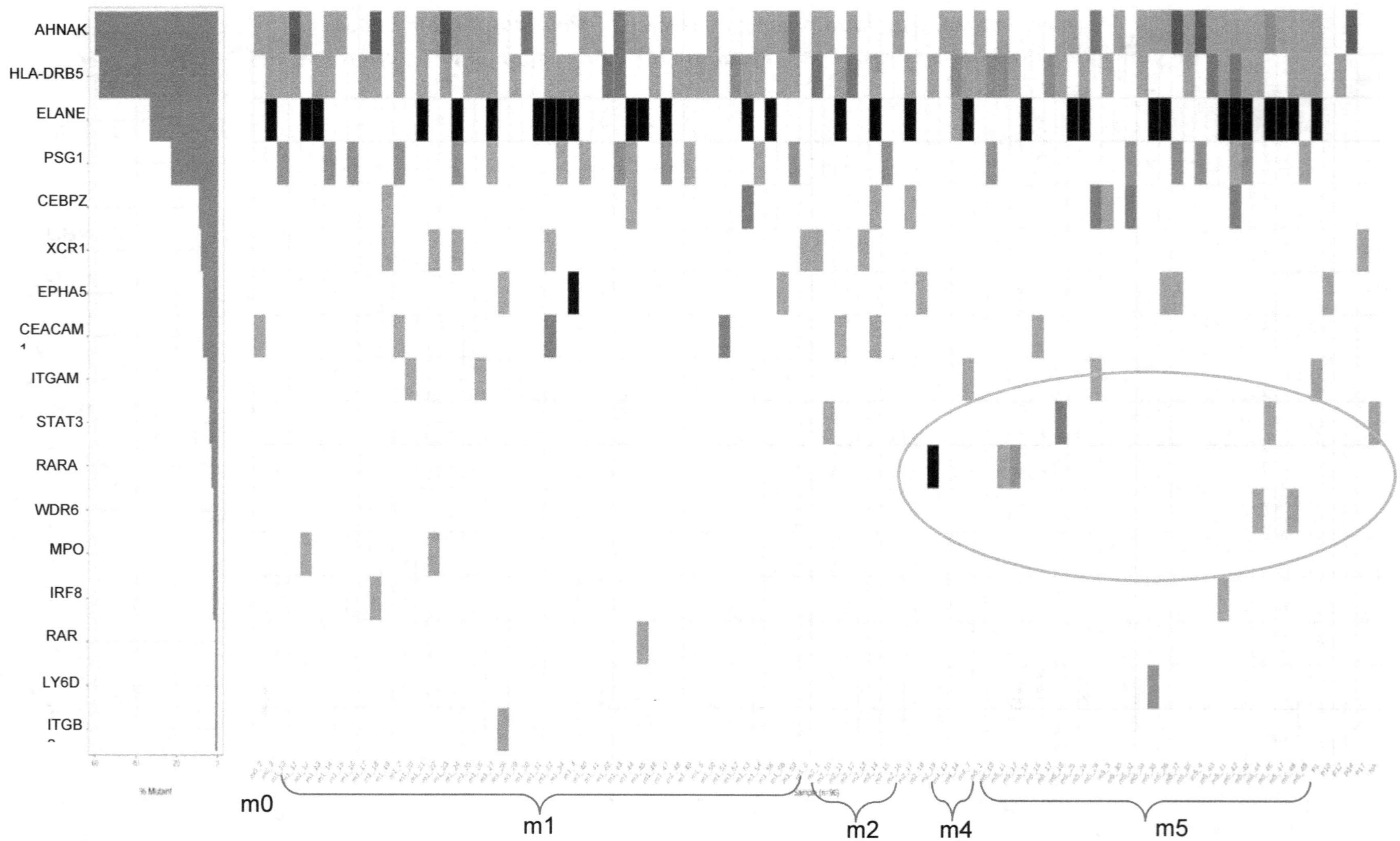

Figure 3.5: A waterfall plot showing mutation frequency of genes known to be implicated in neutropenia/granulopoiesis across different subtypes with discernable subtype specific patterns

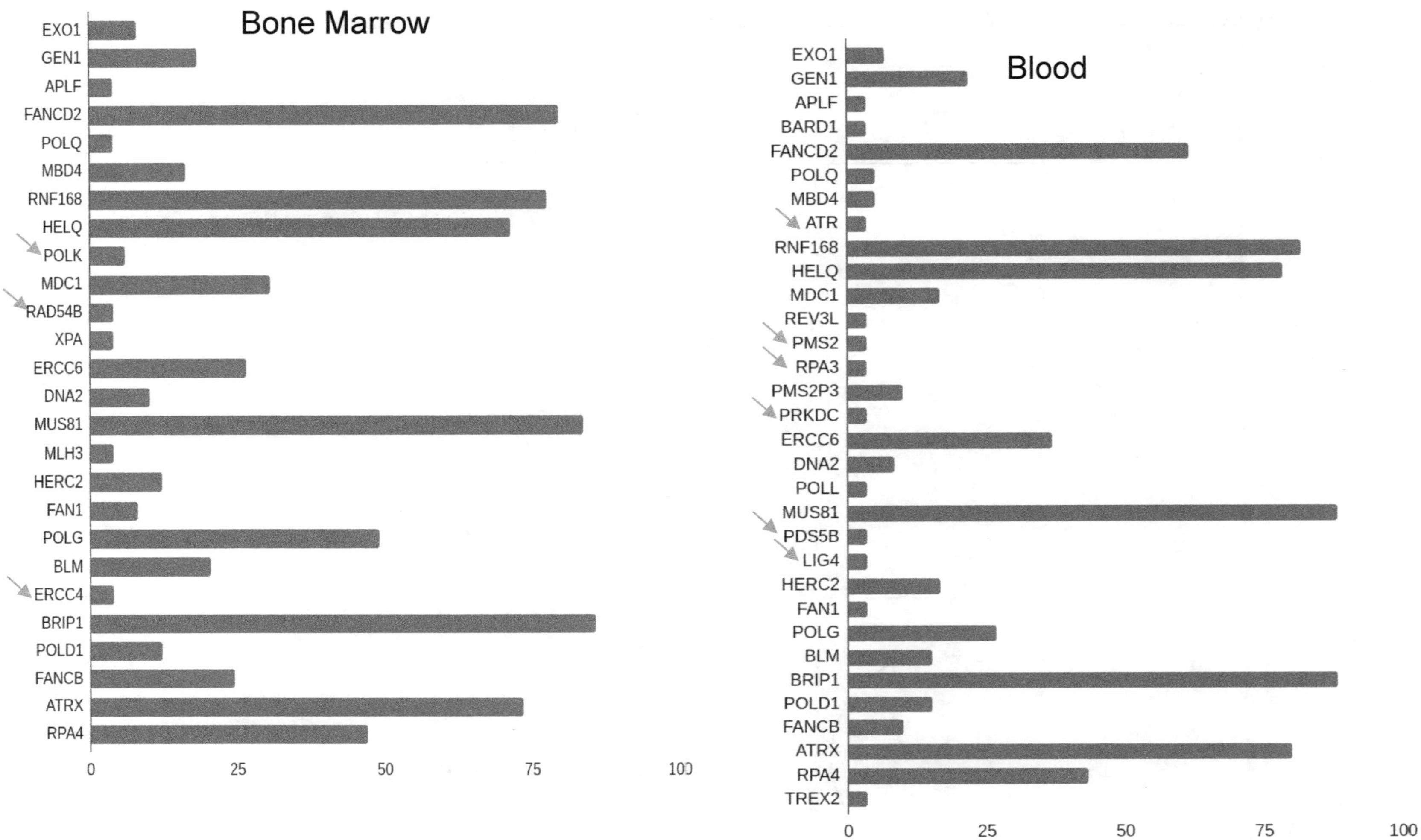

Figure 3.6: Two bar graphs showing mutation frequency of DDR genes in Bone marrow (left) vs Blood (right). It can be seen that 63% of genes with mutations are common to blood and bone marrow, while 11% is unique to bone marrow (HR and Excision repair) and 26% unique to blood (NHEJ)

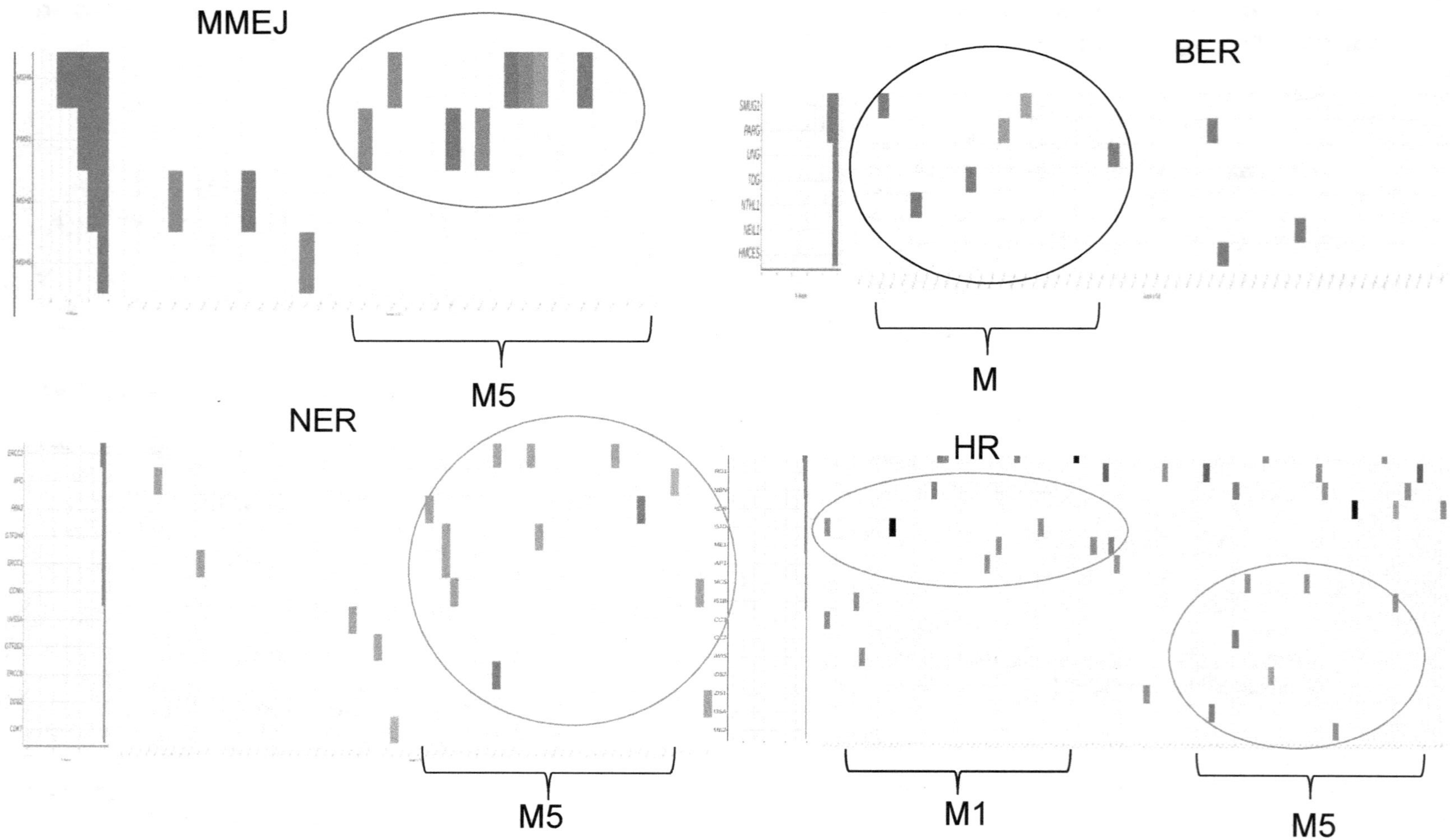

Figure 3.7: DDR pathway Waterfall plots - Top to bottom; left to right HR, NER, BER and MMEJ across different AML subtypes

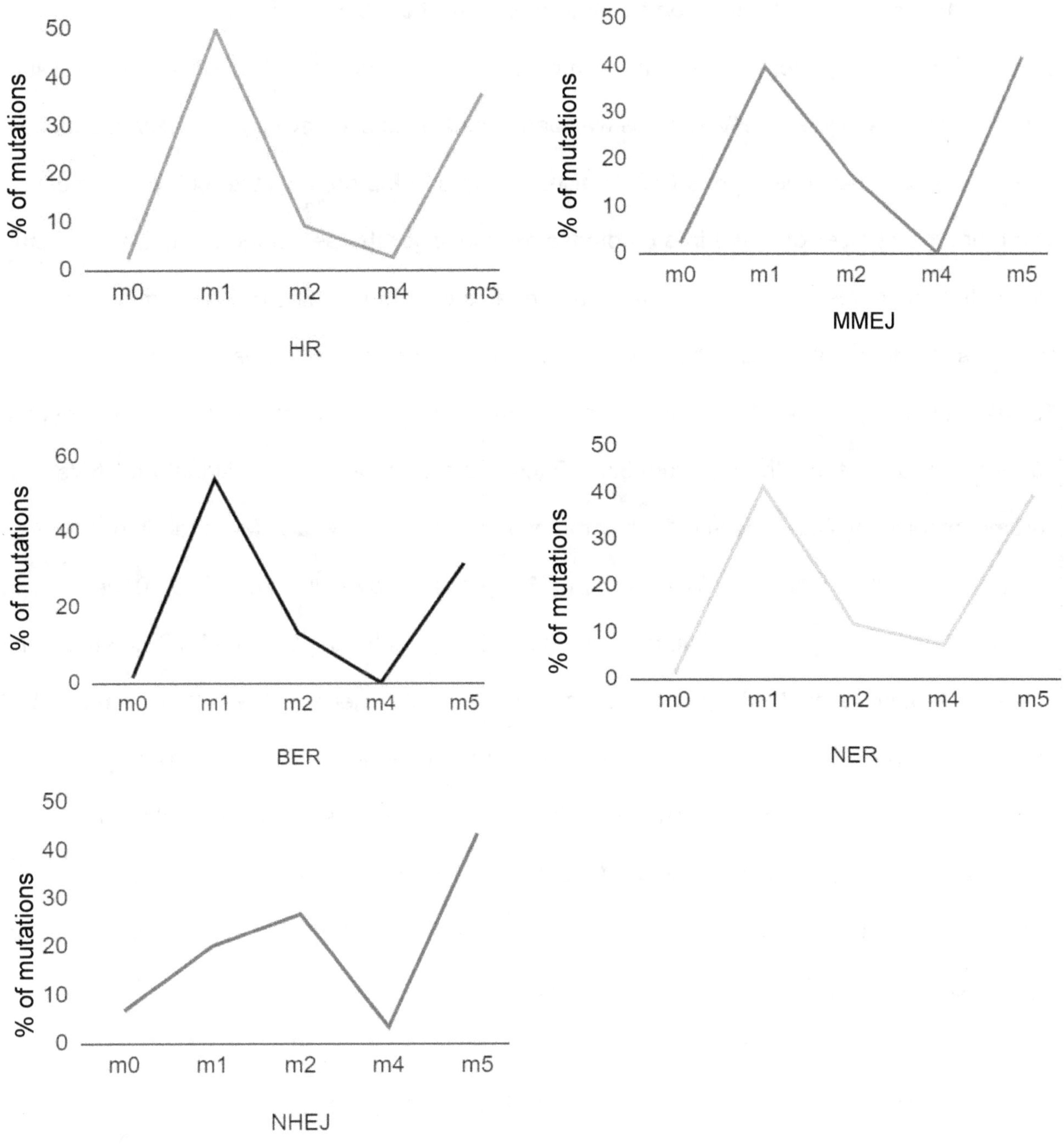

Figure 3.8: Cumulative line plots of percentage of mutations in various DDR pathways across all the subtypes. It can be seen that there are pathway specific subtype signatures. M1 and M5 carry the maximum number of mutations and the M4 subtype is the least mutated.

3.2.3. Copy number analysis shows distinct profiles in M2 and M4Eo and a ubiquitous pattern of 3'-UTR copy number alterations in the DDR genes.

To identify deletions, insertions, and gene amplifications observed in AML and identify any pattern associated with subtypes, CNV analysis was performed using exomeCopy and CNVkit packages. The exomeCopy package reports CNV profiles in terms of the normal state of the chromosome. The more the number of CNVs in a chromosome, the lower the percentage of the normal state. On plotting the percentage of the normal state of all the chromosomes across samples of all the subtypes, a subtype-specific pattern of copy number variation in chromosomes was observed (Table). M2 (12%) and M4Eo (10%) subtypes showed the lowest normal states in chromosomes 10,19 and 1, 8,11 respectively (Figure 3.9). Each of the subtypes showed signature CNVs at the chromosomal level. Chromosome 11 is common between M0, M4, and M4Eo subtypes and Chr 22 in M1 and M5A (table 5.1). The 14.4% (3137 genes) of overall genes (9131 genes) having CNVs in their UTR region were common among all subtypes having 3-prime UTR deletion, while for genes that were involved in the DNA repair pathway (232 genes), it was 20% (3-prime UTR deletion) (Figure 3.10a, b). The 31.3% (1476 genes) of overall unique genes (4721 genes) had 5-prime UTR deletion that was unique to a subtype, while for genes that were involved in the DNA repair pathway (49 genes), it was 38.8% (5-prime UTR deletion) (Figure 3.10c, d). indicating that DNA repair genes are getting selected over others in 3-prime UTR deletion in common CNVs and 5-prime UTR deletion for unique cnvs. (Figure 3.10b).

3.2.4. 3'-UTR signatures in DDR genes across AML subtypes

3.2.4.1. Chromosome-wise distribution of UTR variants signatures in DDR genes across AML subtypes

As observed both 5' and 3'UTR alterations were predominantly deletions in the DNA damage repair gene, and the fraction of UTRs remaining were analyzed for the presence of SNV. First, categories; 1) a chromosome-wise distribution of all the variants and 2) UTR variants in DDR

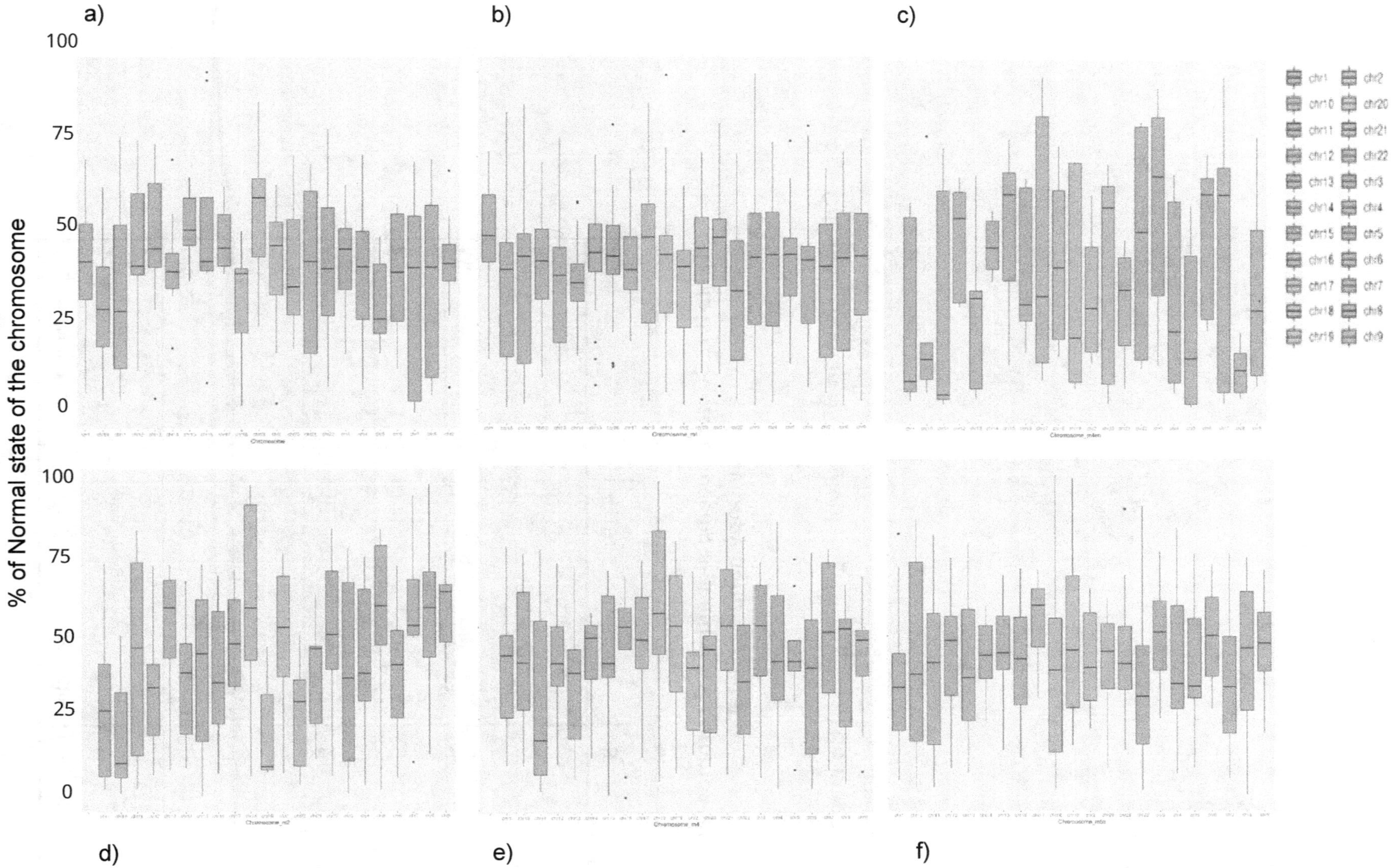

Figure 3.9: Chromosomal state in terms of CNV, lower normal state (y axis) indicates higher CNVs in chromosome.
a) Normal state of chromosomes in M0 subtype, b) Normal state of chromosomes in M1 subtype, c) Normal state of chromosomes in M2 subtype,d) Normal state of chromosomes in M4 subtype,e) Normal state of chromosomes in M4Eo subtype, f) Normal state of chromosomes in M5 subtype.

FAB subtype	Most affected chromosomes	Lowest normal state (%)
M0	5, 10, 11	30
M1	14, 22	37
M2	10, 19	12
M4	11	20
M4Eo	1, 11, 8	10
M5A	1, 22	35
M5B	2, 19	38

Table 3.1: Subtype specific signatures of chromosomes affected by Copy number alteration

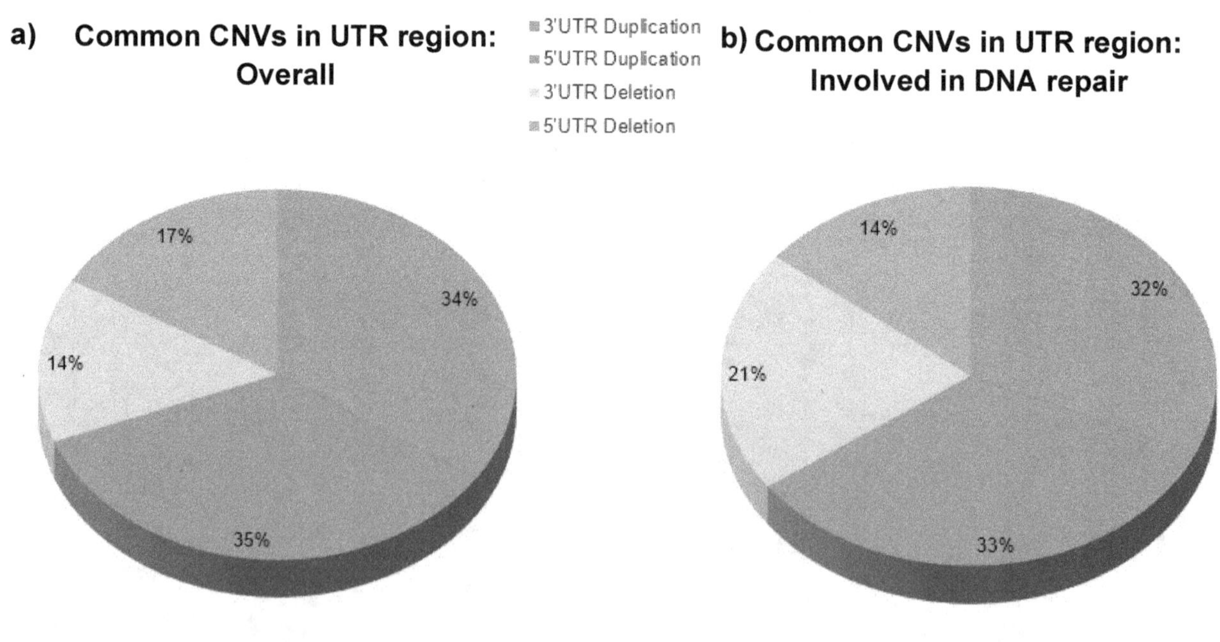

c) **Unique Genes having CNVs in UTR: Overall**

d) **Unique Genes having CNVs in UTR: Involved in DNA repair**

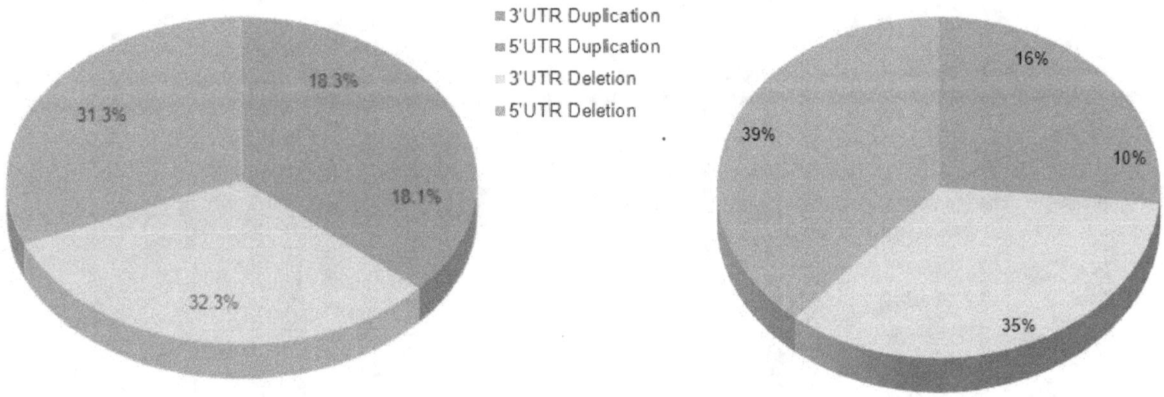

Figure 3.10: Distribution of common and unique genes having CNV in their UTR region. a) Overall distribution of common genes having CNV in their UTR region, b) Overall distribution of common genes involved in DNA repair, having CNV in their UTR region, c) Overall distribution of unique genes having CNV in their UTR region, d) Overall distribution of unique genes involved in DNA repair, having CNV in their UTR region

The representation of a subtype through different chromosomes follows a similar pattern, i.e, the percentage difference in a subtype is ~1-4%. However, chromosome M (mitochondrial chromosome) would be an exception to this norm. The most intriguing patterns were in chr4 where there were variants only in the M5A subtype, and in chr16 where the representation was limited to M1 and M5 (A and B) subtypes. There were no mutations in chr20, 21, and chrY, which could be because of bias as there are no DDR genes in these chromosomes (Figure 3.11 a and b). On contrary, subtype-specific differences in the pattern for DNA repair - 3' UTR variants were observed.

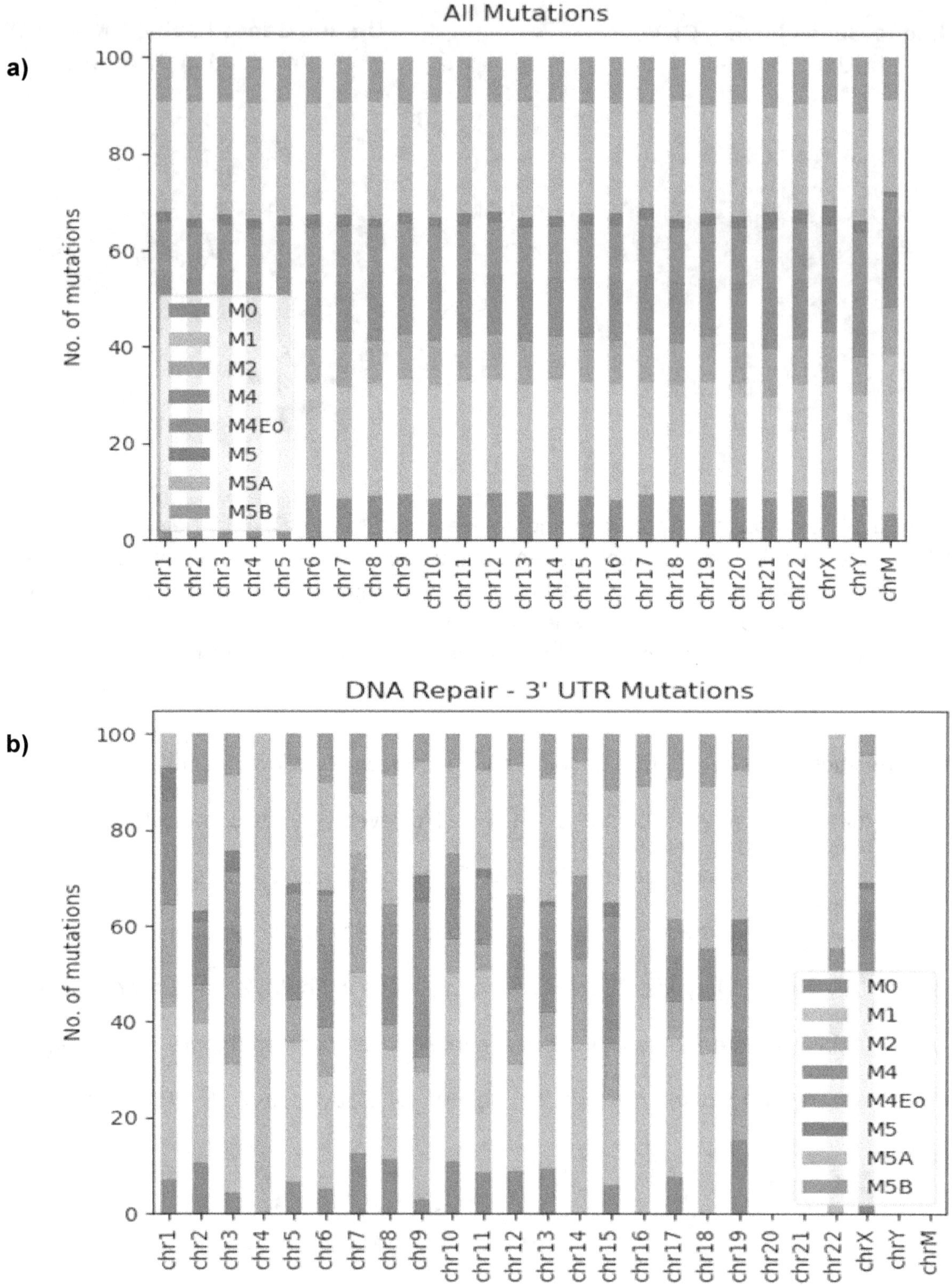

Figure 3.11: Mutation frequency plot per subtype per chromosome, A) Plot for the entire variant dataset; B) Plot for the filtered DNA repair – 3'UTR variants

3.2.4.2. Frequency of UTR variants in DDR genes common to AML subtypes

We shifted our analysis from the chromosome level to the genic level and the very first step was to screen variants in UTRs of DDR genes present across all the subtypes and mutations which persisted in both, bone marrow and blood samples. We observed that certain genes involved in inter-strand cross-link repair, NER, BER, and MMR pathways, namely FANCF, XPC, TDG, GTF2H5, and RAD23B had 3'UTR variants with a >90% frequency (Figure 3.12). Further, we kept a cut off of the variants being in at least 40% of the samples. Keeping this criterion, a set of 15 genes was obtained, FANCF, XPC, TDG, GTF2H5, RAD23B PDS5B, FANCB, NEIL2, ERCC6, MRE11A, BARD1, RPA4, FANCI, ATRX, and POLH. Most of the genes that were included in the subset didn't have any notable variants in their coding region, apart from ATRX, RPA4, and ERCC6. The details of all these mutations are mentioned in Table 3.2 This observation helped strengthen the hypothesis of finding a gene variant at the 3' UTR region which could serve as a potential signature in AML, as the gene has a higher chance of being regulated by miRNA.

3.2.4.3. Subtype specific 3-UTR variant signatures in DDR genes

After obtaining variants common to the majority of the samples it was important to find subtype-specific variants. We made a subset of unique variants pertaining to only one subtype and used it for further analysis on subtype-specific signatures. With the intent of removing the sampling bias, the absolute variant numbers were normalized for each subtype set. It was found that before normalization, every subtype was showing UTR mutations while the maximum number of UTR mutations were in M1 and M5A as the sample size for both of these subtypes was large. After normalization, 62 genes having unique mutations within subtype were found to be present in more than 25% of samples (Figure 3.13).

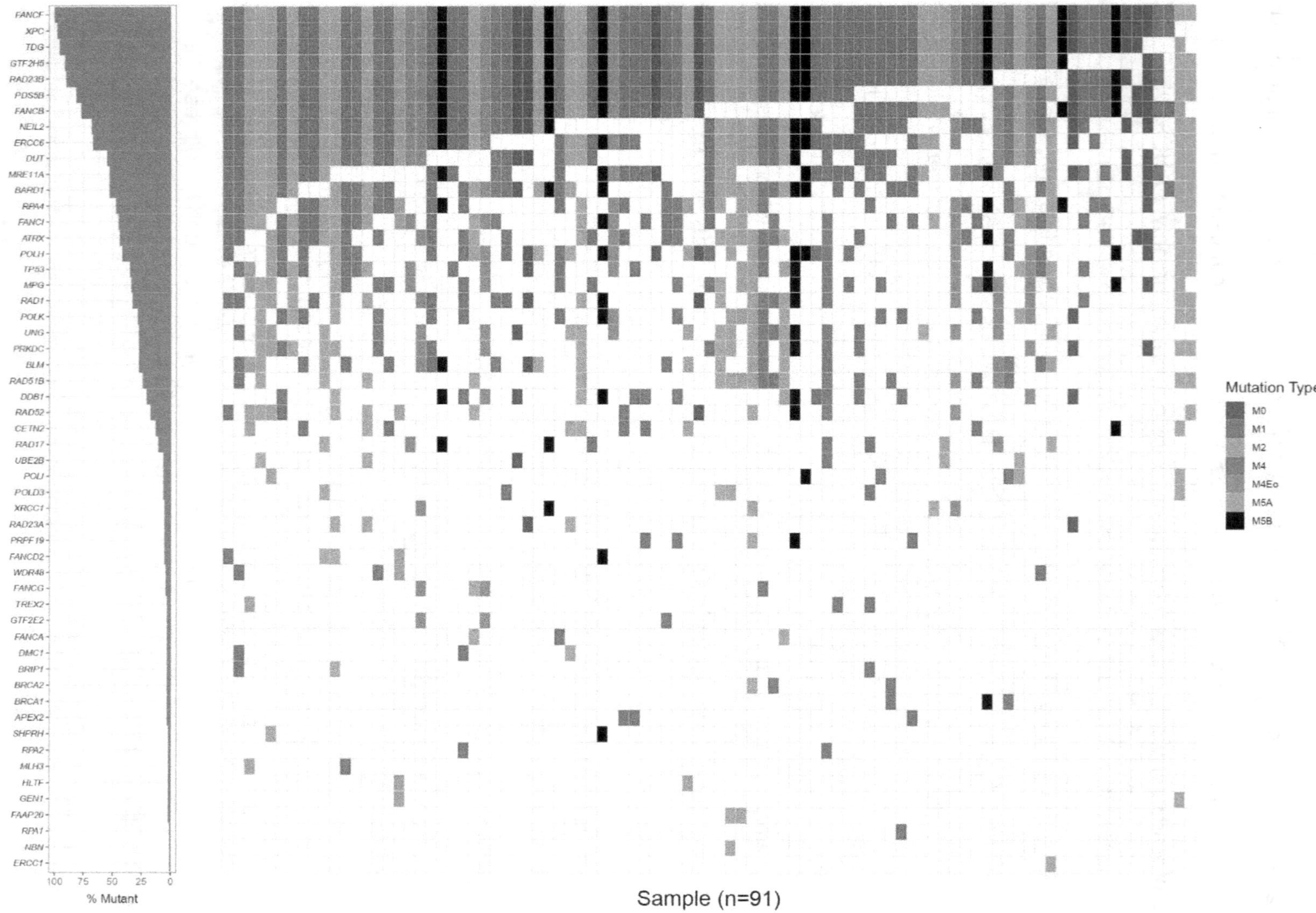

Figure 3.12: Mutation status of genes found to be common across different AML samples. The samples are differentiated with respect to their AML subtype

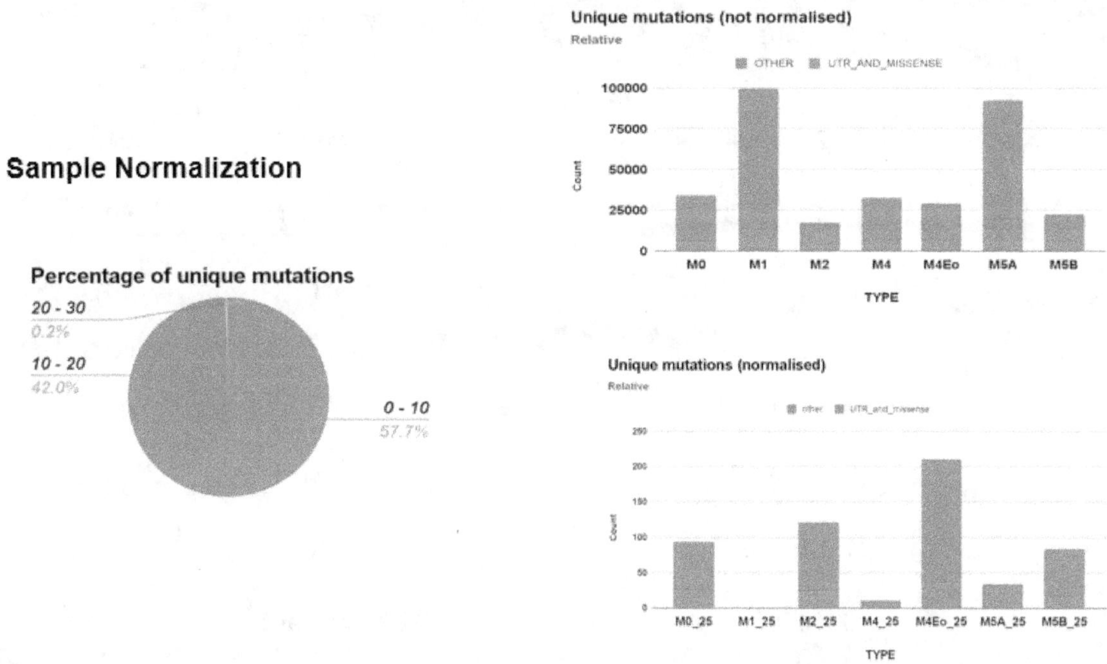

Figure 3.13: Before and after normalization of unique mutation count. a) Pie chart representing the overall distribution (%) of unique mutations after normalization. b) Unique utr (blue) and other (red) mutation's relative distribution (%) across different FAB subtype before normalization. c) Relative distribution of unique utr (blue) and other (red) mutations across subtype which are present in at least 25% of samples (within subtype).

A subset of variants unique to every subtype was curated for further analysis. After normalizing for the number of samples per subtype, a set of 15 genes was obtained with 3; -UTR variants specific to a subtype; M0 - RIF1, NEIL2, DCLRE1A; M1- MRE11A, RAD1, UBE2A, and GTF2H5; M2- RCQI5 and HLTF; M4Eo- OGG1 and DMC1; RNFB and DCLRE1B; M5A PDS5B and ATRX. Screening further for frequency of the variants, we considered only those cases where the same variant was present in at least 25% of the samples in a subtype and absent in any other subtype. Results showed that MRE11A, RAD1, and GTF2H5 specific to M1, HLTF specific to M2, and PDS5B specific to M5A fit the criteria well (Figure 3.14).

Gene	Mutation (Most Prevalent)	Mutation Type	No. of Samples	Any Prote Coding Variants
FANCF	g.22623347_22623348insT	3' UTR variant	91	No
XPC	g.14145257C>G	3' UTR variant	89	No
TDG	g.103965869G>A	5' UTR variant	80	No
	g.103965899A>G	5' UTR variant	63	
	g.103966001C>T	Premature start codon variant	64	
GTF2H5	g.158192343delA	3' UTR Variant	37	No
	g.158195142delT	3' UTR Variant	33	
RAD23B	g.107331074insT	3' UTR variant	82	No
PDS5B	g.32775097insT (1-9)	3' UTR variant	73	Yes(13 samples)
NEIL2	g.11786628_11786630insCT	3' UTR Variant	10	No
	.11786628_11786631insCTT	3' UTR Variant	10	
ERCC6	g.49458582delA	3' UTR variant	44	Yes(38 samples)
DUT	g.48342122delA or g.48342122insA	3' UTR Variant	50	No
MRE11A	g.94418381insT(1-2)	3' UTR Variant	35	No
BARD1	g.214728537insT(1-3)	3' UTR Variant	37	No
RPA4	g.96885184delT	3' UTR Variant	35	Yes(41 samples)
FANCI	g.89316701insC	3' UTR Variant	41	No
ATRX	g.77508201delA	3' UTR Variant	32	Yes(75 samples)
POLH	g.43618961delG	3' UTR Variant	17	No
	g.43618961insG	3' UTR Variant	13	

Table 3.2: Genes involved in DNA Repair with the most mutations observed at UTR locations.

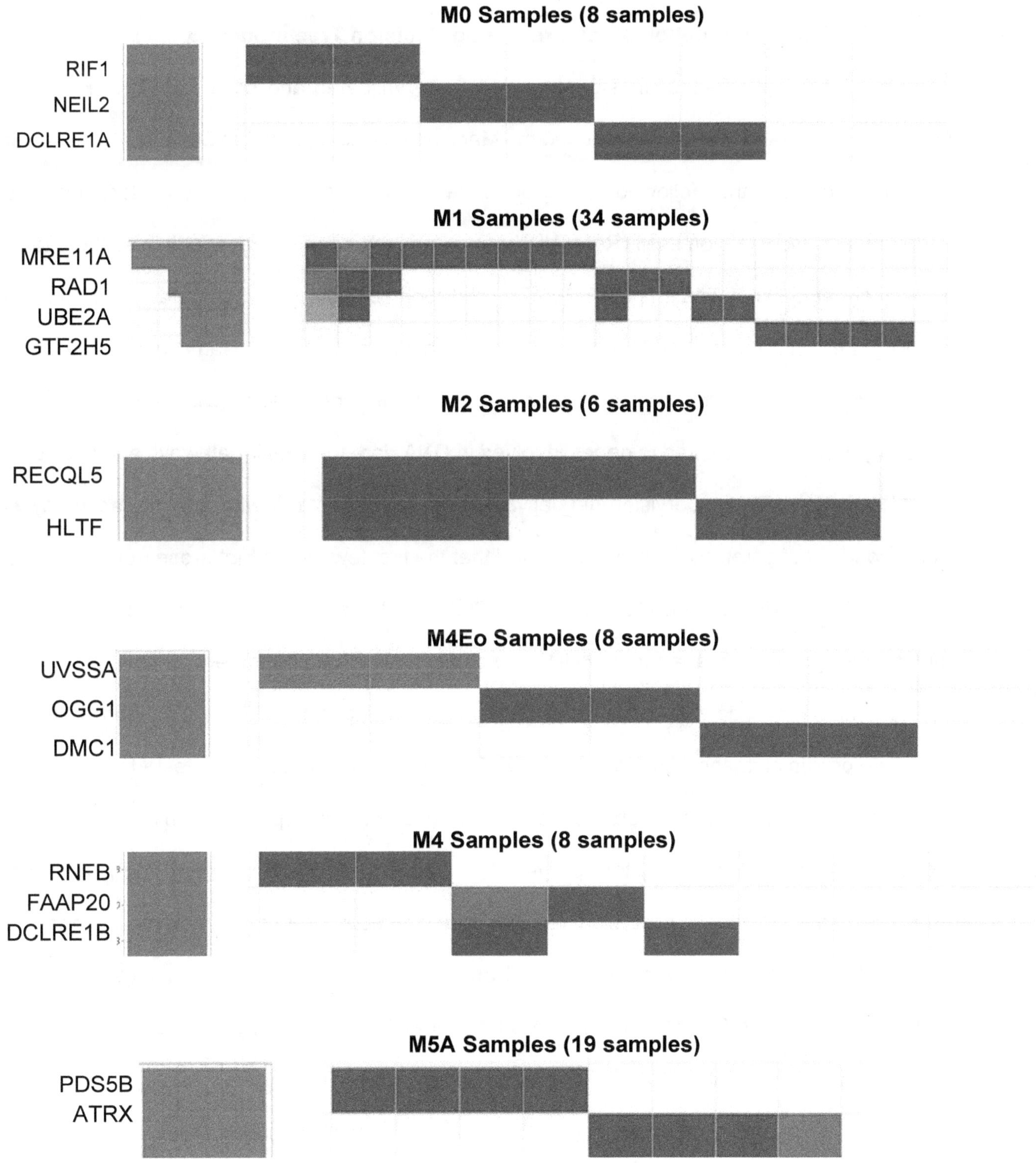

Figure 3.14: Genes observed with most unique mutations (mutations absent in other subtypes) for each subtype

3.2.5. Validation of mutation signatures using Decision Tree modeling

To check if the subtype-specific signatures could be validated and could be used as potential predictive markers for a subtype, we used the Machine Learning algorithm Decision Tree modeler. For every iteration that followed, the independent variables were the gene, location of the variation, and the variation itself (Ref->Alt change), and the dependent variable was the subtype. The initial dataset that was employed for the prediction consisted of 4955 data points consisting of the genes with most 3' UTR variants (min. 15 data points for the same gene). Due to the variability of the data, the best accuracy that the model could reach was 41%. To increase accuracy, data was restricted to genes involved in DNA damage repair pathways and showcased a 3' UTR variant. This supervision did deliver a slightly better result with a 51.5% accuracy with the second set of parameters. It is to be noted that the first few genes that arose from the root are ATRX, RIF1, HLTF (g.149031159delA), and OGG1. These genes were also observed in the mutation frequency but, apart from HLTF, the other genes contain different variants in the same subtype. Lastly, the data was further supervised by selecting the 15 genes found as per the subtype-specific mutation frequency analysis. This supervised dataset was tested with both sets of parameters. The first set of parameters ("Gene", and "Position") provided an accuracy of 80%, while the second set of parameters delivered an accuracy of 64.28%. Interestingly, both these trees had a root of MRE11A in M1; the tree that used the second set of parameters also mentioned position 94419465, which was also present as a part of the waterfall plot analysis. Since the mutation is robust in MRE11A and involves a large stretch of the sequence being inserted, it could be a potential target for regulation. The other classifying factor obtained was UBE2A from M1 which was the first gene that branched out after MRE11A (Figure 3.15).

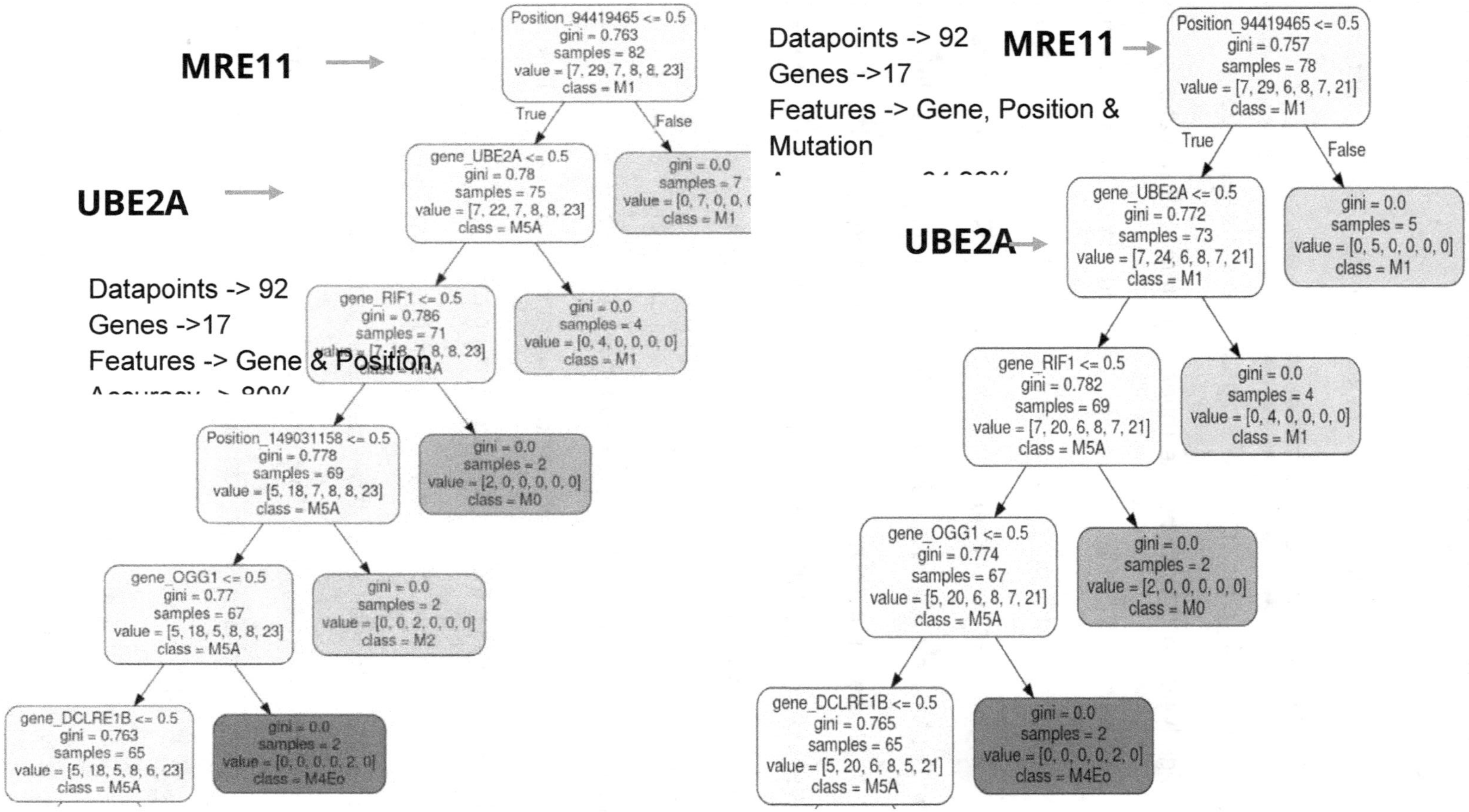

Figure 3.15: Decision tree with different parameters, the first tree (left) has 3 parameters, used for prediction, “Gene” and “Position”, the second tree (right) uses an additional parameter “Mutation” to predict the subtype. The models show an accuracy of 80% (left) and 64.28% respectively. Both the trees give out MRE11A and UBE2A M1 subtype specific signatures

3.3 DISCUSSION

Exome analysis of the AML samples returned the three most frequently (20-40%) mutated genes DNMT3A, NPM1, and FLT3. Although recurrent, mutations in these are largely present in only a quarter of the AML patients reported[21], indicating heterogeneity in the disease despite common cytogenetic abnormality signifying each subtype. As reported before, the mutations which co-occur are NPM1, FLT3, and IDH2 with DNMT3A mutations, and this combination of co-mutations has been of importance in personalized prognostic therapeutics[21,22]. There were only two genes that showed any subtype-specific signatures, ASXL1, and TP53. ASXL1 mutation was found to be present in all but M2 and M4 subtypes, with a high frequency in the M5 subtype. It has been shown in earlier studies that ASXL1^{mut} AML is inversely correlated to the FAB M4 subtype and has a high frequency in the M5 subtype, and this result points to a possible subtype signature for AML M4 and M5 in an inverse manner[23,24]. TP53, showing a generally low frequency of mutations, was absent in the M1 subtype.

The three most frequently mutated genes (50-60% frequency) were AHNAK, HLA-DRB5, and ELANE. AHNAK is a protein that is associated with cellular migration and invasion. It is known to have an ambiguous role, where it could either act as a tumor suppressor, while its overexpression, as an inflammation marker, is linked to poor survival in Laryngeal carcinoma[25–27]. A high frequency of mutation with a further analysis of the expression profile could help understand its role in AML. HLA-DRB5 variants have been liked to childhood ALL[28], showing a high frequency of AML mutations in our study, indicating that it can play an oncogenic role when mutated. An interesting observation is of ELANE mutations. It is known that mutations in this elastase gene are associated with neutropenia in leukemic patients[29]. Apart from ELANE, a mutation in STAT3 and RARA was observed only in the M5 subtype of AML indicating defective granulopoiesis as in all subtypes of AML but mutations in the genes indicative of subtype-specific signatures. Mutations of STAT3 and overexpression of RARA are associated with AML[30]. Also, MPO showed a mutation in a subtype-specific manner in M0, M1, and M5. MPO is in use to differentiate the AML subtype based on the expression[31]. Mutations in the genes associated with granulopoieses such as XCR1, CEACAM1, and ITGAM was found to be present only in blood across the subtypes indicating the use of these mutations as a biomarker for prognosis, which requires to be validated in a larger sample and experimentally. In this regard, attempts to identify markers of impaired neutrophils and assay for the minimal residual disease have shown a significant impact of the blood-based presence of mutations in the AML genes to be associated with a worse prognosis [32]. HAX1 mutation was observed only in bone marrow samples. To decipher the status of AML complete remission, standard practice is to use bone marrow samples, and blood-based assays, and the sensitivity of the assays in predicting treatment outcome and relapse is warranted. A marker that has been studied in this regard is WT1, and we observed WT1 mutations in 8% of the samples.[33] We have tried to fish out markers in the DNA damage repair which can differentiate subtypes of AML and mutations in the blood which can be used to guide the prognosis discussed below.

Studies have shown that neutrophilic granulocytes can promote genomic instability by inhibiting DNA repair and they display a lack of repair in cancerous conditions[34,35]. It has also been shown that there is impaired DNA repair in Neutropenia patients[14]. A major focus was the study of mutational profiles of DNA repair genes across tissue and subtype groups. It was seen that 63% of the DNA repair mutations were common to blood and bone marrow samples, while 11% were unique to Bone marrow belonging to HR and Base Excision repair, and 26% mutations, specific to NHEJ, unique to blood, indicating that while majorly common, there are possible mutational signatures of DNA repair in clonal populations, in the bone marrow, and the differentiated population in blood. On performing an individual analysis of all the DNA repair pathways across all the subtypes, we observed that mutations in the M1 subtype were enriched in the HR and BER pathways, whereas M5 was mutated in NER, HR, and MMEJ pathways. Cumulatively we observed a uniform trend where the least mutated DDR pathways were observed in M4 and M0 whereas, M1 showed the highest frequency of mutations in HR, BER, and NER and M5 showed the highest mutation frequency in NHEJ and MMEJ. There are no reports of mutational profiles across AML subtypes. Subtype-specific coding mutation signatures in DDR pathways could help explain the differences in the genetic predisposition for every subtype of AML. Several studies have shown HR to be important for lymphocyte maturation, and in hematopoietic stem cells in the bone marrow for normal lymphocyte development[36,37]and a comparison of repair mechanisms between blood and bone marrow showed NHEJ to be prevalent in blood and HR in bone marrow [38]. . The M1 subtype results due to loss of HR early in the differentiation process whereas M5 due to mutations in the NHEJ pathway indicating usage of different therapeutic targets in these two subtypes of leukemia. Mutations in the HR pathway genes correlated with a higher mutational burden, which also signifies heterogeneity to be higher in bone marrow than in blood. TMb has been considered a factor for marking clonal evolution in many cancers and specifically in AML[39,40]. AML being a disease of the bone marrow essentially, a higher TMb in bone marrow can be expected and it also suggests that there is a clonal selection happening wherein the number of mutations decreases when entering the blood. Despite the Tmb being low, there is a specific mutation recorded in the blood. Cumulatively we observed a uniform trend of mutations in DDR pathway genes, where M4 and M0 were the least mutated across all pathways. Subtype-specific coding mutation signatures in DDR pathways could help explain the differences in the genetic predisposition for every subtype of AML.

Results obtained from the CNV analysis and mutation frequency analysis suggests that there are regions in the Leukemic genome that are often subjected to faulty DNA repair mechanism[41], furthermore, the mutation in DNA repair - 3' UTR genes do not have any established pattern across chromosomes, suggesting a subtype-specific pattern in 3'UTR of DDR genes.

The most frequently mutated 3' UTR was in the FANCF gene. FA pathway is known to have a role in preventing AML, and an aberration is observed in this pathway in AML patient samples[42], moreover, FANCF silencing has been correlated with early leukemogenesis [43].

Unfortunately, when we checked its corresponding sequence post introduction of the variant, it was flanked with a 3' poly T region, ruling out the possibility of a new miRNA binding site. The other two genes which were of interest to us were RAD23B and XPC, both proteins belonging to the XPC complex, involved in the NER pathway. The additive consequence of SNPs in these genes was previously noted to affect the DNA Repair capacity in breast cancer patients[44], while in AML XPC SNPs coding for a faulty protein have been associated with shorter survival[45]. The variant analysis in our study showed a significant number of patients having mutations in both XPC and RAD23B (80 samples) in the 3' UTR region, without having any other variants in their protein-coding region. The combinatorial effect of these genes on survival was shown to be noteworthy, thus it would be interesting if any miRNA binding site was generated in XPC due to g.14145257C>G substitution, possibly downregulating the expression of XPC.

The subtype-specific variant analysis was the penultimate step to determining a biomarker for a specific subtype. From the list of the genes that were observed in this analysis. Two genes came forth as plausible subtype signatures for the M1 AML subtype with possible miRNA regulation, MRE11A, and UBE2A. MRE11A, a pivotal component of the MRN(MRE11-RAD50-NBS1) complex involved in homologous recombination, is a major pathway to repair DSBs. Although the role of MRN complex and MRE11 has not been well established in the case of AML, it has been contemplated to play a dual role in cancers. MRE11 is essential to stop the early onset of cancer due to DNA damage and acts as a tumor suppressor[46], however, it can also prolong tumorigenesis as a response to oncogenic-mediated stress[47]. The consequences of the change in the miRNA binding and expression are discussed in the next chapter.

3.4 Conclusion

Variant Analysis revealed M1 and M5 specific ASXL1 signature along with bone marrow specific HAX1 mutations. This can be tapped into towards a guided therapeutic approach in a granulopoiesis dependent manner. DDR analysis revealed that M4 is the least mutated subtype whereas M1 and M5 are the most mutated. M1 subtype patients revealed non-coding signatures in MRE11A and UBE2A genes which can be pivotal in developing M1 specific therapeutic targets.

3.5 REFERENCES

1. Khwaja A, Bjorkholm M, Gale RE, Levine RL, Jordan CT, Ehninger G, et al. Acute myeloid leukaemia. Nat Rev Dis Primers. 2016;2: 16010.

2. Sung H, Ferlay J, Siegel RL, Laversanne M, Soerjomataram I, Jemal A, et al. Global Cancer Statistics 2020: GLOBOCAN Estimates of Incidence and Mortality Worldwide for 36 Cancers in 185 Countries. CA: A Cancer Journal for Clinicians. 2021. pp. 209–249. doi:10.3322/caac.21660

3. Davis AS, Viera AJ, Mead MD. Leukemia: an overview for primary care. Am Fam Physician. 2014;89: 731–738.

4. Website. Available: Website. Available: Blumenreich MS. The White Blood Cell and Differential Count. In: Walker HK, Hall WD, Hurst JW, editors. Clinical Methods: The History, Physical, and Laboratory Examinations. 3rd edition. Boston: Butterworths; 1990. Chapter 153. Available from: https://www.ncbi.nlm.nih.gov/books/NBK261/

5. Arora RS, Arora B. Acute leukemia in children: A review of the current Indian data. South Asian J Cancer. 2016;5: 155–160.

6. Savage SA, Walsh MF. Myelodysplastic Syndrome, Acute Myeloid Leukemia, and Cancer Surveillance in Fanconi Anemia. Hematol Oncol Clin North Am. 2018;32: 657–668.

7. Vandenberghe P, Beel K. Severe congenital neutropenia, a genetically heterogeneous disease group with an increased risk of AML/MDS. Pediatr Rep. 2011;3 Suppl 2: e9.

8. Hasan S, Naqvi AR, Rizvi A. Transcriptional Regulation of Emergency Granulopoiesis in Leukemia. Front Immunol. 2018;9: 481.

9. Website.

10. Greenberg PL, Nichols WC, Schrier SL. Granulopoiesis in acute myeloid leukemia and preleukemia. N Engl J Med. 1971;284: 1225–1232.

11. de Oliveira Lisboa M, Brofman PRS, Schmid-Braz AT, Rangel-Pozzo A, Mai S.

Chromosomal Instability in Acute Myeloid Leukemia. Cancers . 2021;13. doi:10.3390/cancers13112655

12. Gumy-Pause F, Wacker P, Sappino A-P. ATM gene and lymphoid malignancies. Leukemia. 2004. pp. 238–242. doi:10.1038/sj.leu.2403221

13. Severe congenital neutropenias. Nature Reviews Disease Primers. 2017. doi:10.1038/nrdp.2017.33

14. Mir P, Klimiankou M, Dannenmann B, Zeidler C, Schulze-Osthoff K, Kanz L, et al. Impaired DNA Damage Repair in Severe Congenital Neutropenia Patients. Blood. 2016. pp. 1334–1334. doi:10.1182/blood.v128.22.1334.1334

15. Gabellier L, Bret C, Bossis G, Cartron G, Moreaux J. DNA Repair Expression Profiling to Identify High-Risk Cytogenetically Normal Acute Myeloid Leukemia and Define New Therapeutic Targets. Cancers . 2020;12. doi:10.3390/cancers12102874

16. Schuster SL, Hsieh AC. The Untranslated Regions of mRNAs in Cancer. Trends in Cancer. 2019. pp. 245–262. doi:10.1016/j.trecan.2019.02.011

17. Ziebarth JD, Bhattacharya A, Cui Y. Integrative analysis of somatic mutations altering microRNA targeting in cancer genomes. PLoS One. 2012;7: e47137.

18. Percival M-E, Lai C, Estey E, Hourigan CS. Bone marrow evaluation for diagnosis and monitoring of acute myeloid leukemia. Blood Rev. 2017;31: 185–192.

19. de Rooij JDE, Zwaan CM, van den Heuvel-Eibrink M. Pediatric AML: From Biology to Clinical Management. J Clin Med Res. 2015;4: 127–149.

20. Klco JM, Miller CA, Griffith M, Petti A, Spencer DH, Ketkar-Kulkarni S, et al. Association Between Mutation Clearance After Induction Therapy and Outcomes in Acute Myeloid Leukemia. JAMA. 2015;314: 811–822.

21. DiNardo CD, Cortes JE. Mutations in AML: prognostic and therapeutic implications. Hematology Am Soc Hematol Educ Program. 2016;2016: 348–355.

22. Ley TJ, Ding L, Walter MJ, McLellan MD, Lamprecht T, Larson DE, et al. DNMT3A mutations in acute myeloid leukemia. N Engl J Med. 2010;363: 2424–2433.

23. Pratcorona M, Abbas S, Sanders MA, Koenders JE, Kavelaars FG, Erpelinck-Verschueren CAJ, et al. Acquired mutations in ASXL1 in acute myeloid leukemia: prevalence and prognostic value. Haematologica. 2012;97: 388–392.

24. Rose D, Haferlach T, Schnittger S, Perglerová K, Kern W, Haferlach C. Subtype-specific patterns of molecular mutations in acute myeloid leukemia. Leukemia. 2017;31: 11–17.

25. Zardab M, Stasinos K, Grose RP, Kocher HM. The Obscure Potential of AHNAK2. Cancers . 2022;14. doi:10.3390/cancers14030528

26. Schoch C, Kohlmann A, Schnittger S, Brors B, Dugas M, Mergenthaler S, et al. Acute myeloid leukemias with reciprocal rearrangements can be distinguished by specific gene expression profiles. Proc Natl Acad Sci U S A. 2002;99: 10008–10013.

27. Dumitru CA, Bankfalvi A, Gu X, Zeidler R, Brandau S, Lang S. AHNAK and inflammatory markers predict poor survival in laryngeal carcinoma. PLoS One. 2013;8: e56420.

28. Urayama KY, Thompson PD, Taylor M, Trachtenberg EA, Chokkalingam AP. Genetic variation in the extended major histocompatibility complex and susceptibility to childhood acute lymphoblastic leukemia: a review of the evidence. Front Oncol. 2013;3: 300.

29. Makaryan V, Zeidler C, Bolyard AA, Skokowa J, Rodger E, Kelley ML, et al. The diversity of mutations and clinical outcomes for ELANE-associated neutropenia. Curr Opin Hematol. 2015;22: 3–11.

30. Larrue C, Heydt Q, Saland E, Boutzen H, Kaoma T, Sarry J-E, et al. Oncogenic KIT mutations induce STAT3-dependent autophagy to support cell proliferation in acute myeloid leukemia. Oncogenesis. 2019;8: 39.

31. Kim Y, Yoon S, Kim SJ, Kim JS, Cheong J-W, Min YH. Myeloperoxidase expression in acute myeloid leukemia helps identifying patients to benefit from transplant. Yonsei Med J. 2012;53: 530–536.

32. Yanada M, Borthakur G, Garcia-Manero G, Ravandi F, Faderl S, Pierce S, et al. Blood counts at time of complete remission provide additional independent prognostic information in acute myeloid leukemia. Leuk Res. 2008;32: 1505–1509.

33. Zeijlemaker W, Kelder A, Oussoren-Brockhoff YJM, Scholten WJ, Snel AN, Veldhuizen D, et al. Peripheral blood minimal residual disease may replace bone marrow minimal residual disease as an immunophenotypic biomarker for impending relapse in acute myeloid leukemia. Leukemia. 2016;30: 708–715.

34. Bui TM, Butin-Israeli V, Wiesolek HL, Zhou M, Rehring JF, Wiesmüller L, et al. Neutrophils Alter DNA Repair Landscape to Impact Survival and Shape Distinct Therapeutic Phenotypes of Colorectal Cancer. Gastroenterology. 2021;161: 225–238.e15.

35. Ponath V, Heylmann D, Haak T, Woods K, Becker H, Kaina B. Compromised DNA Repair and Signalling in Human Granulocytes. J Innate Immun. 2019;11: 74–85.

36. Caddle LB, Hasham MG, Schott WH, Shirley B-J, Mills KD. Homologous recombination is necessary for normal lymphocyte development. Mol Cell Biol. 2008;28: 2295–2303.

37. Desai A, Gerson SL, Qing Y. Hematopoietic Stem Cells Are Dependent On Homologous Recombination Only During Active Cell Cycle in Nuclease-Mutant Exonuclease1mut mice. Blood. 2012. pp. 1225–1225. doi:10.1182/blood.v120.21.1225.1225

38. Biechonski S, Olender L, Zipin-Roitman A, Yassin M, Aqaqe N, Marcu-Malina V, et al. Attenuated DNA damage responses and increased apoptosis characterize human hematopoietic stem cells exposed to irradiation. Sci Rep. 2018;8: 6071.

39. Grove CS, Vassiliou GS. Acute myeloid leukaemia: a paradigm for the clonal evolution of cancer? Dis Model Mech. 2014;7: 941–951.

40. Lam VK, Zhang J. Blood-based tumor mutation burden: continued progress toward personalizing immunotherapy in non-small cell lung cancer. Journal of thoracic disease. 2019. pp. 2208–2211.

41. Hastings PJ, Lupski JR, Rosenberg SM, Ira G. Mechanisms of change in gene copy number. Nat Rev Genet. 2009;10: 551–564.

42. Xie Y, de Winter JP, Waisfisz Q, Nieuwint AW, Scheper RJ, Arwert F, et al. Aberrant Fanconi anaemia protein profiles in acute myeloid leukaemia cells. Br J Haematol. 2000;111: 1057–1064.

43. Tischkowitz M, Ameziane N, Waisfisz Q, De Winter JP, Harris R, Taniguchi T, et al. Bi-allelic silencing of the Fanconi anaemia gene FANCF in acute myeloid leukaemia. Br J Haematol. 2003;123: 469–471.

44. Morales L, Alvarez-Garriga C, Matta J, Ortiz C, Vergne Y, Vargas W, et al. Factors associated with breast cancer in Puerto Rican women. J Epidemiol Glob Health. 2013;3. doi:10.1016/j.jegh.2013.08.003

45. Strom SS, Estey E, Outschoorn UM, Garcia-Manero G. Acute myeloid leukemia outcome: role of nucleotide excision repair polymorphisms in intermediate risk patients. Leuk Lymphoma. 2010;51: 598–605.

46. Kim JH, Grosbart M, Anand R, Wyman C, Cejka P, Petrini JHJ. The Mre11-Nbs1 Interface Is Essential for Viability and Tumor Suppression. Cell Rep. 2017;18: 496–507.

47. Spehalski E, Capper KM, Smith CJ, Morgan MJ, Dinkelmann M, Buis J, et al. MRE11 Promotes Tumorigenesis by Facilitating Resistance to Oncogene-Induced Replication Stress. Cancer Res. 2017;77: 5327–5338.

Chapter 4: Profile and study the global transcriptome patterns of DNA repair pathways in Acute Leukemia samples.

4.1. INTRODUCTION

In the previous chapter, we discussed the cytogenetic and genetic abnormalities which can differentiate between subtypes of AML. The impact of these abnormalities can be studied at the transcriptional level at the global scale using RNA-seq, which can be used for risk stratification and guided therapeutics. Despite the information gathered on AML pathogenesis, most categories of AML (except for acute promyelocytic leukemia, APL) recurrence and relapse are common[1,2]. However, the impact of technological gains has led to identifying mechanisms and targets for therapy [2].

Transcriptome analysis has progressed from using a relatively small set of gene panels for diagnostics to whole transcriptome sequencing to gain more benefits[3]. Amongst all the sequencing strategies, transcriptome profiles come closest to representing the functional status of the cell[4]. RNA-seq analysis is the most relevant in terms of diagnostics and clinical correlation[3]. AML is a heterogeneous disease due to its various genetic alterations [5]. Studies have exploited the availability of large-scale transcriptome datasets to categorize and identify subtype-specific expression patterns[5,6]. Large scale genomic projects like TCGA, BEAT AML, Target - AML, etc.,[6,7] have taken efforts to perform not only massively parallel transcriptome sequencing of 100s of AML patients, but along with cataloging their clinical features to derive useful diagnostic correlations.

Newman et al. developed a method to fractionate the immune cells using gene expression, CIBERSORT (Cell type Identification By Estimating Relative Subsets Of known RNA Transcripts) [8]. It has been utilized in AML patients to predict inferior event-free survival (EFS) and overall survival (OS) and identified a novel prognostic [9]. The relative presence of M0 vs M2 macrophages predicted the relapse. Apart from the available markers of risk stratification, the immune cell scoring system (ICSS) can be used as an independent prognostic predictor [9].

Co-expression analysis to understand disease pathogenesis has been widely used[10]. Recent studies have utilized Weighted gene co-expression network analysis (WGCNA) to identify co-expressed groups of genes from RNA-seq[11], which is based on higher-order relationships and integrated function of gene modules[12,13].

To gain a more comprehensive understanding of the genetic landscape, integrating WES and RNA-seq data is required[14,15]. Identifying genetic variants alone is not enough, understanding its functional impact and the biological effect is equally essential to understanding the phenotype of disease[16].

In adult patients, remission/ relapse in subtypes of AML can be linked to the expression of genes involved in stem cell-like properties[17–20]. However, coding gene-based analysis alone cannot provide insights into the processes underlying relapse potential and has limited the targets for intervention. Also, the heterogeneity observed cannot be linked to one factor guiding the treatment outcomes.

The role of non-coding regions of the genome in gene regulation is progressing, and their role in driving various diseases is expanding[21–23]. Therefore, the progression of AML cannot only be explained in terms of coding mutations and expression [24–26]. The role of miRNAs in the pathogenesis of AML is well established[27–29]. miRNAs are 18-21 nucleotide sequences that regulate gene expression by binding to 3'UTR off mRNA [30]. miRNAs are known to express in a subtype-specific manner and are also cell type-specific, therefore adding value to prognosis and classifying patients into smaller groups.

The clinical relevance of the role of LncRNAs in AML has been reviewed [31]. Long noncoding RNA can regulate gene expression in multiple ways (refer to the literature review); its regulatory role as a sponge is of particular significance. The involvement of 3'UTR in gene regulation in cancer (refer to the review of literature section, page no) is also established. The integrated action of lincRNA and miRNA in gene regulation can be used to stratify the patient groups within a subtype to predict disease status and therapeutic intervention better.

This study has profiled the expression patterns of genes associated with granulopoiesis and DDR pathways. We laid out the immune cell fractions of samples distributed into tissue and subtype categories using CIBERSORTx. We attempted to understand the correlation between gene expression and FAB subtypes using WGCNA, profiled DDR gene expression patterns across all the subtypes, and identified gene expression differences between samples with and without mutations. Significant differences were seen in the expression patterns of MRE11A and UBE2A and built a prediction model. To correlate our findings from the variant analysis, we checked for interruption or introduction of miRNA binding sites in the 3'UTR. We also performed LASSO-COX regression analysis and identified 4 alive signature genes, DCLRE1C, PMS2, DNTT, RAD51B, and 3 dead signature genes, H2AX, MUTYH, and FAAP20.

4.2. RESULTS

4.2.1. Downregulated transcription factors implicated in AML mark the M5 subtype of AML, whereas upregulated IRF8 is a marker of M4 and M5 subtypes

Transcriptome analysis was performed for 109 exome-matched transcriptome samples from the publicly available studies PRJNA214592 (42 samples), PRJNA229548 (27 samples), and PRJNA263397 (40 samples) with an average of 220 million reads (100 bp read length) and 93.2 % alignment to the human genome. On plotting a heatmap of the expression values of genes mutated in AML, clustering of the subtypes was observed, indicating similar expression changes due to translocation or mutation-specific to subtypes. Transcription factors, KIT, WT1, NPM1, RUNX1, DNMT3A, FLT3 ASXL1, and KRAS, were downregulated in the M5 subtype (Figure 4.1) Transcriptome profiles of Neutropenia associated genes were investigated across AML subtypes. MPO, one of the markers of mature neutrophils, was expressed least in the M0 subtype and mild in the M1 and M2 subtypes. The expression values were highest in M4/M4Eo subtype with low in M5A and M5B subtypes (Figure 4.2).

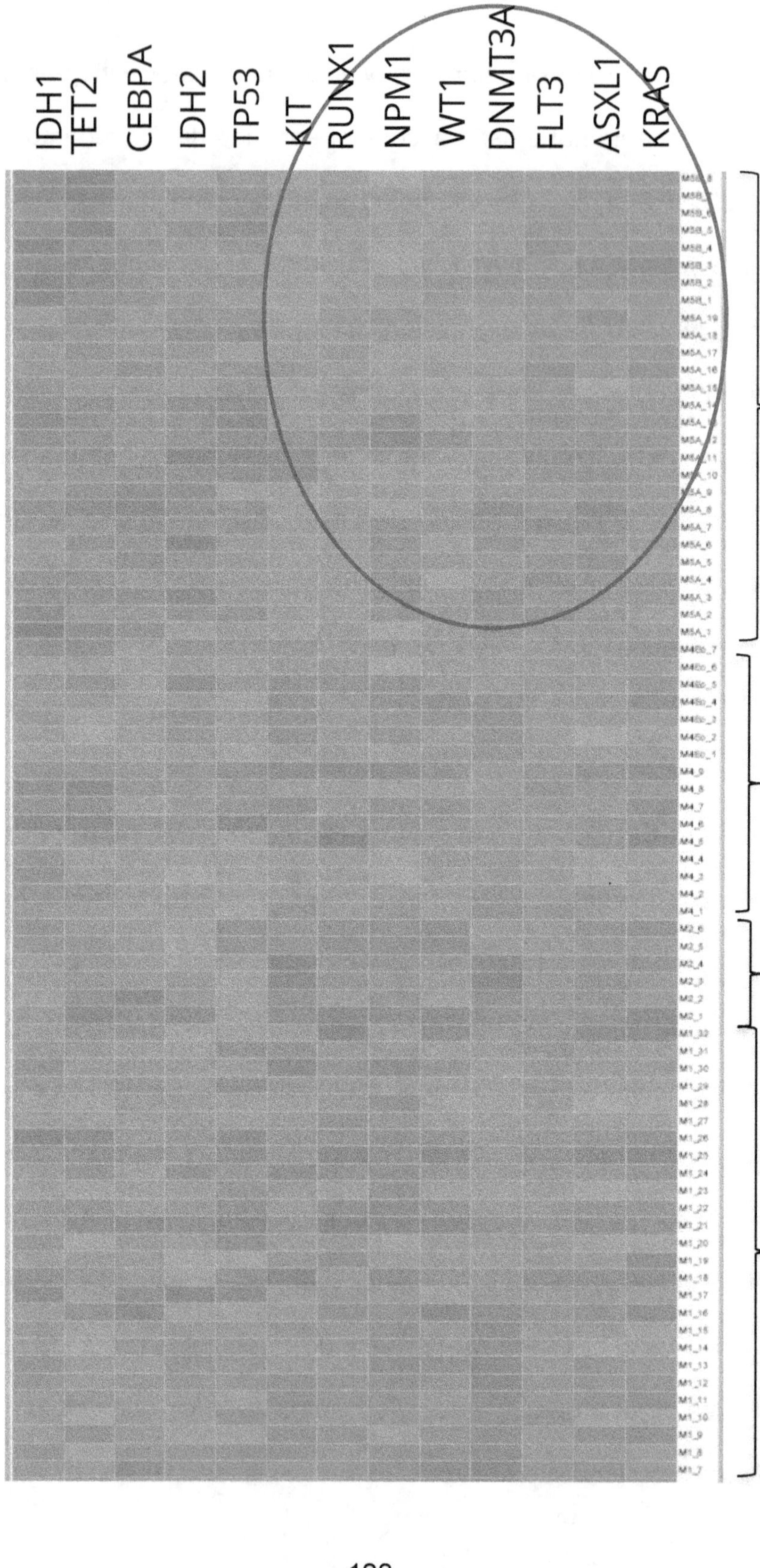

Figure 4.1: A heatmap representing the expression profiles of genes known to be implicated in AML. The blue circle highlights the expression patterns of a subset of genes in M5 subtype

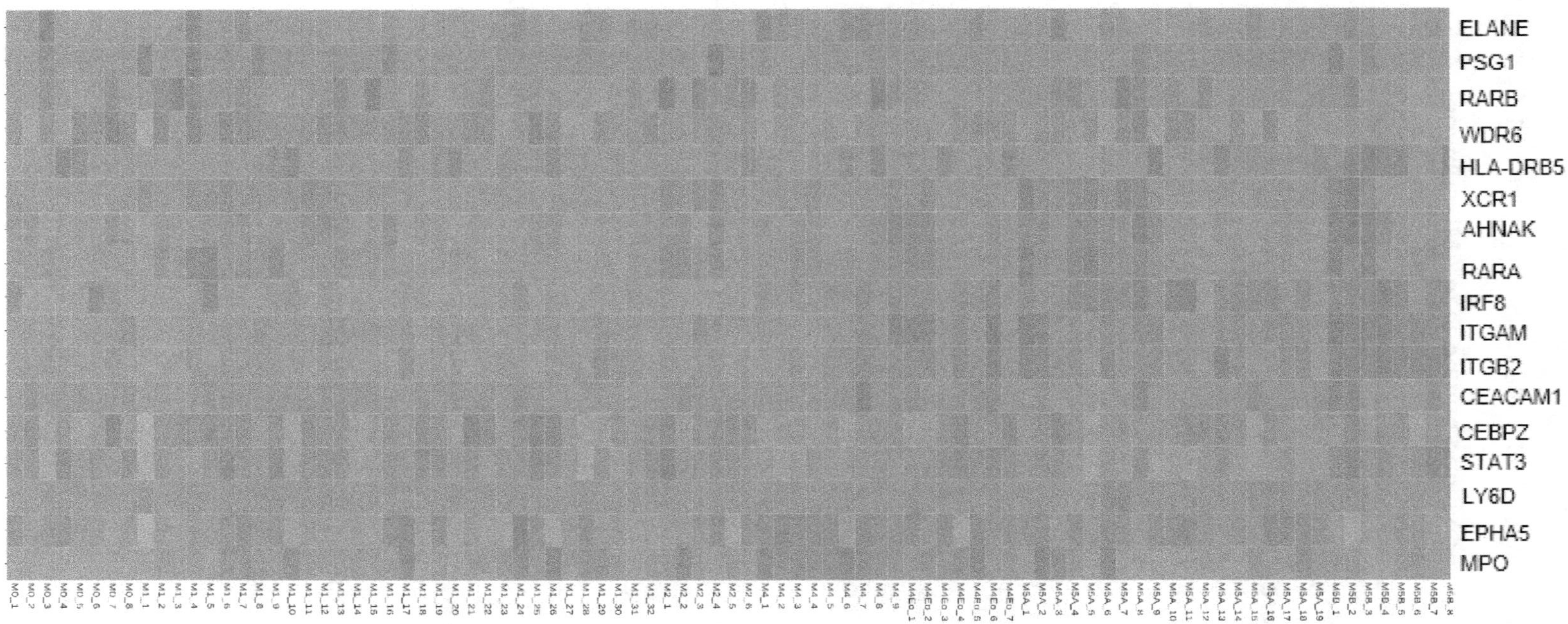

Figure 4.2: A heatmap representing the expression profiles of granulopoiesis transcription factors across AML subtypes.

To assess the levels of immune cell types in the subtypes of AML due to altered expression of transcription factors regulating hematopoiesis and check if there was any difference in the immune cell fractions between blood and bone in AML subtypes, CIBERSORTx was used.

4.2.2. Immune cell profiles of the blood and bone marrow AML patients reveal differential Tregs and M2 Macrophages.

CIBERSORTx is an online interface that calculates the fractions of immune cell profiles in a given set of samples based on their transcriptome profiles. The tool has its own set standard of expression values of genetic markers that define various immune cell profiles in the Lm22 expression matrix file. The output of CIBERSORTx is a bar graph that represents the fraction of immune cells per sample (Figure 4.2). We used transcriptome profiles of two normal whole blood samples as control and 60 blood and 49 bone marrow samples of AML patients. On performing the analysis between blood and bone marrow of AM samples, we observed a higher fraction of Macrophage M0 in bone marrow samples (t-test: t-value -1.5, p-value=0.06) vs a higher fraction of T-regulatory cells in blood samples (t-test: t-value 2.12, p-value=0.017). Also, although deficient in general, there was a higher neutrophil fraction in Bone marrow samples (Figure 4.4). The monocyte fraction was the largest among all blood types in AML compared to the control blood, where the neutrophil fraction was the largest.

4.2.3. Differential Immune cell fractions among AML subtypes

To investigate immune cell fraction across AML subtypes, we compared the total WBC counts between normal samples and AML subtypes. M2 and M5 subtypes showed the lowest deviation of WBCs from normal samples, which correlates with survival trends of AML subtypes, where it is known that M2 and M5 show the best survival (Figure 4.5). Further, we investigated the immune cell profiles across AML subtypes using CIBERSORTx. The largest fraction of immune cells, neutrophils, was negligible/absent in M1, M4, and M5 (Fig 4.6)., and it was seen that the fraction of Monocytes was higher in M4 and M5 subtypes as compared to M0-M2, Tregs fraction: M0-M2 > M4-M5, Neutrophils: M0 and M2 vs all others (Fig 4.6) Neutrophil, the largest fraction of immune cells, was negligible/absent in M1, M4, and M5, and M0 and M2 had a relatively higher fraction of neutrophils but not comparable to normal (Fig 4.6). Macrophage Mo was highest in M2, low in M0, and absent in M1 and M4Eo. M2 macrophages were highest in M5A and least in the M2 subtype.

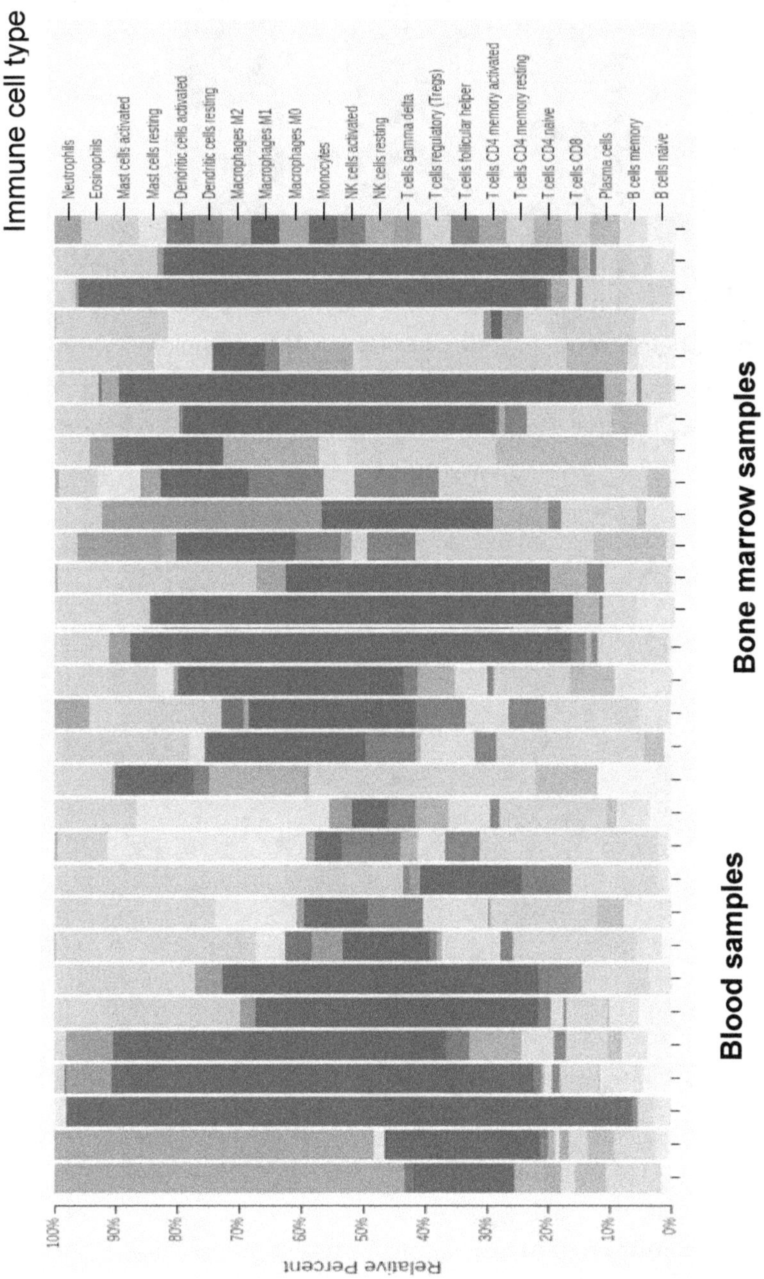

Fig 4.3: Representative result of CIBERSORTx. The Y-axis on the right shows the immune cell categories, y-axis on the left shows Relative fraction of the immune cells

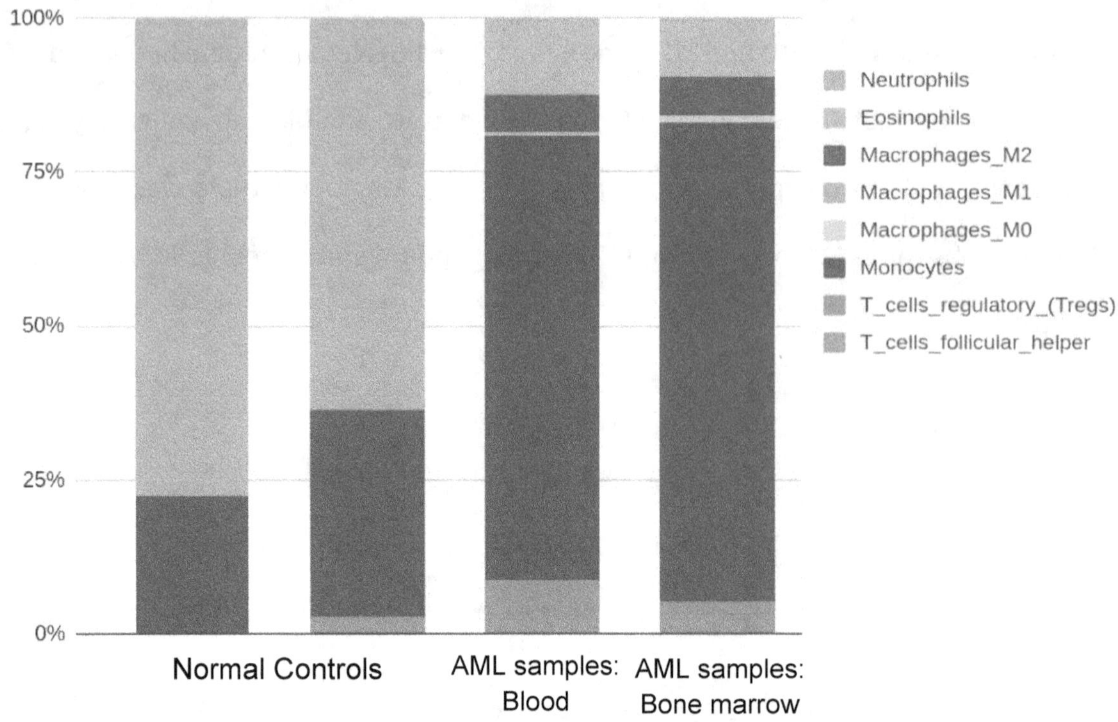

Figure 4.4: A bar plot showing the average immune cell fractions in blood and bone marrow samples.

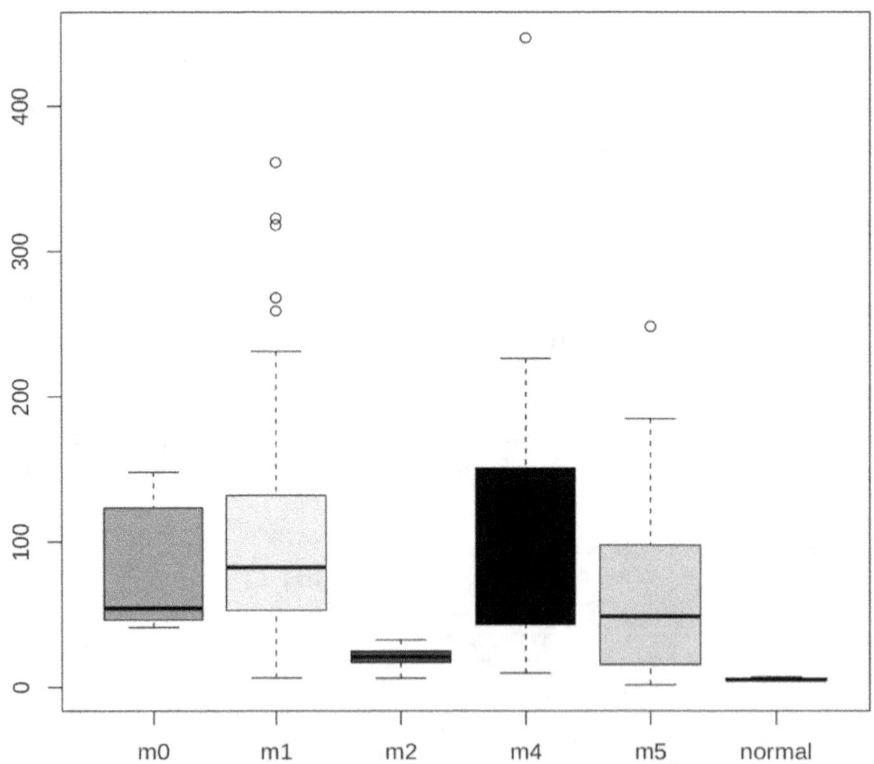

Figure 4.5: Average WBC count across all the subtypes

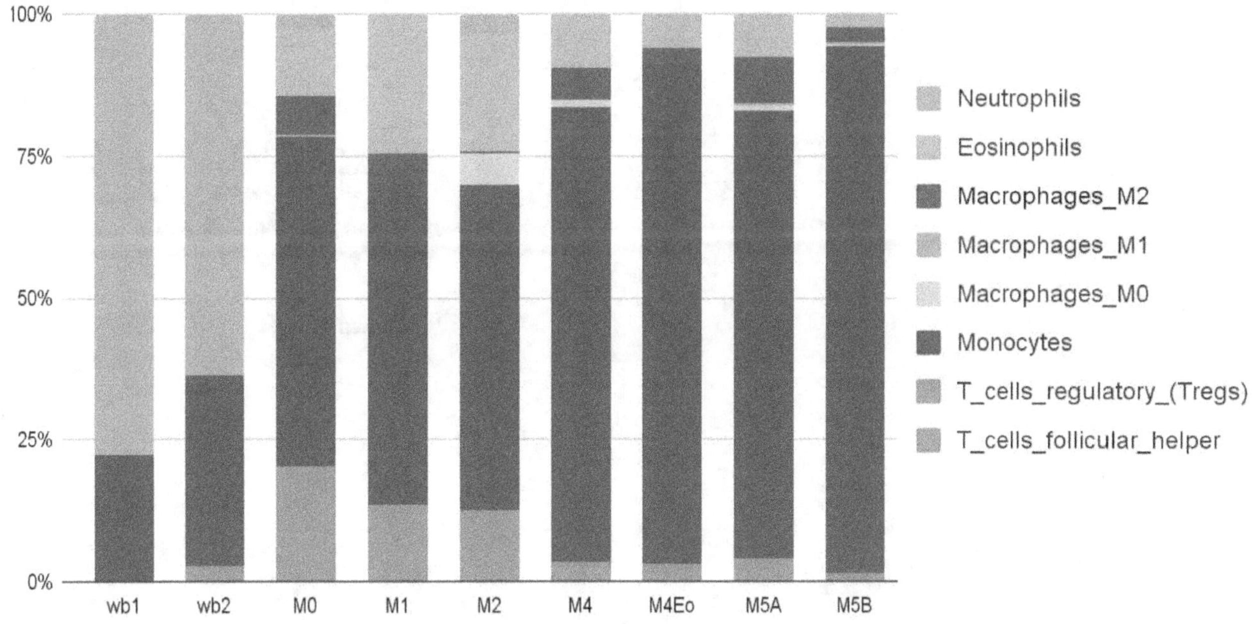

Figure 4.6: Relative percentage of immune cells across AML subtypes

4.2.4. Identification of Hub Genes Associated with AML subtypes Using Weighted Gene Co-expression Network Analysis

To investigate genes/modules enriched in blood vs bone marrow of AML, co-expression analysis using WGCNA (R package) was performed. WGCNA starts by creating clusters/modules, characterized by colors, based on the co-expression of genes and correlates them with traits/clinical data using the Pearson correlation test, all based on vector elements of linear algebra. WGCNA analysis of bone marrow samples showed a significantly high correlation of a cyan color module (Pearson correlation value r=0.9, p-value = 3e-18). Gene ontology analysis of the genes in the Cyan module revealed the Neutrophil degranulation pathway enriched in the bone marrow. The genes in the cyan module were given as input to stringdb, and a network was created (Fig 4.7).

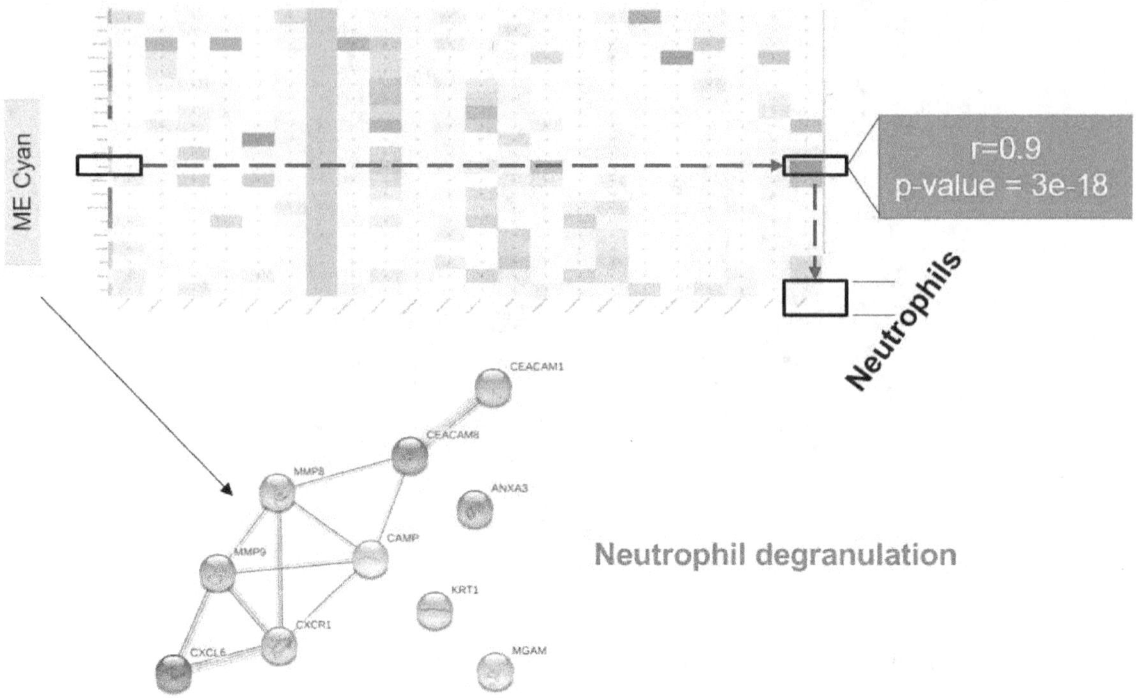

Fig 4.7: Significant correlation of the Cyan module with neutrophils. Pathway analysis of genes of the significantly correlated module shows neutrophil degranulation

Further, to identify enriched gene expression networks in the AML subtypes, WGCNA was performed using FAB classification as a trait. The first correlation was performed by taking all the FAB subtypes together as a single trait. On analyzing the co-expression and trait correlation matrix, it was seen that the grey module showed a significant inverse correlation with the traits. Analysis of genes in the module revealed genes associated with the regulation of neutrophil migration, differentiation of hematopoietic cell lineage, and proliferation of T cells (Fig 4.8). Following the clubbed analysis, we performed a WGCNA analysis with all the subtypes as separate traits. Each sample was marked for the subtype it belonged to and, correspondingly, 7 traits were considered, one for each subtype (M0, M1, M2, M4Eo, M4, M5A, and M5B). The module-trait correlation was obtained, and significantly correlated modules were identified for each subtype (**Table 4.1**).

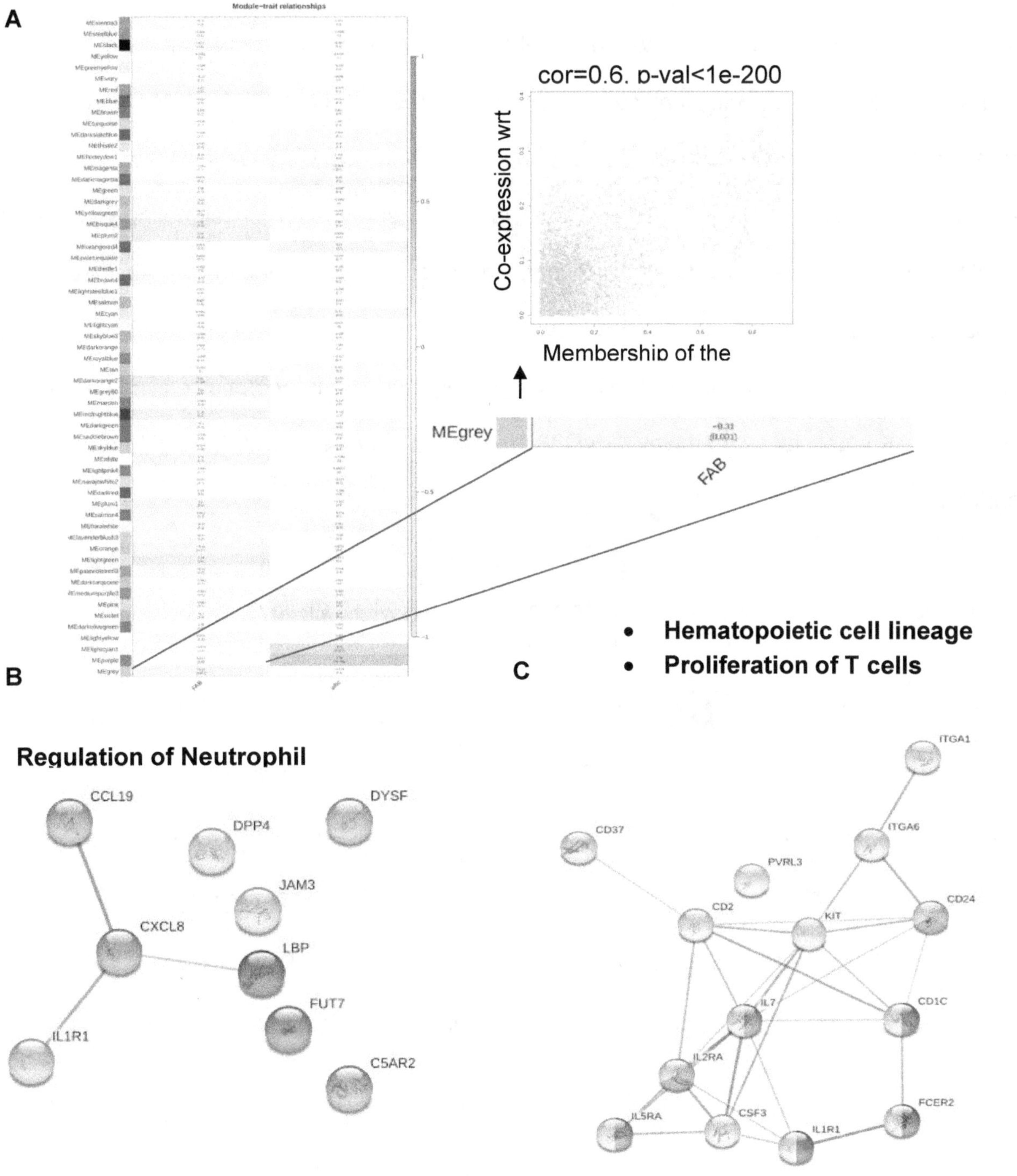

Figure 4.8: A) Module vs trait relation of between gene expression of AML samples and FAB subtypes with the most significantly module being grey, B) and C) show pathway analysis of the genes from the grey module.

The most significantly correlated modules for each subtype are as follows; M0: black, M1: pink, M2: dark grey, M4: light pink4, M4Eo: steel blue, M5A: grey, M5B: yellow. The module-trait correlation values and their significance values are given in **Table 4.1.** Genes from the most significant modules were extracted and subjected to pathway analysis. Based on the most significant FDR value (False Discovery Rate), in the M1 subtype GPCR signaling was enriched, the M2 subtype was enriched with TLR signaling and NK-cell signaling, M4 showed olfactory signaling pathway, M4Eo was enriched with cell-cell communication, M5A subtype was enriched in ECM receptor signaling, PI3-Akt signaling, and Hematopoietic cell lineage, and M5B shows IRAK4 deficiency pathway, MyD88 deficiency pathway, and Innate Immune system enrichment.

Subtype	Module colour	Correlation value	P-value	Pathways
M0	Black	0.36	2e-04	SREBP signalling
M1	Pink	0.29	0.03	GPCR signalling
M2	Dark grey	0.4	3e-05	TLR signalling, NK-cell signalling
M4Eo	Steel blue	0.47	4e-07	Cell-cell communication
M4	Light pink4	0.3	0.002	Olfactory signalling
M5A	Grey	0.62	2e-12	ECM receptor signalling
M5B	Yellow	0.62	1e-12	IRAK4 and MyD88 deficiency, Innate Immune system

Table 4.1: Subtype specific significantly correlated genes modules from WGCNA. The first column has AML subtypes, the second column contains the correlated gene, the 3rd column shows the Pearson correlation coefficient, the 4th column shows the significance values and the last column contains their corresponding pathways.

4.2.5. Subtype specific lncRNA-mRNA pairs reveal unique pathways

We checked for coding genes in the vicinity of the subtype specific lncRNA to check for subtype

Figure 4.9: Expression profiles of lncRNA unique to subtypes

specific lncRNA-mRNA pairs and the pathways that are enriched by them (Figure 4.9). From the upregulated set, we obtained 46 M0, 43 M1, 42 M2, 16 M4, 71 M5 lncRNA-mRNA pairs, and from the downregulated set, we obtained 33 M0, 20 M1, 32 M2, 19 M4, 27 M5 pairs. To obtained pathways

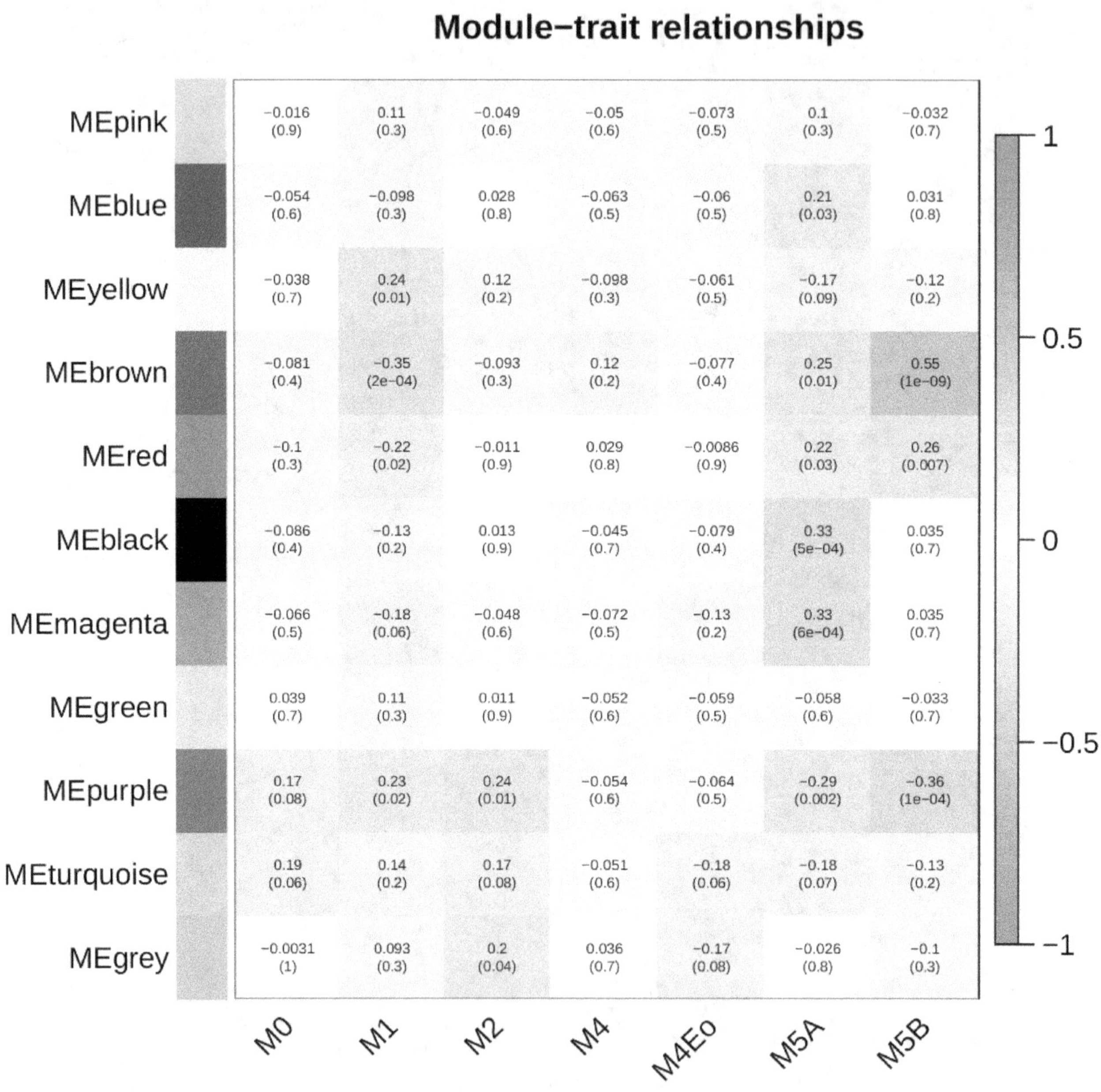

Figure 4.10: Module-trait correlation heatmap between lncRNA-mRNA co-expression and AML subtypes.

from the co-expressed lncRNA-mRNA pathways we ran a WGCNA analysis on subtype specific pairs with the subtypes as traits. The module-trait correlation heatmap is given in Figure 4.10. The subtypes M0 and M4Eo were enriched with NOD1/2 and TNF signaling pathway, M1 subtype was positively associated with FGFR1 signaling and negatively associated with Apoptosis pathway. M2 shows enrichment with Slit/Robo signaling pathway, which was negatively associated with M5B subtype. M5A was positively enriched with Cytokine signaling. M5B was also positively enriched with Apoptosis signaling. M4 subtype did not have any significant correlations. We also extracted the lncRNA-mRNA pairs common to all the subtypes and on conducting a pathway analysis, we obtained upregulation of HOX genes regulation pathway and downregulation IFN signaling pathway (Table 4.3).

Subtypes	**Enrichment**	**Pathways**
M0	0.19 (p=0.06)	NOD1/2 and TNF signaling
M1	0.24 (p=0.01)	FGFR1 signaling
M2	0.24 (p=0.01)	Slit/Robo signaling pathway
M4Eo	-0.18 (p=0.06)	NOD1/2 and TNF signaling
M5A	0.33 (p=6e-04)	Cytokine signaling
M5B	0.55 (p=1e-09)	Apoptosis
Common to all	Upregulated	HOX genes regulation
	Downregulated	IFN signaling

Table 4.2: Significant HUB pathways specific to subtypes based on unique lncRNA-mRNA pairs along with Enrichments highlighted with module colors.

In Chapter 3, we observed 3'UTR variants in DDR genes as AML subtype-specific signatures. In continuation of those results, we checked for any correlation between the 3'UTR variants to gene expression changes and their association with overall survival.

4.2.6. Identification of miRNAs binding to the 3'UTR of the DDR genes

DDR genes with a mutation in the 3'UTR in AML subtypes (FANCF, XPC, TDG, RAD23B, GTF2H5, PDS5B, NEIL2, DUT, BARD1, MRE11A, RPA4, FANCI, ATRX, POLH, TP53, RAD1, UNG, POLK, PRKDC, and RAD51B) (Chapter 3) were checked for miRNA binding in their variant regions using a python script, using UTR information from UCSC browser and the miRNA binding information from miRWalk and miRDB. From this analysis, we found 149 unique miRNAs that had binding sites in only 5 genes (Table 4.3).

Gene	Position	Number of unique miRNAs
BARD1	214728537	1
GTF2H5	158193149	24
GTF2H5	158193282	1
GTF2H5	158195141	1
MRE11A	94419465	80
POLH	43617916	22
POLH	43618961	21
POLH	43619364	20
POLH	43620553	1
RAD1	34908171	1

Table 4.3: Quantifying the number of unique miRNAs that were observed to have an original binding function at the mutation site for particular genes in the non-subtype-specific dataset.

The top genes that showed alteration in miRNA binding to the UTR site belonged to the subtype M1. 134 unique miRNAs were observed for the gene variants in this subtype. Neither of the subtypes had any gene variant where miRNA binding was observed. To check whether the miRNAs with the binding site at the altered 3'UTR sites expressed in AML. miRNAs involved in Leukemia were identified using the miRNACancer database [32]. Of interest were 2 miRNAs hsa-mir-125a-3p (MRE11A, position 94418724), and hsa-mir-23b-5p (GTF2H5, 158193149). At the site of the altered base in the miRNA binding site of MRE11A, at least 80 unique miRNA binding was observed, of which only 2 miRNA expression was reported in AML. hsa-mir-125a-3p is a tumor suppressor miRNA downregulated in AML [33]. hsa-642a-5p, also a TSmiRNA, cannot bind to the 3'UTR of MRE11A due to insertional mutation at 3'UTR (Fig 4.15 A). The low expression of hsa-mir-125a-3p cannot be correlated with disruption in MRE11A, and its high expression is observed in AML subtype M1. The levels of hsa-642a-5p in AML are not known and are under investigation.

FANCF was another exciting gene to explore whether a novel miRNA binding site was created due to the variant or if there was any miRNA binding loss, as this particular variant was observed in all the samples. FANCF and other genes involved in Fanconi Anemia have been previously reported to play a role in preventing AML [34]. It was of interest to understand the consequence of the variant. However, as per the sequence, the A at position 22623347 is flanked by Ts on its 3' region (Kent et al., 2002) (Figure 4.15 A); hence of no consequence.

4.2.7. MRE11A, UBE2A, and BARD1 show a difference in expression between samples with and without the 3'UTR variant

Having observed a possible interruption of the miRNA binding site due to a 3'UTR variant, we wanted to check for changes in expression patterns that could accompany the presence of the variant.

A

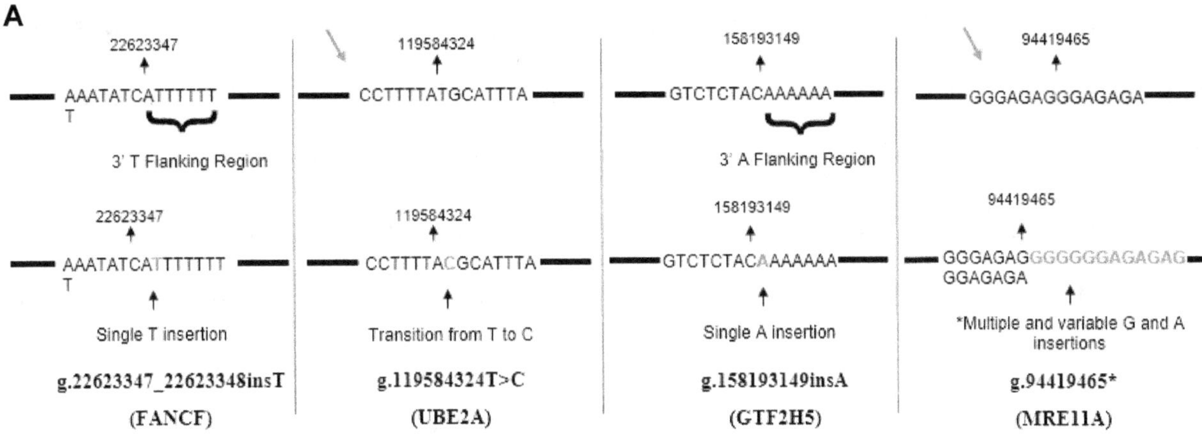

B

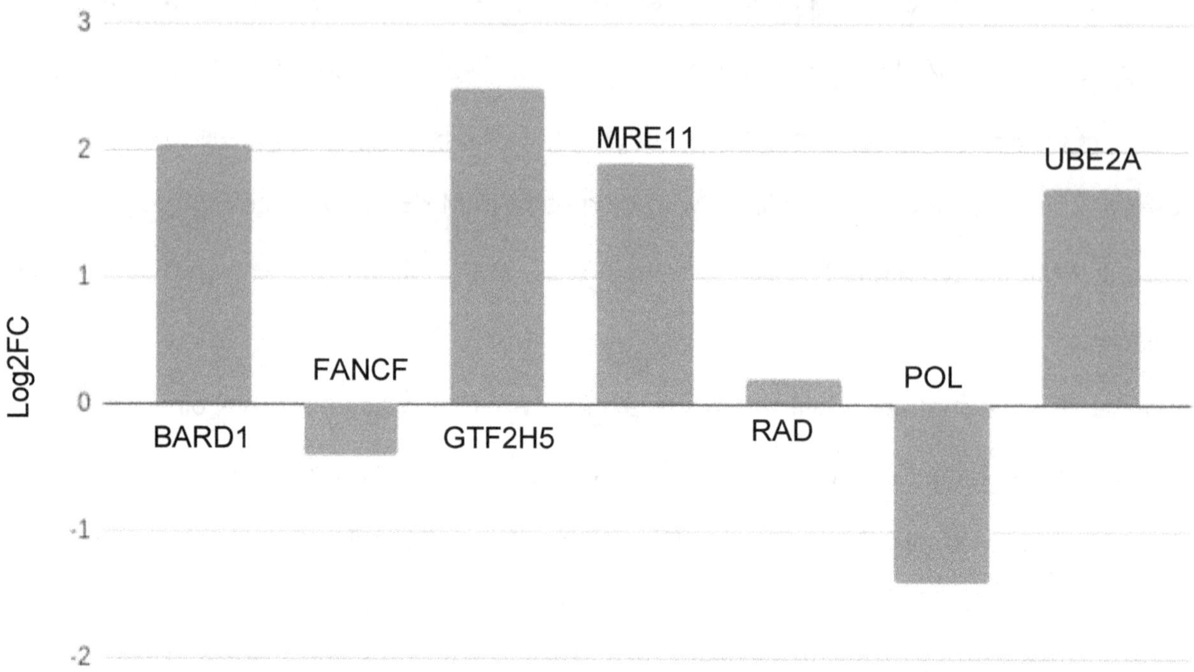

Fig 4.11: A) 3'UTR variants in FANCF, UBE2A, GTF2H5 and MRE11A which could possibly interrupt miRNA binding sites, B) Bar graph with relative expression of candidate genes in AML samples as compared to normal samples

We took two approaches, 1) Difference in expression between AML patients and normal samples, and 2) Difference in expression between patients with and without the mutation.

BARD1, GTF2H5, UBE2A, and MRE11 were significantly downregulated in normal samples compared to AML bone marrow and blood samples. Significant upregulation of RAD1 was observed (Figure 4.11). The gene expression per subtype shows that BARD1 was highly downregulated in M1 compared to any other subtype. (Figure 4.11). Overall expression differences for genes of interest between samples mutated in miRNA binding sites versus those not mutated were not very significant, except for UBE2A, where mild significance was observed (p=0.06) in the M1 subtype. UBE2A is significantly upregulated in samples having a mutation at the miRNA binding site than in samples with no mutation. BARD1 showed a significant upregulation (p=0.03) in expression concerning samples with the 3'UTR mutation

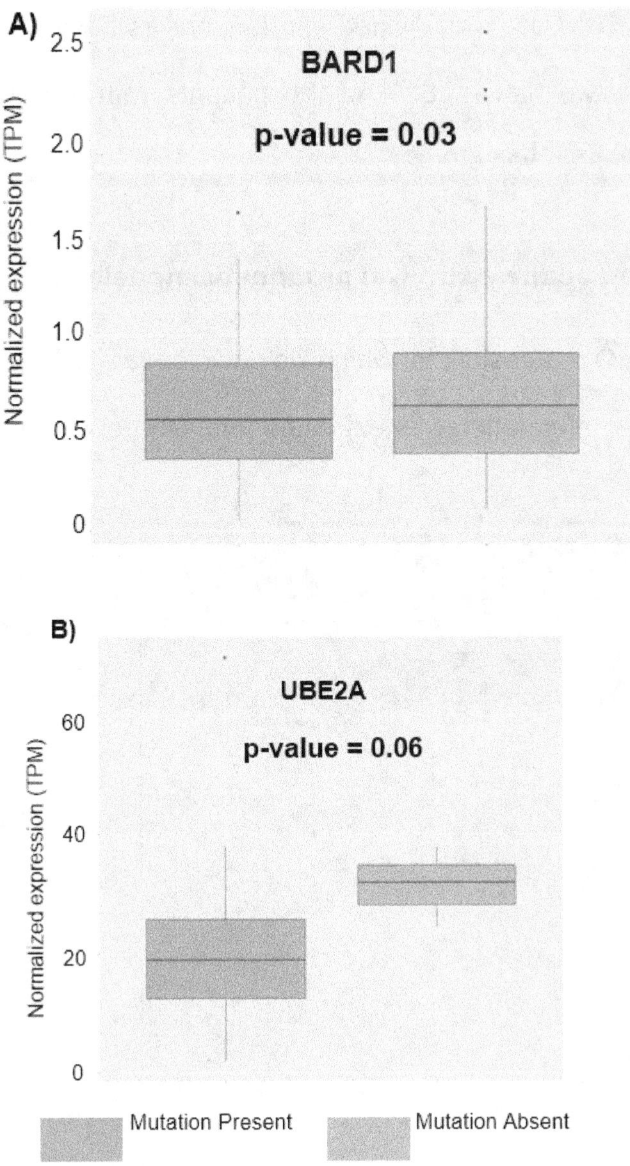

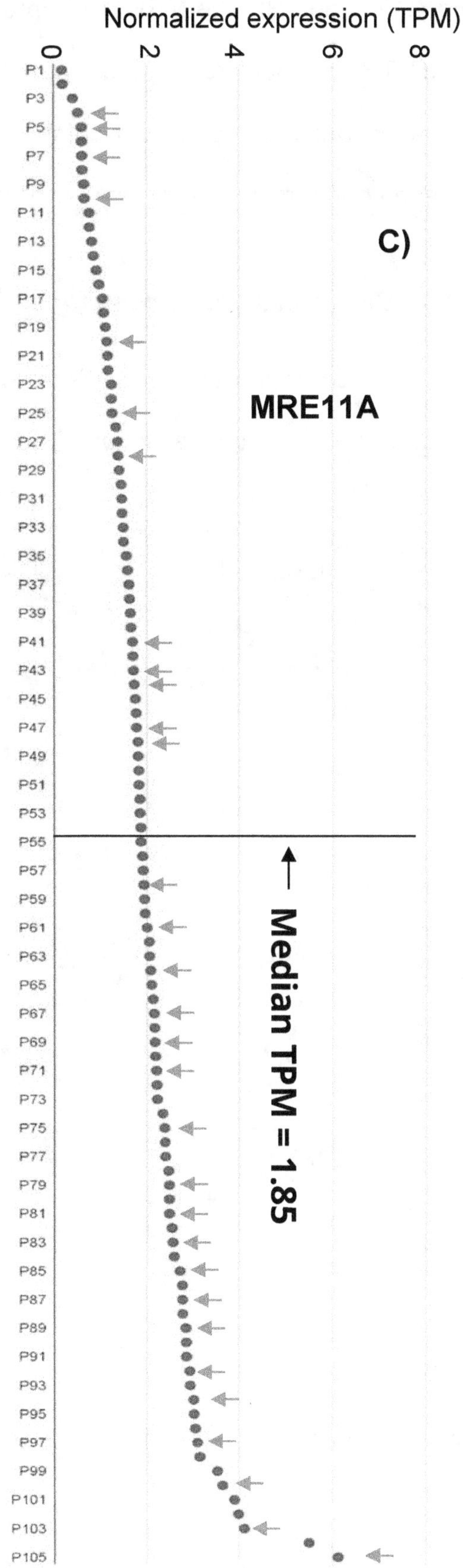

Figure 4.12: Difference in expression between samples with and without mutation for A) BARD1 and B) UBE2A. C) Expression values of MRE11A in an increasing order with patients with mutations marked in red

(Fig 4.12 A and B). The MRE11A expression was plotted in increasing order, and samples with the 3'UTR variant were marked (Fig 4.12 C). The data was divided into two halves based on a median expression value. On comparing the two halves, 61% of the patients with the UTR mutation had a relatively higher expression (t-test: p-value 0.02).

4.2.8. DNA repair genes pose for significant additive survival prognostic models

To screen for prognostic genes, we used LASSO regression, for which we downloaded TARGET-AML survival and expression data. The survival information was extracted for DDR genes, on

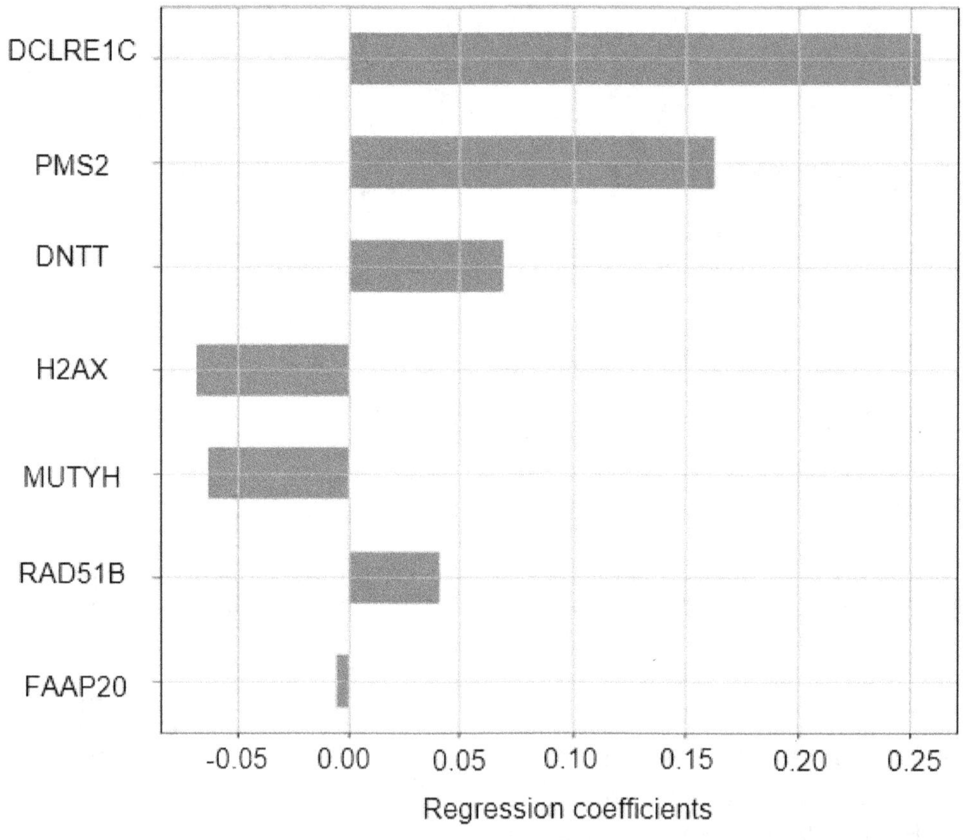

Figure 4.13: Lasso regression model for genes with discernable Regression coefficients. Negative coefficients signify dead signatures and positive coefficients signify alive signatures

which this analysis was performed. The dataset was analyzed using python's Scikit-learn module. The data was processed using 100 random penalty values (penalty) for 1000 iterations to obtain the best set of coefficients. Lasso-cox regression analysis provided features/signatures that are significant compared to others. These signatures were both dead and alive signatures for survival according to their coefficient values. DCLRE1C (0.255), PMS2 (0.16), DNTT (0.07), and RAD51B (0.045) are alive signatures, and H2AX (-0.065), MUTYH (-0.06), and FAAP20 (-0.005) are dead signature (Figure 4.13). Among

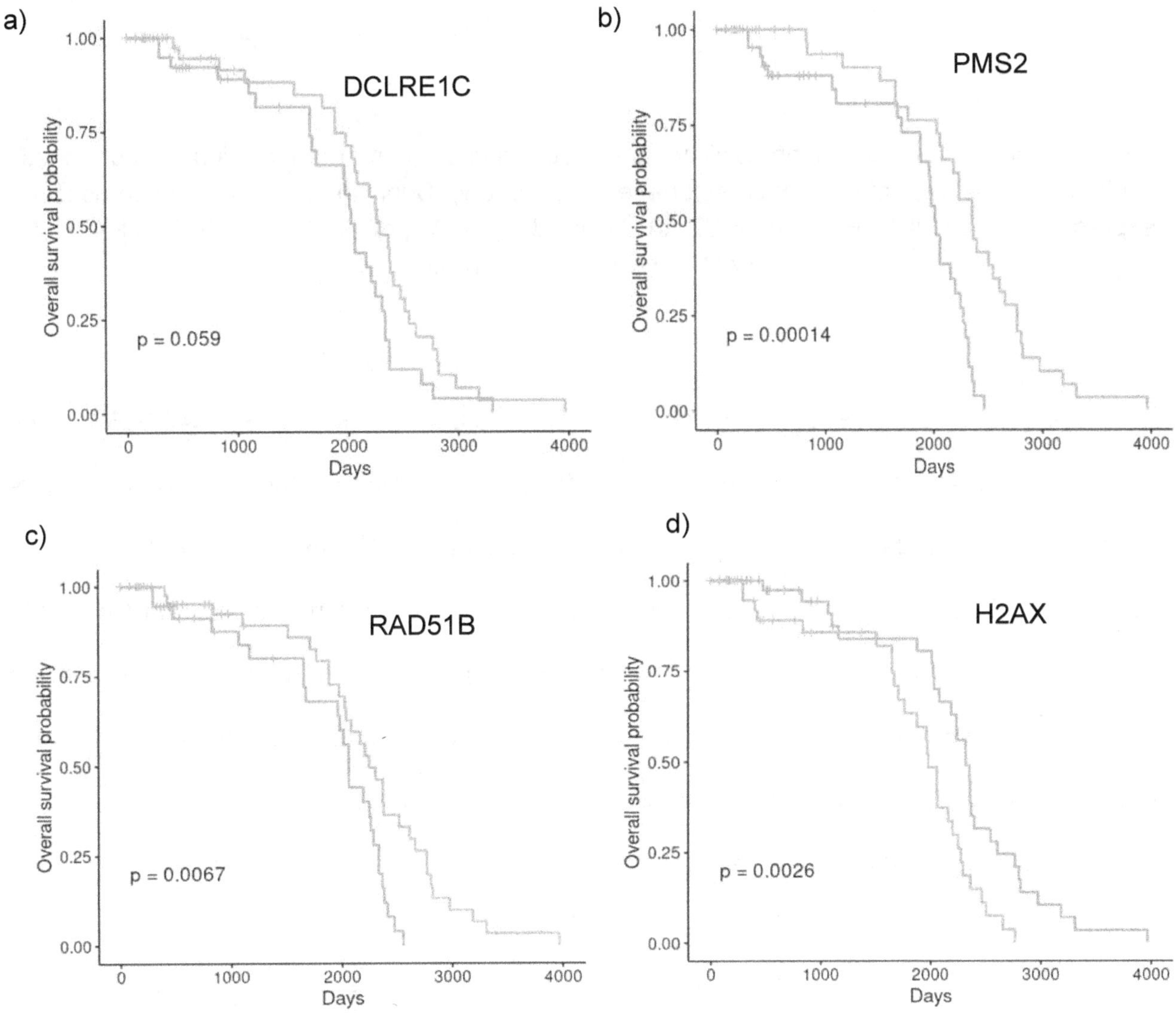

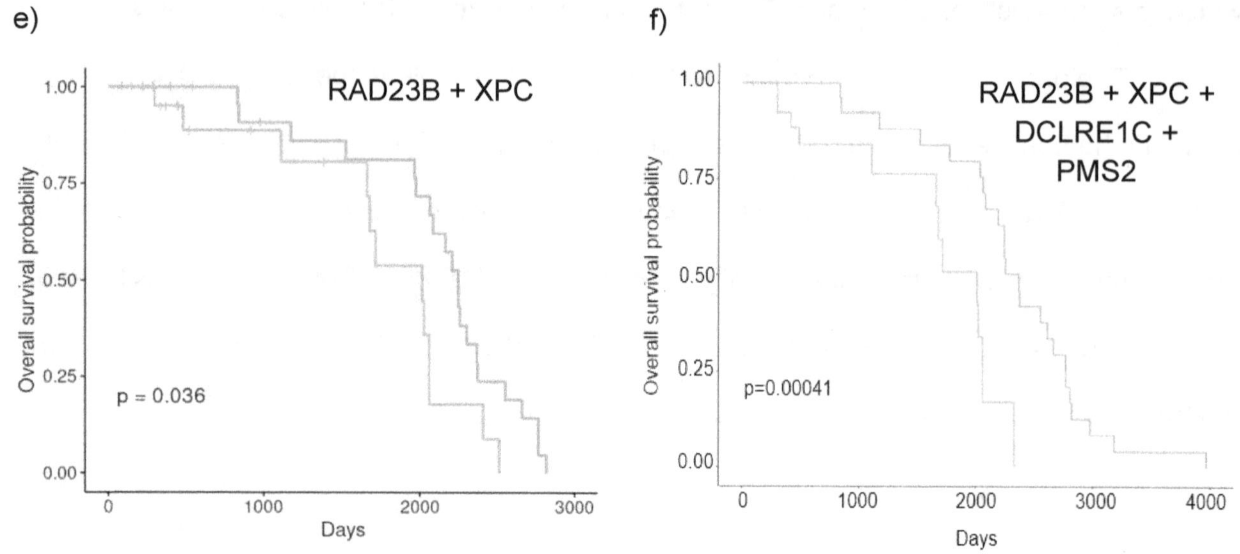

Figure 4.14: Overall survival probability plotted per gene of interest or combinations of genes of interest with respect to its expression (i.e., high or low). Survival curve of high versus low expression for: a) DCLRE1C, b) PMS2, c) RAD51B, d) H2AX, e) RAD23B + XPC, f) RAD23B + XPC+ DCLRE1C + PMS2.

these signatures, DCLRE1C (p=0.059), PMS2 (p=0.00014), RAD51B (p=0.0067), and H2AX(p=0.0026) showed significant predictability for survival in terms of their expression (Figure 4.14 a-d). Apart from the above-mentioned genes, we screened for additional DDR genes and saw that XPC in combination with RAD23B gave a significant difference in survival (p=0.036). RAD23B with XPC, PMS2, and DCLRE1C forms a DNA repair complex, which gives a significant (p=0.00041) combinatorial effect in predicting patients' survival (Figure 4.14 e and f). Additionally, using the survival data we evaluated the survival data of the genes mentioned, as risk factors using multivariate cox proportional hazard ratio analysis in a forest plot It was seen that of all the genes, expression difference in MUTYH and DNTT were significant risk factors for patient death (Figure 4.15). Further, we used Damage-Net, a tool that can be used to analyze data related to DDR genes in TCGA cancer datasets, and one utility of the tool is differential survival analysis. Out of all the genes discussed above, we could see that low expression of DCLRE1C (p=0.04) and PMS2 (p=0.04) correlates significantly with lower survival, while higher expression of FAAP20 (p=0.01) and MUTYH (p=0.01) correlates with better survival (Figure 4.16 a-d). Neither the lasso regression nor the individual KM (Kaplan-Meier) analysis yielded significant results for MRE11A, UBE2A, or BARD1, because of which we decided to check for combinatorial prognostic models using ROC analysis (Receiver Operating Characteristics). Interestingly, MRE11A and UBE2A showed 61.5% accuracy in predicting patients' survival, while the accuracy of 65.5% was achieved when BARD1 was included (Figure 4.16 e and f).

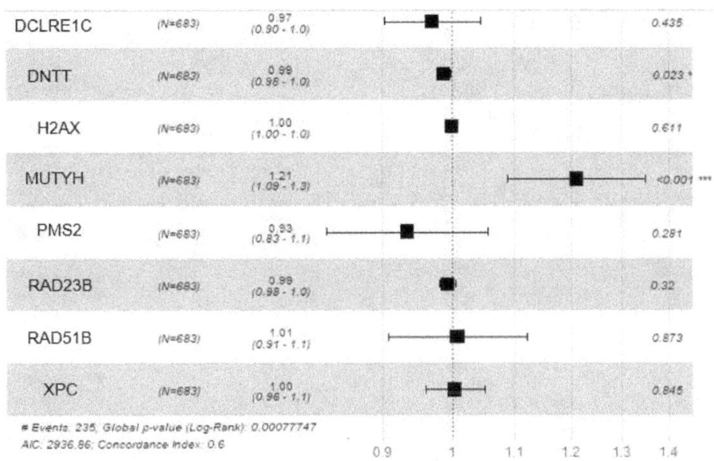

Figure 4.15: A forest plot representing Hazard Ratios of DDR Genes, with respect to their correlation of expression and survival status

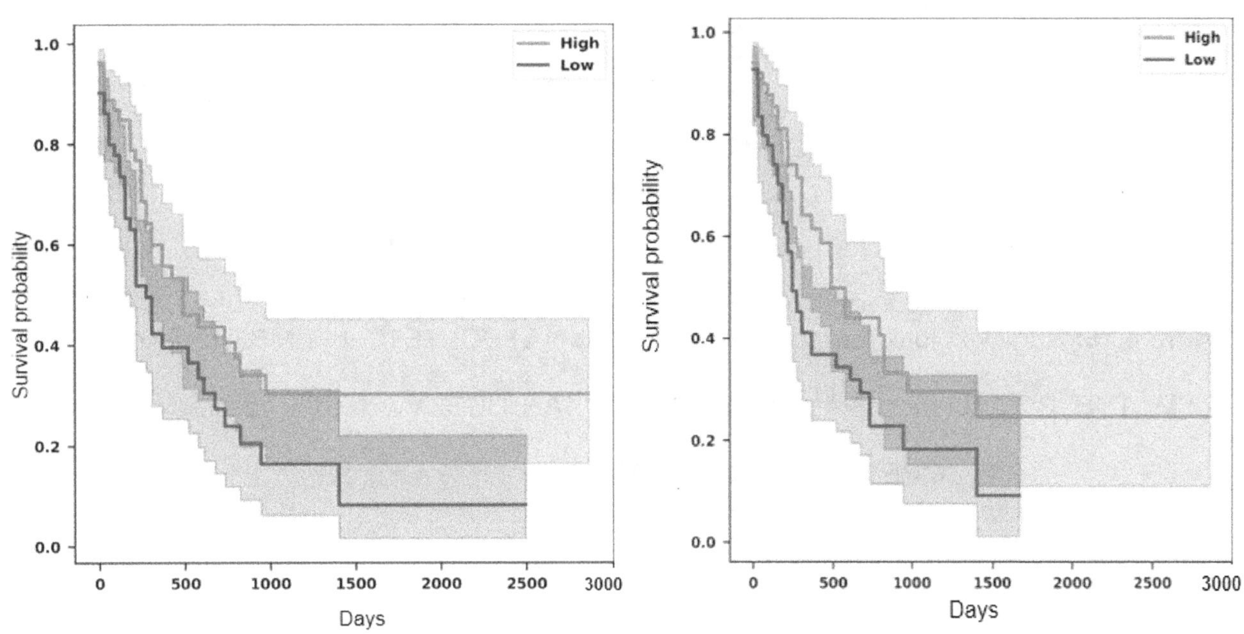

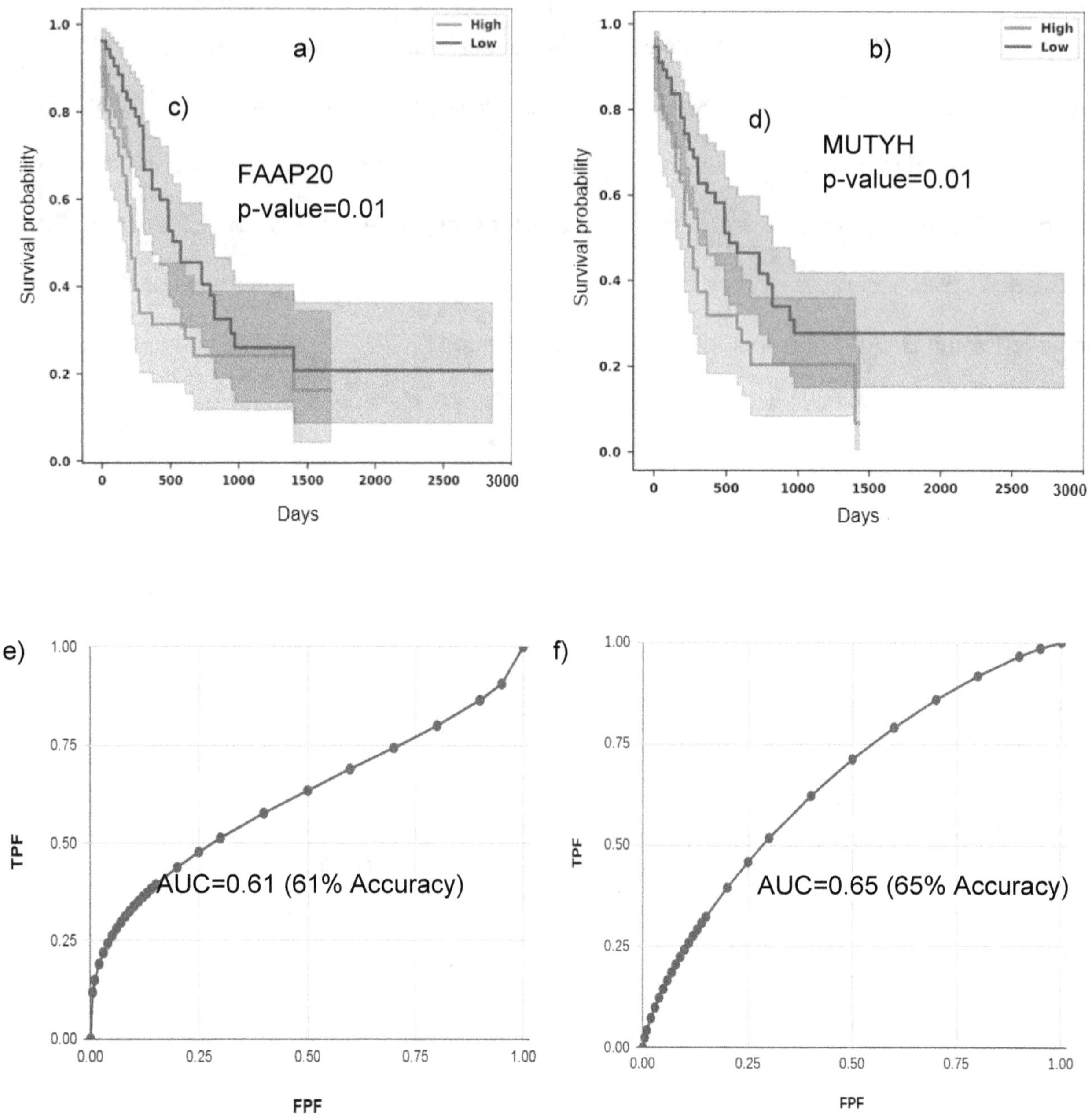

Figure 4.16: Survival plots from the Damage-Net tool a) DCLRE1C, b) PMS2, c) FAAP20 and d) MUTYH. ROC curves represented in e) MRE11A + UBE2A with 61% accuracy and in f) MRE11A + UBE2A + BARD1 with 65% accuracy

4.2.9. LncRNA CASC15 has 35 binding sites for hsa-miR-642a-5p 13 for has-miR-125a-3p and is upregulated in the M1 subtype

The understanding that lincRNA can act as sponges to prevent it from binding to the mRNA may regulate gene expression. We observed 2 miRNAs that could regulate MRE11a, of which hsa-mir-125a-3p has been reported to be upregulated in AML [35]. There are no reports on hsa-miR-642a-5p in AML but is expressed in bone marrow [36]. Since both hsa-miR-642a-5p and miR-125a-3p was known to express in hematopoietic system, and miR-125a-3p is upregulated in AML, we decided to check for the possible sponges expressed in AML samples. To check for the sponging activity of any potential lncRNA with miR-642a-5p and miR-125a-3p, we started by profiling all the differentially expressed lncRNA. LincRNA profiling across all the subtypes showed subtype-specificity.58 up and 38 downregulated lncRNA specific to the M0 subtype was observed. In M1; 62 unique upregulated, 26 unique downregulated, M2; 46 unique upregulated, 39 unique downregulated, M4; 35 unique upregulated and 37 unique downregulated, M5; 91 unique upregulated and 48 unique downregulated (Figure 4.15) lncRNA was observed suggesting subtype-specific signature lncRNAs. Since MRE11A and its variant were specific to the M1 subtype and MRE11A expression is upregulated in patients, we extracted the lncRNA that were upregulated in M1 and checked if the 8-mer seed sequence of miR-642a-5p bound to any of them with a high frequency.

CASC15 is a lincRNA reported to have an oncogenic role in childhood AML[37] . Out of the total 637 upregulated lncRNA, the hsa-mir-642a seed sequence was present on 293 lncRNA, and the maximum number of 35 binding sites was on lncRNA CASC15. CASC15 was also upregulated in M0 and M2 subtypes apart from the M1 subtype. To predict a more robust binding of the miRNA and lincRNA, we used IntaRNA. IntaRNA is a program for the fast and accurate prediction of interactions between two RNA molecules. We took a 1000 bp region of CASC15 where we had found multiple matches to the 8-mer miR-642a-5p seed sequence and gave it as an input to IntaRNA along with the mature sequence of miR-642a-5p. Results predicted the miRNA binding to the target lncRNA region at multiple locations with a maximum total negative energy of -22.64 kcal/mol at one region with multiple adjacent sites. Other predicted regions also showed a negative binding energy. This is represented in the heatmap (Figure 4.17) where the blue regions show strong binding and the intensity peak plot (Figure 4.18)

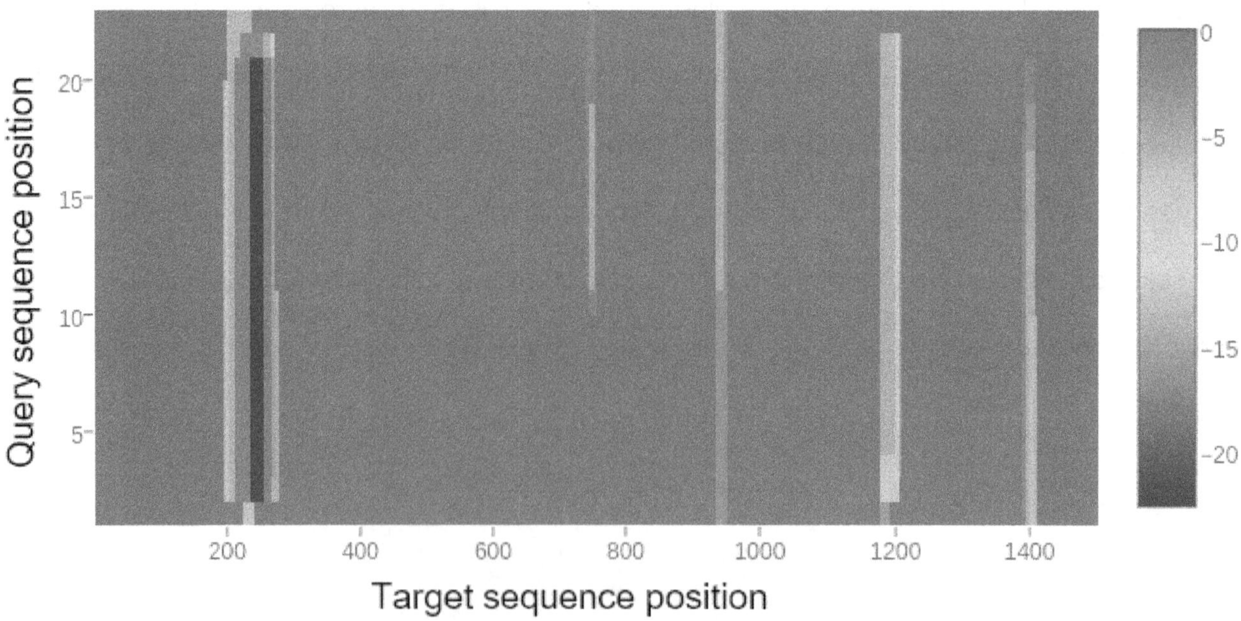

Figure 4.17: Heatmap representing the binding of miR-642a-5p onto the target sequence from CASC15 lincRNA. The intensity of the blue colour corresponds to the strength of binding

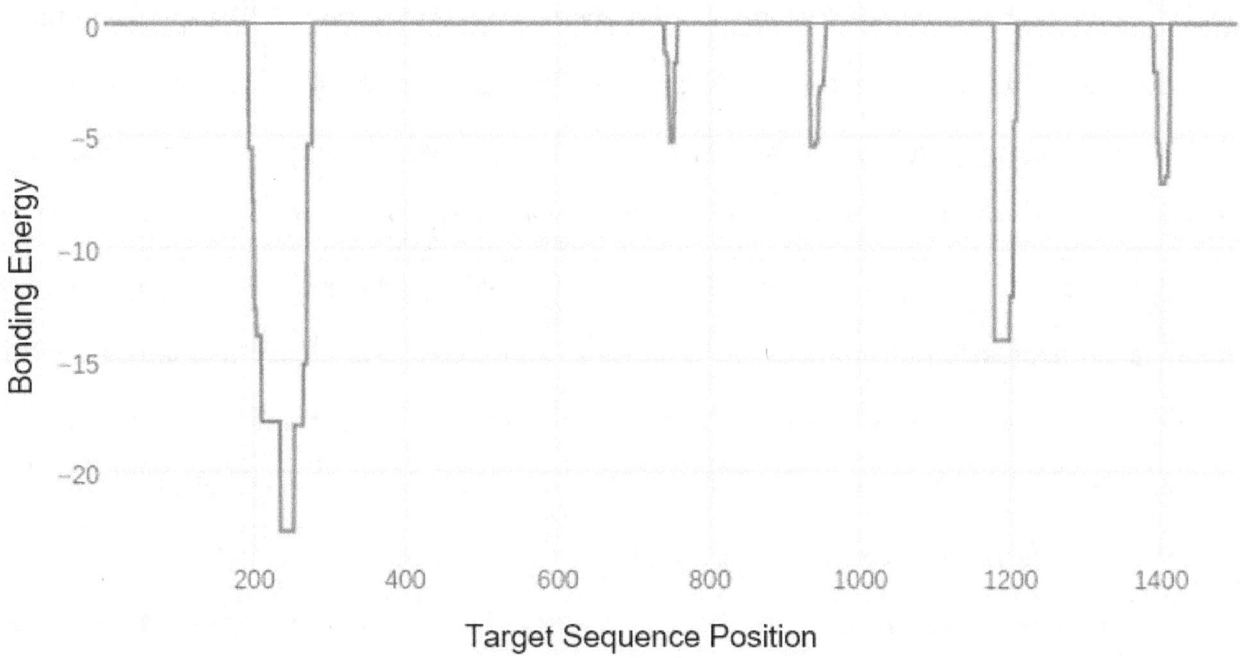

Figure 4.18: Peaks showing the binding energy of miR-642a-5p at various locations of the target sequence from CASC15 lincRNA. Height of the peak corresponds to the binding energy- the more negative the value, better, stronger the binding

4.3. DISCUSSION

AML is a highly heterogeneous disease characterized by cytogenetic, genetic, and transcriptional alterations associated with phenotype neutropenia. Neutrophils are the first line of defense and belong to the innate immune system. The absence of neutrophils leads to microbial infections, commonly observed in AML. Mutations in the genes ELANE, HAX1, and CEBP essential for neutrophil differentiation and maintenance have been described in Chapter3. Integration of the mutation with expression will shed light on the pathogenesis of AML. Many studies describe molecular signatures specific to AML subtypes and prognostic markers, but few studies correlate mutation with expression[38,39]. In terms of clinical correlation, RNA-seq has provided a better assessment than WES or WGS analysis [3]. To understand if granulopoiesis has a similar pattern across subtypes, we immune profile the samples and found subtype-specific patterns. However, a common feature was the absence of neutrophils. MPO expression had a subtype-specific pattern, lowest in the M0 subtype and highest in the M4 subtype. Higher-than-average expression status in M1 and M2 and low in the M5 subtype, in concordance with phenotyping of the AML subtypes based on MPO activity assay, where M0 and M5 are MPO -ve subtypes and M1, M2, and M4 are MPO +ve subtypes[40]. M4 and M5 subtypes showed upregulation expression of 3 genes, IRF8, ITGAM, and ITGB2. No mutation was observed in ITGB2, but samples with ITGAM and IRF8 carried the mutation were expressed, which correlated with slight differences in immune cell types. Among the most significant ones was IRF8. IRF8 is a transcription factor that plays a significant role in the hematopoietic system[41]. In leukemia, it is known to have a dual role as a tumor suppressor[42] as well as an oncogene[41], where its overexpression is linked to poor survival outcomes [43,44]. In the myeloid lineage, it is known to drive the cells towards the macrophage stage, and in concordance with this role, we found IRF8 to be highly upregulated in the M4 and M5 stages, where the cells are in the monocyte stage[45]. Hence IRF8, indicative of an oncogenic function, can be a potential therapeutic target for the M4 and M5 stages.

Neutropenia refers to the degradation and death of neutrophils, commonly linked to AML[46]. Neutrophils are produced in the bone marrow; they mature over time and move into the blood circulation[47,48]. To check if there were any differentiating signatures between bone marrow and blood that could point to Neutropenia, CIBERSORTx was used to profile the patient's immune cells from the blood and bone marrow. A mildly but appreciable increase in the neutrophil fraction in bone marrow compared to blood. We also checked for a difference in the immune cell profiles between FAB subtypes, and as expected, it was seen that M4 and M5 subtypes were enriched in the monocyte population. Tregs and neutrophils were the highest in M0 and M2 stages.

Gene expression profiles of the genes associated with neutrophil formation and differentiation have helped us identify subtype-specific granulopoiesis markers. Interestingly, this subtype specificity correlates with the survival trends where M4 and M5 show a poor prognosis vs good prognosis in M0-M2[49]. Despite the Tregs and neutrophil fraction in Mo and M2, the ratio of neutrophil to lymphocyte was the high and hence favorable prognosis, but any therapy that would alter this ratio despite a particular genotype might alter the survival. Low NLR has been associated with longer OS and DFS in AML[50]. High M2 macrophage is associated with poor outcomes in AML[51].

To correlate gene expression with neutropenia phenotype and if there is a difference between blood and bone marrow and subtypes that could explain differences in the immune cells observed, WGCNA was performed. WGCNA analysis of bone marrow samples showed that the most significant module in terms of co-expression of genes correlated to the neutrophil degranulation pathway. Studies have used immune cell profiling and co-expression analysis to develop prognostic markers using transcriptome profiles[52,53]. Neutropenia in AML patients was due to degranulation of neutrophils, a feature specific to Bone marrow in leukemia[54]. All the above observations of correlation of immune cell profiles with OS and the gene signatures where mutation and expression correlate vs where there was no clear correlation between mutation and expression has to be considered for prognosis and calculating therapeutic responses or minimal residual disease. As mentioned above, immune profiles can be used as signatures to understand AML progression[55].

Among the genes implicated in translocation in subtypes of AML, it was observed that the M5 subtype showed downregulation of transcription factors. One of the genes is RUNX1, playing a pivotal role in malignant hematopoiesis and a gene partner in a characteristic translocation RUNX1-RUNX1T1 in AML. It has been established that RUNX1 suppression induces myeloid proliferation and differentiation, and its knockdown leads to apoptosis in AML cells[5,56]. The finding that RUNX1 was downregulated in the M5 subtype suggests that RUNX1 could play a pivotal role in cell differentiation. FLT3, known to play a key role in AML classification and a part of the FLT3-ITD translocation subtype, was also downregulated in the M5 subtype. A recent study showed that overexpression of FLT3 is a high-risk factor and correlates to poor prognosis in AML patients[53]. Another study shows that FLT3 expression is closely associated with the M5 subtype[39]. KRAS, a vital SIGNALING FACTOR whose overexpression leads to adverse prognosis in AML patients[57], was also seen to have low expression in the M5 subtype, indicating that differentiation of the monocyte lineage is dependent on the function of all the genes, with particular emphasis on FLT3 which is a frequent mutation observed in M5 and is associated with poor prognosis. It is clear that it is multifactorial, and the genes involved in hematopoietic stem cell differentiation are underexpressed in M5. Therefore, the treatment that could alter the levels of HSC proliferation and differentiation genes and alter monocyte number would be an ideal phenotypic change to observe.

Further, to check if the AML subtypes can be differentiated based on gene expression, pathway analysis was performed following WGCNA analysis across different subtypes. Interestingly, distinct networks were enriched in each subtype. A previous study has shown that SREBP expression is absent in acute leukemia cells [58], but the M0 subtype was enriched with SREBP metabolism in our study. In another study, targeting genes of the SREBP regulated pathway has boosted drug-mediated apoptosis in leukemias[59], suggesting that targeting the SREBP pathway can benefit AML-M0 patients. M1 patients showed enrichment of GPCR signaling, and upregulation of GPCRs has been linked to poor prognosis in AML[60]. In the M2 subtype, TLR signaling was obtained, and a previous study has shown the inductive effect of TLR activation in AML differentiation using M2 subtype cells[61]. M2 also showed enrichment of NK cell signaling. NK-cell-based immunotherapy has been extensively adopted in haematological malignancies, and TLRs play a role in NK-cell-based immunotherapy in leukemias[62,63]. An intriguing case was the M4 subtype that displayed an upregulation of Olfactory signaling. A recent study discusses the ectopic expression of olfactory genes on AML cells, and hence it is of a novel potential therapeutic implication[64]. The M5A subtype correlated with the ECM signaling pathway, which is known to characterize leukemic cells and promote AML cell survival[65,66], while the M5B subtype shows a correlation with IRAK4 and MyD88 deficiency. It is known that TLRs recruit IRAK4 and MyD88 in bone marrow cells[62][67]. Ongoing studies are exploring the role of IRAK1/4 inhibitors in MDS clones, but IRAK's role in AML has not been well established yet[68]. These results suggest that AML subtypes show the enrichment of various inter-related pathways. All the subtypes can be explored for their specific drug targets. Each subtype with specific alteration in pathways can also be correlated with immune profile and the OS and DFS, which is an ongoing part of the study.

Despite the use of technologies that have enhanced our understanding of AML and treatment strategies that show CR, traces of the disease remain, also called minimal residual disease, which is the reason for relapse; the field is open to understanding gene regulation perturbations which would get rid of MRD. This study has investigated the role of lincRNA and performed co-expression analysis to identify perturbed pathways which could explain the clonal expansion of the cells which are not targeted by the chemotherapeutic drugs. A particular focus of this study has been on gene regulation of the DDR genes by miRNAs and its correlation with survival.

lincRNA in AML has been reviewed, and its role in prognosis has also been established. The connection between lincRNA and miRNA has also been performed (Frontiers in oncology). However, there are not many studies which have explored lincRNA-mRNA in a subtype-specific manner. Subtype specific lncRNA-mRNA pairs were obtained based on their location on the chromosome, and the criteria were set to within 2000bp of mRNA, and WGCNA was performed for the same. Pathway analysis of subtype-specific significant modules was conducted, and distinct pathways were obtained. M0 and M4E0 subtypes showed the enrichment of NOD1/2 signaling and TNF signaling. NOD2 gene is known to be expressed in hematopoietic cells and has not previously been directly linked to hematological malignancies. However, it has been demonstrated that NOD1 could upregulate CD44, which subsequently activates the PI3K-Akt pathway and is undoubtedly associated with survival in leukemia cells[69-71]. Therefore, although indirect, there does seem to be an M0 subtype-specific correlation between AML and NOD1/2 singalling. As to TNF-α's role in AML, there have been conflicting studies concerning whether it is an oncogene or a tumor suppressor[72], but previous studies have seen its high expression in AML and are correlated to adverse survival. [73,74]. FGFR kinases are majorly involved in hematological regulation, and their elevation promotes AML proliferation[75]. There is also evidence of lncRNA mediated regulation of FGFR1 in Cancer [76], so its enrichment in the M1 subtype suggests lncRNA regulated FGFR1 mediated proliferation of the M1 subtype. We also found an enrichment of the SLIT/ROBO signaling in the M2 subtype. Studies discussing the role of this pathway in leukemia are minimal, but recently ROBO expression has been revealed to be associated with AML in an angiogenic manner[77]. Our study showing the enrichment of lncRNA governed SLIT/ROBO pathway suggests its subtype-specific role in AML. M5 subtype shows lncRNA mediated significant co-expression of genes belonging to Cytokine signalling and Apoptosis pathways. Cytokines have a critical effect on leukemia progression, and they are characteristic features in AML and its classification. One classic example is BCR-ABL, a fusion involving a non-receptor cytokine tyrosine kinase, a CML signature[78]. Cytokines govern AML via multiple signalling pathways, like PI3K-Akt/mTOR, JAK-STAT, MAPK signaling[79], etc. [80]., where they have also been associated with lncRNA mediated regulation and have proven to be promising therapeutic targets in the M5 subtype[81]. Apoptosis has been a famously targeted pathway for drug studies in leukemia via inhibitors of various genes like TP53[82], BCL2[83,84], MDM2[85], and MCL1[86], etc. Elevated expression levels of apoptosis genes are associated with poor prognosis in the M5 subtype[87], and our results show an M5 subtype-specific enrichment of the apoptosis pathway. Therefore, it can be seen that except for the M5 subtype, our results reveal lncRNA-mRNA mediated subtype-specific pathways that have not been investigated thoroughly and open up promising avenues for therapeutics related to regulatory mechanisms in a subtype-specific manner.

Further, we focussed on the role of DDR genes and their regulation by alterations in the 3'UTR, which is known to have a role in CRC [88]. There are no reports of 3'UTR mutations correlating with subtypes of AML. We have integrated 3'UTR mutations and expression with survival to unravel subtype specificity. To check associations between 3'UTR variants and expression differences, we picked up from the last part of chapter 3, where 3'UTR mutation signatures were obtained in AML subtypes. We correlated the presence of 3'UTR variants with possible miRNA-mediated regulation of gene expression. The hypothesis is as follows; A 3'UTR variant could interrupt a miRNA binding site and perform aberrant up-regulation of an otherwise inhibited protein, or on the flip-side, a variant could introduce a miRNA binding site and block the expression of a gene[30,89,90].

As AML is a very subtype-specific disorder, it is essential to note that there was a significant upregulation of MRE11A compared to the normal samples in the M1 subtype. Among the patients, 61% of those with the UTR mutation had a relatively high expression. Correlating it to our miRNA findings in MRE11A, the apparent upregulation in MRE11A could be due to the disruption of a miRNA binding site due to the presence of the variant. UBE2A upregulation in the samples could be due to loss of miRNA binding too. To check the sensitivity and specificity of this observation, ROC was performed, and accuracy of 61% and 65% were obtained for MRE11A+UBE2A and

MRE11A+UBE2A+BARD1. In all three genes, no coding mutations were observed in the samples. An increase can improve the accuracy of the data points. In the dataset, clinical details as in survival were not available for all samples. The role of DDR in leukemogenesis is well established, and the correlation between the 3'UTR variants and expression of the genes has been attempted for the first time. The function of these genes is described in Chapter3.

Using the survival data and all the DDR genes whose 3'UTR was found to have the mutation, a lasso regression model was built using R and python. 4 alive signature genes, DCLRE1C, PMS2, DNTT, RAD51B, and 3 dead signature genes, H2AX, MUTYH, FAAP20 were obtained. Upon survival analysis, it was found that DCLRE1C, PMS2, RAD51B, and H2AX were significant players in survival. Of all the survival gene signatures, expression of PMS2 and MRE11A has previously been linked with a bad prognosis in cytogenetically normal AML samples[91]. The miRNA binding site disrupted on MRE11A was hsa-miR-125a-5p and has-miR-642a. Both miRs expressed in the hematopoietic system and hsa-miR-125a-5p [92] are expressed highly in AML. hsa-miR-642a is a known tumour suppressor in Prostate cancer [93] and is known to regulate the cell cycle. The status of expression in AML is not known. Because of the loss of miRNA binding, MRE11A was overexpressed in samples with a mutation in 3'UTR. The samples without mutation also had higher levels than the normal. To explain the result, we checked for the sponging activity of the lincRNA. We identified CASC15, a survival-associated oncogenic lincRNA in adult and childhood AML [37,94]. We found a possible sponging activity of this lncRNA with miR-125a-5p and miR-642a-5p, which has not been reported earlier. The IntaRNA interaction tool supported this sponging activity, which showed a significant binding.

4.4. Conclusion

The results from Chapter 1 and Chapter 2 suggest multiple targets from the Neutropenia and DDR pathways. Tissue and Subtypes specific enrichment of immune cell fractions was obtained that delineates the involvement of different immune cells in different stages of myeloid cell maturation. WGCNA analysis revealed subtype-specific enrichment of signaling pathways. The most exciting finding is in the case of DDR genes, which were predicted as potential prognostic survival models in AML patients. We could predict M1 subtype-specific 3'UTR variant signatures MRE11A and UBE2A using machine learning algorithms, and by combining the transcriptome and exome data, we were able to hypothesize a regulatory mechanism of these genes via the presence of 3'UTR variants that could alter miRNA binding sites and result in differences in the expression levels. MREA11A, UBE2A and BARD1 together also make an accurate prognostic model. These results need to be validated further. This was the scenario in the Caucasian population. The Indian population scenario is presented in Chapter 6.

4.5.REFERENCES

1. Verma D, Kantarjian H, Faderl S, O'Brien S, Pierce S, Vu K, et al. Late relapses in acute myeloid leukemia: analysis of characteristics and outcome. Leuk Lymphoma. 2010;51: 778–782.
2. Ngo S, Oxley EP, Ghisi M, Garwood MM, McKenzie MD, Mitchell HL, et al. Acute myeloid leukemia maturation lineage influences residual disease and relapse following differentiation therapy. Nat Commun. 2021;12: 6546.
3. Docking TR, Parker JDK, Jädersten M, Duns G, Chang L, Jiang J, et al. A clinical transcriptome approach to patient stratification and therapy selection in acute myeloid leukemia. Nat Commun. 2021;12: 2474.
4. Handschuh L. Not Only Mutations Matter: Molecular Picture of Acute Myeloid Leukemia Emerging from Transcriptome Studies. J Oncol. 2019;2019: 7239206.
5. Mou T, Pawitan Y, Stahl M, Vesterlund M, Deng W, Jafari R, et al. The transcriptome-wide landscape of molecular subtype-specific mRNA expression profiles in acute myeloid leukemia. Am J Hematol. 2021;96: 580–588.
6. Burd A, Levine RL, Ruppert AS, Mims AS, Borate U, Stein EM, et al. Precision medicine treatment in acute myeloid leukemia using prospective genomic profiling: feasibility and preliminary efficacy of the Beat AML Master Trial. Nat Med. 2020;26: 1852–1858.
7. Farrar JE, Schuback HL, Ries RE, Wai D, Hampton OA, Trevino LR, et al. Genomic Profiling of Pediatric Acute Myeloid Leukemia Reveals a Changing Mutational Landscape from Disease Diagnosis to Relapse. Cancer Res. 2016;76: 2197–2205.
8. Newman AM, Liu CL, Green MR, Gentles AJ, Feng W, Xu Y, et al. Robust enumeration of cell subsets from tissue expression profiles. Nat Methods. 2015;12: 453–457.
9. Wang Y-H, Hou H-A, Lin C-C, Kuo Y-Y, Yao C-Y, Hsu C-L, et al. A CIBERSORTx-based immune cell scoring system could independently predict the prognosis of patients with myelodysplastic syndromes. Blood Adv. 2021;5: 4535–4548.
10. Sundarrajan S, Arumugam M. Weighted gene co-expression based biomarker discovery for psoriasis detection. Gene. 2016;593: 225–234.
11. Clarke C, Madden SF, Doolan P, Aherne ST, Joyce H, O'Driscoll L, et al. Correlating transcriptional networks to breast cancer survival: a large-scale coexpression analysis. Carcinogenesis. 2013;34: 2300–2308.
12. Zhao W, Langfelder P, Fuller T, Dong J, Li A, Hovarth S. Weighted gene coexpression network analysis: state of the art. J Biopharm Stat. 2010;20: 281–300.

13. Kadarmideen HN, Watson-Haigh NS. Building gene co-expression networks using transcriptomics data for systems biology investigations: Comparison of methods using microarray data. Bioinformation. 2012;8: 855–861.

14. Hu Y, Zhang X, Wang O, Cui M, Li X, Wang M, et al. Integrated Whole-Exome and Transcriptome Sequencing of Sporadic Parathyroid Adenoma. Front Endocrinol . 2021;12: 631680.

15. Codina-Solà M, Rodríguez-Santiago B, Homs A, Santoyo J, Rigau M, Aznar-Laín G, et al. Integrated analysis of whole-exome sequencing and transcriptome profiling in males with autism spectrum disorders. Mol Autism. 2015;6: 21.

16. Desai SS, K RR, Jain A, Bawa PS, Dutta P, Atre G, et al. Multidimensional Mutational Profiling of the Indian HNSCC Sub-Population Provides IRAK1, a Novel Driver Gene and Potential Druggable Target. Front Oncol. 2021;11: 723162.

17. Eppert K, Takenaka K, Lechman ER, Waldron L, Nilsson B, van Galen P, et al. Stem cell gene expression programs influence clinical outcome in human leukemia. Nat Med. 2011;17: 1086–1093.

18. Levine JH, Simonds EF, Bendall SC, Davis KL, Amir E-AD, Tadmor MD, et al. Data-Driven Phenotypic Dissection of AML Reveals Progenitor-like Cells that Correlate with Prognosis. Cell. 2015;162: 184–197.

19. Gentles AJ, Plevritis SK, Majeti R, Alizadeh AA. Association of a leukemic stem cell gene expression signature with clinical outcomes in acute myeloid leukemia. JAMA. 2010;304: 2706–2715.

20. Ng SWK, Mitchell A, Kennedy JA, Chen WC, McLeod J, Ibrahimova N, et al. A 17-gene stemness score for rapid determination of risk in acute leukaemia. Nature. 2016;540: 433–437.

21. Herz H-M, Hu D, Shilatifard A. Enhancer malfunction in cancer. Mol Cell. 2014;53: 859–866.

22. Hnisz D, Schuijers J, Lin CY, Weintraub AS, Abraham BJ, Lee TI, et al. Convergence of developmental and oncogenic signaling pathways at transcriptional super-enhancers. Mol Cell. 2015;58: 362–370.

23. Mansour MR, Abraham BJ, Anders L, Berezovskaya A, Gutierrez A, Durbin AD, et al. Oncogene regulation. An oncogenic super-enhancer formed through somatic mutation of a noncoding intergenic element. Science. 2014;346: 1373–1377.

24. Hnisz D, Abraham BJ, Lee TI, Lau A, Saint-André V, Sigova AA, et al. Super-Enhancers in the Control of Cell Identity and Disease. Cell. 2013. pp. 934–947. doi:10.1016/j.cell.2013.09.053

25. Roadmap Epigenomics Consortium, Kundaje A, Meuleman W, Ernst J, Bilenky M, Yen A, et al. Integrative analysis of 111 reference human epigenomes. Nature. 2015;518: 317–330.

26. Lee TI, Young RA. Transcriptional Regulation and Its Misregulation in Disease. Cell. 2013. pp. 1237–1251. doi:10.1016/j.cell.2013.02.014

27. Esquela-Kerscher A, Slack FJ. Oncomirs - microRNAs with a role in cancer. Nat Rev Cancer. 2006;6: 259–269.

28. Calin GA, Dumitru CD, Shimizu M, Bichi R, Zupo S, Noch E, et al. Frequent deletions and down-regulation of micro- RNA genes miR15 and miR16 at 13q14 in chronic lymphocytic leukemia. Proc Natl Acad Sci U S A. 2002;99: 15524–15529.

29. Dixon-McIver A, East P, Mein CA, Cazier J-B, Molloy G, Chaplin T, et al. Distinctive patterns of microRNA expression associated with karyotype in acute myeloid leukaemia. PLoS One. 2008;3: e2141.

30. Schuster SL, Hsieh AC. The Untranslated Regions of mRNAs in Cancer. Trends in Cancer. 2019. pp. 245–262. doi:10.1016/j.trecan.2019.02.011

31. Gourvest M, Brousset P, Bousquet M. Long Noncoding RNAs in Acute Myeloid Leukemia: Functional Characterization and Clinical Relevance. Cancers . 2019;11. doi:10.3390/cancers11111638

32. Xie B, Ding Q, Han H, Wu D. miRCancer: a microRNA-cancer association database constructed by text mining on literature. Bioinformatics. 2013;29: 638–644.

33. Emamdoost F, Khanahmad H, Ganjalikhani-Hakemi M, Doosti A. The miR-125a-3p Inhibits TIM-3 Expression in AML Cell Line HL-60 In Vitro. Indian J Hematol Blood Transfus. 2017;33: 342–347.

34. Taniguchi T, Tischkowitz M, Ameziane N, Hodgson SV, Mathew CG, Joenje H, et al. Disruption of the Fanconi anemia-BRCA pathway in cisplatin-sensitive ovarian tumors. Nat Med. 2003;9: 568–574.

35. Chen Y, Chen S, Lu J, Yuan D, He L, Qin P, et al. MicroRNA-363-3p promote the development of acute myeloid leukemia with RUNX1 mutation by targeting SPRYD4 and FNDC3B. Medicine . 2021;100: e25807.

36. Stigliani S, Morandi F, Persico L, Lagazio C, Erminio G, Scaruffi P, et al. miRNA expression profile of bone marrow resident cells from children with neuroblastoma is not significantly different from that of healthy children. Oncotarget. 2018;9: 19014–19025.

37. Grasedieck S, Ruess C, Krowiorz K, Lux S, Pochert N, Schwarzer A, et al. The long non-coding RNA *Cancer Susceptibility 15* (*CASC15*) is induced by isocitrate dehydrogenase (IDH) mutations and maintains an immature phenotype in adult acute myeloid leukemia. Haematologica. 2020. pp. e448–453. doi:10.3324/haematol.2019.235291

38. Pratcorona M, Abbas S, Sanders MA, Koenders JE, Kavelaars FG, Erpelinck-Verschueren CAJ, et al. Acquired mutations in ASXL1 in acute myeloid leukemia: prevalence and prognostic value. Haematologica. 2012;97: 388–392.

39. Kuchenbauer F, Kern W, Schoch C, Kohlmann A, Hiddemann W, Haferlach T, et al. Detailed analysis of FLT3 expression levels in acute myeloid leukemia. Haematologica. 2005;90: 1617–1625.

40. Austin GE, Chan WC, Zhao W, Racine M. Myeloperoxidase gene expression in normal granulopoiesis and acute leukemias. Leuk Lymphoma. 1994;15: 209–226.

41. Liss F, Frech M, Wang Y, Giel G, Fischer S, Simon C, et al. IRF8 Is an AML-Specific Susceptibility Factor That Regulates Signaling Pathways and Proliferation of AML Cells. Cancers . 2021;13. doi:10.3390/cancers13040764

42. Gaillard C, Surianarayanan S, Bentley T, Warr MR, Fitch B, Geng H, et al. Identification of IRF8 as a potent tumor suppressor in murine acute promyelocytic leukemia. Blood Adv. 2018;2: 2462–2466.

43. Scheller M, Schönheit J, Zimmermann K, Leser U, Rosenbauer F, Leutz A. Cross talk between Wnt/β-catenin and Irf8 in leukemia progression and drug resistance. J Exp Med. 2013;210: 2239–2256.

44. Pogosova-Agadjanyan EL, Kopecky KJ, Ostronoff F, Appelbaum FR, Godwin J, Lee H, et al. The prognostic significance of IRF8 transcripts in adult patients with acute myeloid leukemia. PLoS One. 2013;8: e70812.

45. Tsujimura H, Nagamura-Inoue T, Tamura T, Ozato K. IFN consensus sequence binding protein/IFN regulatory factor-8 guides bone marrow progenitor cells toward the macrophage lineage. J Immunol. 2002;169: 1261–1269.

46. Hasan S, Naqvi AR, Rizvi A. Transcriptional Regulation of Emergency Granulopoiesis in Leukemia. Front Immunol. 2018;9: 481.

47. Lacy P. Mechanisms of Degranulation in Neutrophils. Allergy, Asthma & Clinical Immunology. 2006. doi:10.1186/1710-1492-2-3-98

48. Rosales C. Neutrophil: A Cell with Many Roles in Inflammation or Several Cell Types? Frontiers in Physiology. 2018. doi:10.3389/fphys.2018.00113

49. Yang Y-L, Jaing T-H, Chen S-H, Liu H-C, Hung I-J, Lin D-T, et al. Treatment outcomes of pediatric acute myeloid leukemia: a retrospective analysis from 1996 to 2019 in Taiwan. Sci Rep. 2021;11: 5893.

50. Zhang Q, Yang Q, Weng Y, Huang Z, Chen R, Zhu Y, et al. Neutrophil-to-lymphocyte ratio correlates with prognosis and response to chemotherapy in patients with non-M3 acute myeloid leukemia. Transl Cancer Res. 2021;10: 1013–1024.

51. Xu Z-J, Gu Y, Wang C-Z, Jin Y, Wen X-M, Ma J-C, et al. The M2 macrophage marker : a novel prognostic indicator for acute myeloid leukemia. Oncoimmunology. 2020;9: 1683347.

52. Wang J, Hao J-P, Uddin MN, Wu Y, Chen R, Li D-F, et al. Identification and validation of inferior prognostic genes associated with immune signatures and chemotherapy outcome in acute myeloid leukemia. Aging . 2021;13: 16445–16470.

53. Chen B, Khodadoust MS, Liu CL, Newman AM, Alizadeh AA. Profiling Tumor Infiltrating Immune Cells with CIBERSORT. Methods Mol Biol. 2018;1711: 243–259.

54. Qu Y, Zhang S, Qu Y, Guo H, Wang S, Wang X, et al. Novel Gene Signature Reveals Prognostic Model in Acute Myeloid Leukemia. Front Genet. 2020;11: 566024.

55. Swatler J, Turos-Korgul L, Kozlowska E, Piwocka K. Immunosuppressive Cell Subsets and Factors in Myeloid Leukemias. Cancers . 2021;13. doi:10.3390/cancers13061203

56. Mill CP, Fiskus W, DiNardo CD, Qian Y, Raina K, Rajapakshe K, et al. RUNX1-targeted therapy for AML expressing somatic or germline mutation in RUNX1. Blood. 2019. pp. 59–73. doi:10.1182/blood.2018893982

57. Zhou J-D, Yao D-M, Li X-X, Zhang T-J, Zhang W, Ma J-C, et al. overexpression independent of mutations confers an adverse prognosis in cytogenetically normal acute myeloid leukemia. Oncotarget. 2017;8: 66087–66097.

58. Varma N, Varma S, Kaul D. Expression of receptor-Ck and SREBP genes in mononuclear cells from acute leukemia patients. Leuk Res. 2000;24: 913–916.

59. Advani AS, Li H, Michaelis LC, Medeiros BC, Liedtke M, List AF, et al. Report of the relapsed/refractory cohort of SWOG S0919: A phase 2 study of idarubicin and cytarabine in combination with pravastatin for acute myelogenous leukemia (AML). Leuk Res. 2018;67: 17–20.

60. Yang J, Wu S, Alachkar H. Characterization of upregulated adhesion GPCRs in acute myeloid leukemia. Transl Res. 2019;212: 26–35.

61. Ignatz-Hoover JJ, Wang H, Moreton SA, Chakrabarti A, Agarwal MK, Sun K, et al. The role of TLR8 signaling in acute myeloid leukemia differentiation. Leukemia. 2015;29: 918–926.

62. Xu J, Niu T. Natural killer cell-based immunotherapy for acute myeloid leukemia. J Hematol Oncol. 2020;13: 167.

63. Gallardo-Zapata J, Maldonado-Bernal C. Role of Toll-like receptors in natural killer cell function in acute lymphoblastic leukemia. Oncol Lett. 2021;22: 748.

64. Manteniotis S, Wojcik S, Brauhoff P, Möllmann M, Petersen L, Göthert JR, et al. Functional characterization of the ectopically expressed olfactory receptor 2AT4 in human myelogenous leukemia. Cell Death Discov. 2016;2: 15070.

65. Izzi V, Heljasvaara R, Pihlajaniemi T. Understanding the extracellular matrix in acute myeloid leukemia. Haematologica. 2017;102: 1807–1809.

66. Yakymiv Y, Augeri S, Bracci C, Marchisio S, Aydin S, D'Ardia S, et al. CD157 signaling promotes survival of acute myeloid leukemia cells and modulates sensitivity to cytarabine through regulation of anti-apoptotic Mcl-1. Scientific Reports. 2021. doi:10.1038/s41598-021-00733-5

67. Akira S, Takeda K. Toll-like receptor signalling. Nat Rev Immunol. 2004;4: 499–511.

68. Bennett J, Starczynowski DT. IRAK1 and IRAK4 as emerging therapeutic targets in hematologic malignancies. Curr Opin Hematol. 2022;29: 8–19.

69. Steelman LS, Abrams SL, Whelan J, Bertrand FE, Ludwig DE, Bäsecke J, et al. Contributions of the Raf/MEK/ERK, PI3K/PTEN/Akt/mTOR and Jak/STAT pathways to leukemia. Leukemia. 2008;22: 686–707.

70. Caruso R, Warner N, Inohara N, Núñez G. NOD1 and NOD2: signaling, host defense, and inflammatory disease. Immunity. 2014;41: 898–908.

71. Hu YW, Wu XM, Ren SS, Cao L, Nie P, Chang MX. NOD1 deficiency impairs CD44a/Lck as well as PI3K/Akt pathway. Sci Rep. 2017;7: 2979.

72. Tian T, Wang M, Ma D. TNF-α, a good or bad factor in hematological diseases? Stem Cell Investig. 2014;1: 12.

73. Kim MS, Kang J-W, Jeon J-S, Kim JK, Kim JW, Hong J, et al. IL-32θ gene expression in acute myeloid leukemia suppresses TNF-α production. Oncotarget. 2015;6: 40747–40761.

74. Tsimberidou AM, Estey E, Wen S, Pierce S, Kantarjian H, Albitar M, et al. The prognostic significance of cytokine levels in newly diagnosed acute myeloid leukemia and high-risk myelodysplastic syndromes. Cancer. 2008;113: 1605–1613.

75. Götte M, Forsberg-Nilsson K. Proteoglycans in Stem Cells: From Development to Cancer. Springer Nature; 2021.

76. Chen S, Guo W, Meng M, Wu D, Zhou T, Wang L, et al. LncRNA SNHG1 Promotes the Progression of Pancreatic Cancer by Regulating FGFR1 Expression via Competitively Binding to miR-497. Frontiers in Oncology. 2022. doi:10.3389/fonc.2022.813850

77. Gołos A, Jesionek-Kupnicka D, Gil L, Braun M, Komarnicki M, Robak T, et al. The Expression of the SLIT–ROBO Family in Adult Patients with Acute Myeloid Leukemia. Archivum Immunologiae et Therapiae Experimentalis. 2019. pp. 109–123. doi:10.1007/s00005-019-00535-8

78. Smith KM, Yacobi R, Van Etten RA. Autoinhibition of Bcr-Abl through its SH3 domain. Mol Cell. 2003;12: 27–37.

79. Laszlo GS, Ries RE, Gudgeon CJ, Harrington KH, Alonzo TA, Gerbing RB, et al. High expression of suppressor of cytokine signaling-2 predicts poor outcome in pediatric acute myeloid leukemia: a report from the Children's Oncology Group. Leukemia & Lymphoma. 2014. pp. 2817–2821. doi:10.3109/10428194.2014.893305

80. Van Etten RA. Aberrant cytokine signaling in leukemia. Oncogene. 2007. pp. 6738–6749. doi:10.1038/sj.onc.1210758

81. Li J, Volk A, Zhang J, Cannova J, Dai S, Hao C, et al. Sensitizing leukemia stem cells to NF-κB inhibitor treatment in vivo by inactivation of both TNF and IL-1 signaling. Oncotarget. 2017;8: 8420–8435.

82. Phillips A, Teunisse A, Lam S, Lodder K, Darley M, Emaduddin M, et al. HDMX-L Is Expressed from a Functional p53-responsive Promoter in the First Intron of the HDMX Gene and Participates in an Autoregulatory Feedback Loop to Control p53 Activity. Journal of Biological Chemistry. 2010. pp. 29111–29127. doi:10.1074/jbc.m110.129726

83. Vartak SV, Hegde M, Iyer D, Gaikwad S, Gopalakrishnan V, Srivastava M, et al. A novel inhibitor of BCL2, Disarib abrogates tumor growth while sparing platelets, by activating intrinsic pathway of apoptosis. Biochem Pharmacol. 2016;122: 10–22.

84. Ashkenazi A, Fairbrother WJ, Leverson JD, Souers AJ. From basic apoptosis discoveries to advanced selective BCL-2 family inhibitors. Nat Rev Drug Discov. 2017;16: 273–284.

85. Long J, Parkin B, Ouillette P, Bixby D, Shedden K, Erba H, et al. Multiple distinct molecular mechanisms influence sensitivity and resistance to MDM2 inhibitors in adult acute myelogenous leukemia. Blood. 2010;116: 71–80.

86. Niu X, Zhao J, Ma J, Xie C, Edwards H, Wang G, et al. Binding of Released Bim to Mcl-1 is a Mechanism of Intrinsic Resistance to ABT-199 which can be Overcome by Combination with Daunorubicin or Cytarabine in AML Cells. Clinical Cancer Research. 2016. pp. 4440–4451. doi:10.1158/1078-0432.ccr-15-3057

87. Testa U, Riccioni R. Deregulation of apoptosis in acute myeloid leukemia. Haematologica. 2007;92: 81–94.

88. Pardini B, Rosa F, Barone E, Di Gaetano C, Slyskova J, Novotny J, et al. Variation within 3'-UTRs of base excision repair genes and response to therapy in colorectal cancer patients: A potential modulation of microRNAs binding. Clin Cancer Res. 2013;19: 6044–6056.

89. Liu P, Zhong Y, Cao T, Sheng X, Huang H. A frequent somatic mutation in the 3'UTR of GAPDH facilitates the development of ovarian cancer by creating a miR-125b binding site. Oncol Rep. 2020;44: 887–896.

90. Lopes-Ramos CM, Barros BP, Koyama FC, Carpinetti PA, Pezuk J, Doimo NTS, et al. E2F1 somatic mutation within miRNA target site impairs gene regulation in colorectal cancer. PLoS One. 2017;12: e0181153.

91. Gabellier L, Bret C, Bossis G, Cartron G, Moreaux J. DNA Repair Expression Profiling to Identify High-Risk Cytogenetically Normal Acute Myeloid Leukemia and Define New Therapeutic Targets. Cancers . 2020;12. doi:10.3390/cancers12102874

92. Dakir E-H, Mollinedo F. Genome-wide miRNA profiling and pivotal roles of miRs 125a-5p and 17-92 cluster in human neutrophil maturation and differentiation of acute myeloid leukemia cells. Oncotarget. 2019;10: 5313–5331.

93. Beveridge DJ, Richardson KL, Epis MR, Brown RAM, Stuart LM, Woo AJ, et al. The tumor suppressor miR-642a-5p targets Wilms Tumor 1 gene and cell-cycle progression in prostate cancer. Sci Rep. 2021;11: 18003.

94. Fernando TR, Contreras JR, Zampini M, Rodriguez-Malave NI, Alberti MO, Anguiano J, et al. The lncRNA CASC15 regulates SOX4 expression in RUNX1-rearranged acute leukemia. Mol Cancer. 2017;16: 126.

Chapter 5: MiRAGDB: A Knowledgebase of RAG Regulators

MiRAGDB; a knowledgebase of RAG regulators

5.1. INTRODUCTION

The translocations observed in leukemia are due to RAG expression in the cells of the lymphoid origin, where antigen diversity is an inherent phenomenon [1–3]. RAGs (RAG1 and RAG2) are expressed in B cell and T cell lineages and create double-strand breaks [4]. In studies in CML and ALL, BCR-ABL1 positive cells that arise from CML-MBC or CML-LBC show increased genomic instability and aberrant RAG expression[5,6]. It is believed that RAG expression leads to additional genomic lesions, which enhances disease progression [5]. It is established that RAG can identify cryptic RSS and cause breaks causing genomic instability, which cells repair by improving the a-NHEJ [7,8]. In the previous chapter, we have shown that components of the DNA repair are aberrantly expressed, and the mechanism of lost control in AML is variants in the 3'UTR, which leads to loss of control of expression and enhanced restoration of aberrant cells, and hence leukemogenesis. While analyzing aberrant miRNA expression in the progression of leukemia and correlating it with increased genomic instability, we chose to map miRNAs that regulate RAG expression, and a database of RAG regulators was developed.

RAG1 (Recombination Activating Gene) along with its partner RAG2, constitutes a lymphoid-specific protein complex involved in initiating V(D)J recombination, a DNA rearrangement-based process that assembles diverse Immunoglobulins and T cell receptor genes[9–11]. These antigen receptor genes are formed by the recombination of variable (V), diversity (D), and joining (J) gene segments in the early stages of developing B and T lymphocytes[4,9,12,13]. Each V, D, and J segment is flanked by specific sequences called recombination signal sequences (RSSs). RAGs cleave the DNA segments using the 12/23 rule in conjunction with the heptamer and nonamer sequences of the respective RSSs (2,8,9).

Inter-chromosomal translocations are a byproduct of V(D)J recombination when RAGs act in a non-physiological state via cleavage at cryptic RSSs and non-B DNA structures[14–18]. The nicks in DNA, form double-stranded breaks, resulting in cell death or translocations leading to aberrant conditions, including leukemias and lymphomas[19][15]. RAG-mediated translocations in humans and mice have been linked to pro-B cell lymphomas, GCB-derived lymphomas, Follicular lymphomas, mantle cell lymphomas, B cell Acute lymphoblastic leukemia, etc[20][21]. A recent study posits that RAG aids in the progression of BCR-ABL1+ leukemic cells[5]. The expression and normal physiological function of RAGs are limited to the early stages of B cell development followed by a decline in expression in mature stages[12,15].

The stage-specific function of RAG1 in lymphoid progenitors and its well-studied role in genomic instability warrants a regulatory mechanism for its expression. A central regulatory mechanism is the involvement of microRNAs. Several studies have linked the regulatory role of miRNAs in lymphoid tissues and their cancers. One of the first reports of miRNA-mediated immune cell regulation talks about the B cell lineage specificity of miR-181 in murine bone marrow[22,23]. The widely studied miR-17-92 cluster is known to induce T cell survival and differentiation by suppressing pro-apoptotic proteins[24]. MiR-29 miRNA family is crucial to the survival and differentiation of lymphoid cells. A recent study has shown that miR-29c regulates RAG1 expression in a developmental stage-specific manner and has an inversion correlation of its expression with that RAG1 in T-ALL and CLL patients[25,26]. This is the story of just one miRNA with its effect on RAG1 and subsequently on the behavior of lymphoid cells, but it is a well-known fact that multiple miRNAs can regulate one common target gene[27,28] and RAG1 need not be an exception, even more so because RAG1 has genome-wide participation and multiple functional modalities.

Having established the fact that RAGs are expressed only in the early stages of B cell development and pose a genome-wide threat in the context of pathological translocations, it is essential to study and collate information on its regulation at the transcriptional and translational level, that is, expression levels of miRNA and transcription factors associated with RAG1. To do so, we have profiled RAG1 and its regulators in normal B and T cells and leukemia in a unique, comprehensive RAG1-specific database, miRAGDB. Apart from the visual representation of existing expression data, the database also offers a utility to upload their data and plot a heatmap. Additionally, there is informative support in the form of links to MGI and UCSC browser databases which contain information on various RAG1 phenotypes.

5.2. DATABASE ORGANIZATION AND ACCESS

Implemented using Shiny-R, miRAGDB is a multi-utility display interface specific to the expression data of RAG1 and its regulators in normal and aberrant B and T cell conditions. The small RNA and Transcriptome data belong to two organisms, mice and humans distributed over various interactive utilities, which are as follows.

5.2.1. Home Page

The database URL lands on the "Home" page. On the left side, there is a navigation panel that lets the user go to whichever next page they want (**Figure 5.1a**). This page displays information about RAG1, its genomic location on chr11, and its role in V(D)J recombination in B and T cells as part of the RAG nuclease complex. This page offers an option for the users to be able to

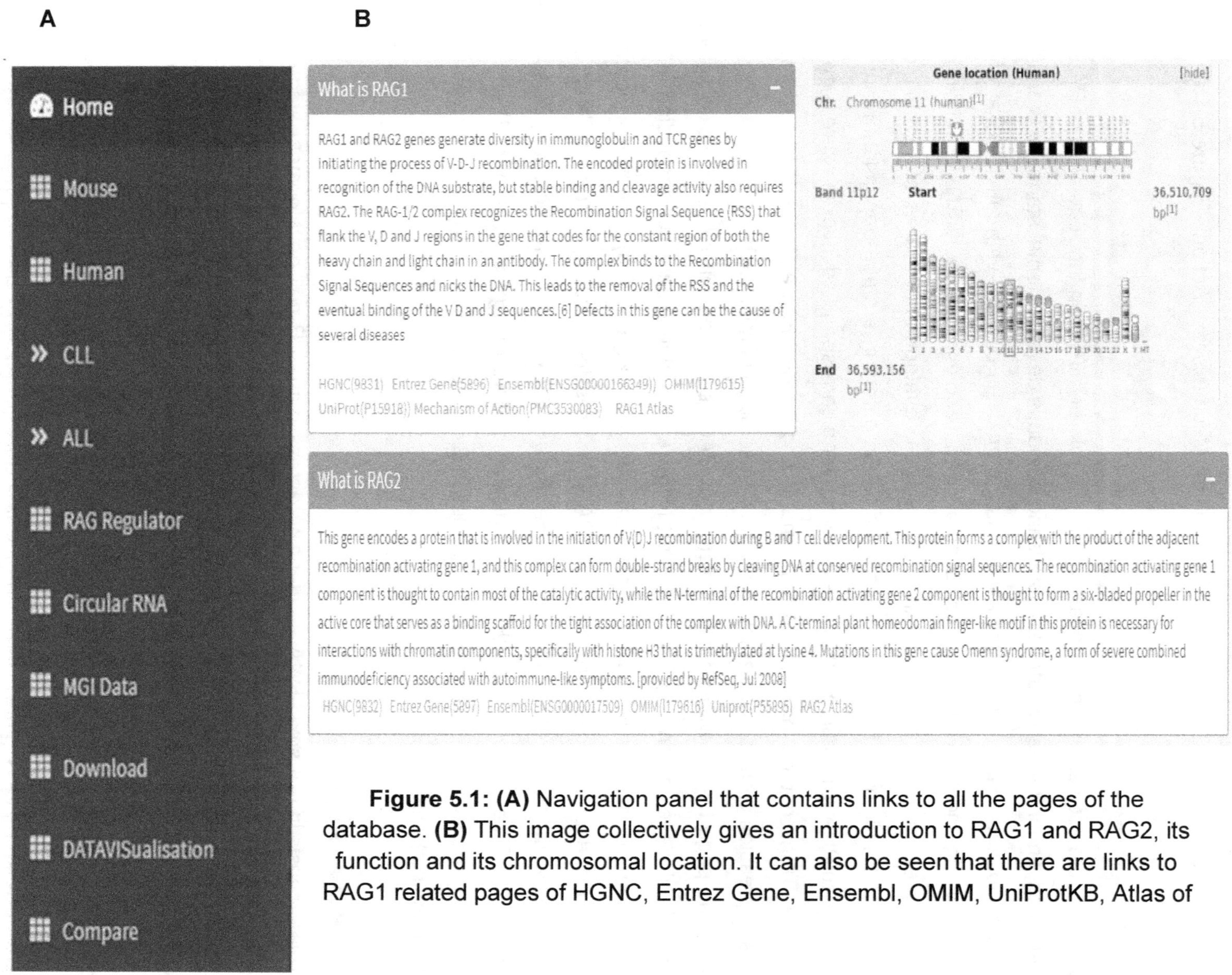

Figure 5.1: (A) Navigation panel that contains links to all the pages of the database. **(B)** This image collectively gives an introduction to RAG1 and RAG2, its function and its chromosomal location. It can also be seen that there are links to RAG1 related pages of HGNC, Entrez Gene, Ensembl, OMIM, UniProtKB, Atlas of

navigate to the RAG1 related pages of HGNC, Entrez Gene, Ensembl, OMIM, UniProtKB, and Atlas of Genetics and Cytogenetics in Oncology and Hematology databases along with a link to a diagram describing RAG mechanism through the "Mechanism of Action" (**Figure 5.1b**).

5.2.2. Mouse Page

Based on a previous study from the lab, where the role of miRNA in the regulation of RAGs was investigated, small RNA-seq datasets consisting of mouse developmental stages of B and T cells were downloaded. Using a standard transcriptome analysis pipeline with mm10 as a reference genome for alignment, followed by calculation of normalized expression, miRNA regulating RAG1 were analyzed for the difference in expression across developmental stages of normal mouse B and T cells. It is known that the expression of RAGs differs in a stage-dependent manner and hence, the miRNA expression data were analyzed for a corresponding inverse expression profile of miRNA. Transcriptome datasets from normal B and T cells were also obtained and analyzed These expression profiles are displayed on the mouse page of miRAGDB.

The page begins with a tabular display of RAG regulating miRNA expression values in normal T cell development stages on the left (**Figure 5.2**) alongside a corresponding heatmap representing the same expression profiles on the right (**Figure 5.3**). Following the miRNA expression, the page moves to tabulated RAG1 expression values in normal T-cell stages followed by a bar graph representing the same (**Figure 5.4 A and B**). In the end, just as it was displayed for T- cells, there is a side-by-side display of RAG1 (**Figure 5.5 A and B**) and RAG2 (**Figure 5.6**) regulating miRNA expression values in B cell development stages on the left and the corresponding heatmap on right.

5.2.3. Human Page

Datasets consisting of small-RNA sequencing across human B cell development stages were downloaded and processed using hg19 as the human reference genome. Similar to the mouse page, this area displays miRNA expression profiles in tabular format (**Figure 5.7A**) along with a visualization in the heatmap (**Figure 5.7B**) and bar graph forms. The difference is that this page is rather interactive. In the beginning, it starts in the same way as the mouse page with miRNA expression values across stages of B cell development in a table on the left and a corresponding heatmap on the right. Going forward, we present the same miRNA B cell data in the form of individual bar graphs available to the users as per their selection from a dropdown list of the miRNAs (**Figure 5.8**). Further, we present a fascinating utility where from a table of expression profiles of miRNA across B-cell development stages, the user can choose any number of miRNAs (at least two) in any order (**Figure 5.9**), and a corresponding heatmap representing the expression profile will be displayed on the right in that specific order (**Figure 5.10**).

Mouse

Normal miRNA Expression T-Cell Stages

Show 10 entries　　Search:

	miRNA	DP	SP_CD4	SP_CD8	SP_nTreg	Th1	Th2	Th17
1	mmu-mir-92b_3p	124.7	172.99	68.15	229.15	137.77	172.97	210.87
2	mmu-mir-382_3p	0.49	1.56	0.6	3.24	0	0	1.03
3	mmu-mir-363_3p	429.01	107.28	155.03	276.86	917.69	77.24	36.82
4	mmu-mir-340_5p	375.32	250.1	1085.63	212.43	1644.72	1250.42	643.92
5	mmu-mir-331_3p	41.24	78	42.84	78.99	155.59	61.4	264.97
6	mmu-mir-330_5p	0.49	5.36	5.18	5.93	13.01	18.49	14.19
7	mmu-mir-326_3p	0	0.89	2.59	5.93	16.69	20.69	19.96
8	mmu-mir-324_5p	1.71	3.58	4.38	22.38	59.41	33.45	25.92
9	mmu-mir-32_5p	0.49	3.58	3.39	4.58	6.51	2.64	4.94
10	mmu-mir-30e_5p	717.7	375.04	457.73	202.46	544.56	364.21	572.12

Showing 1 to 10 of 26 entries　　Previous 1 2 3 Next

Figure 5.2: Mouse page with a tabulated display of RAG1 miRNA expression across T cell development stages

However, the shade of the color corresponding to the expression value in the heatmap for every miRNA for each stage will differ slightly with the addition or removal of every miRNA. In the end, just as in the mouse page, the human page displays expression levels of miRNA against RAG2 in Human B cell development stages (**Figure 5.11 A and B**).

5.2.4. RAG associated miRNA expression in aberrant B and T cell conditions

The next two pages deal with the expression of RAG1 and the miRNA regulating it in two datasets, Chronic lymphocytic leukemia, and T-cell Acute Lymphoblastic Leukemia, respectively.

Both the pages begin by displaying an expression table of RAG1 regulating miRNA across 15 CLL patient samples (17 miRNA spread across two pages) (**Figure 5.12 A and B**) and 48 T-ALL samples (**Figure 5.13 A and B**).

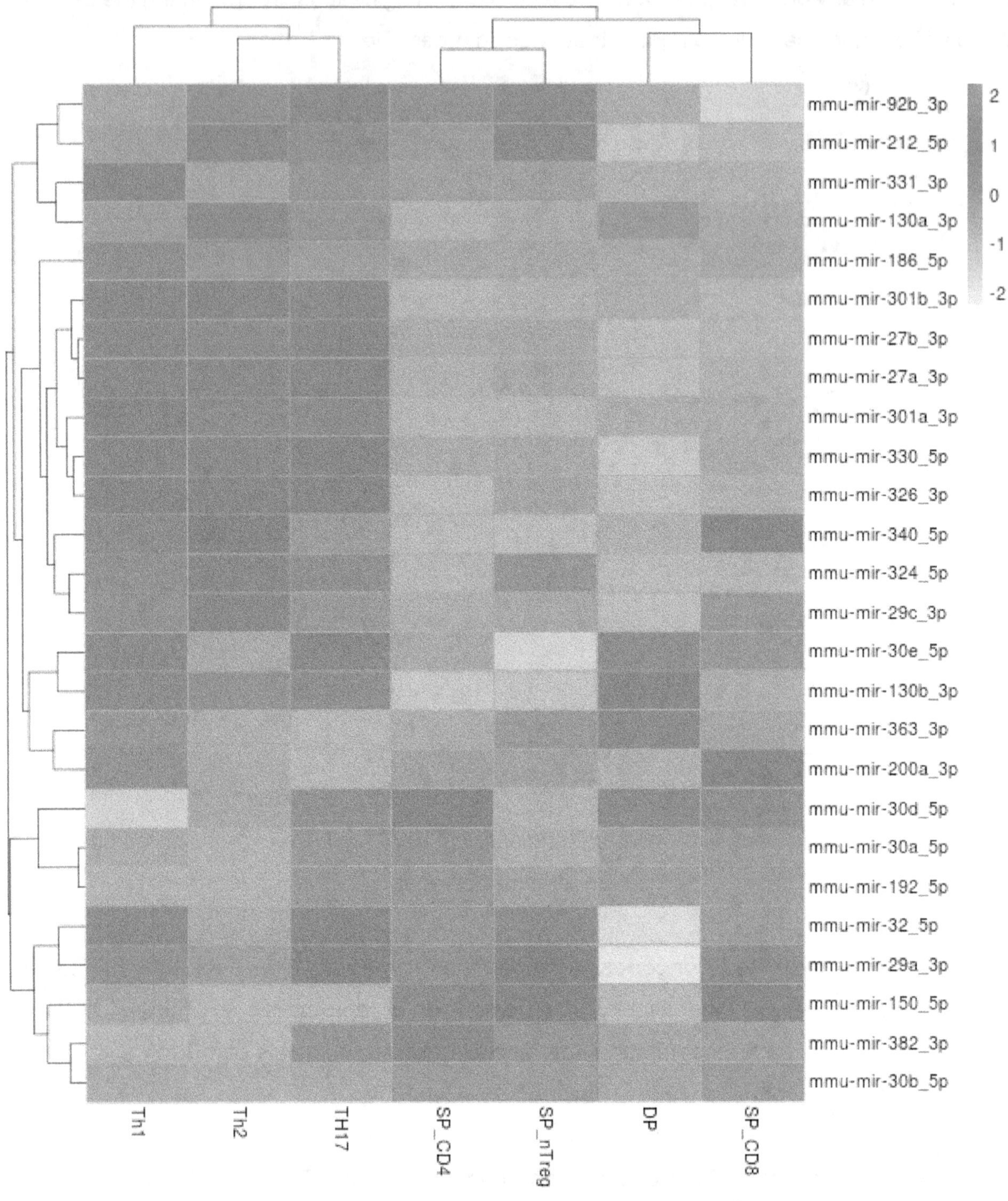

Figure 5.3: Heatmap of RAG1 specific miRNA across T cell development stages in mouse

A

RAG Expression in Normal Condition T-Cell Stages

Show 10 entries Search:

	DN1.R1	DN1.R2	DN2.R1	DN2.R2	DN3.R1	DN3.R2	DN4.R1	DN4.R2
1	0.202539276636068	0.0801706875631093	2.21787715736308	2.01772218847164	2.54332438939102	2.55519800321851	4.04145850072698	4.04957465055061

Showing 1 to 1 of 1 entries Previous 1 Next

B

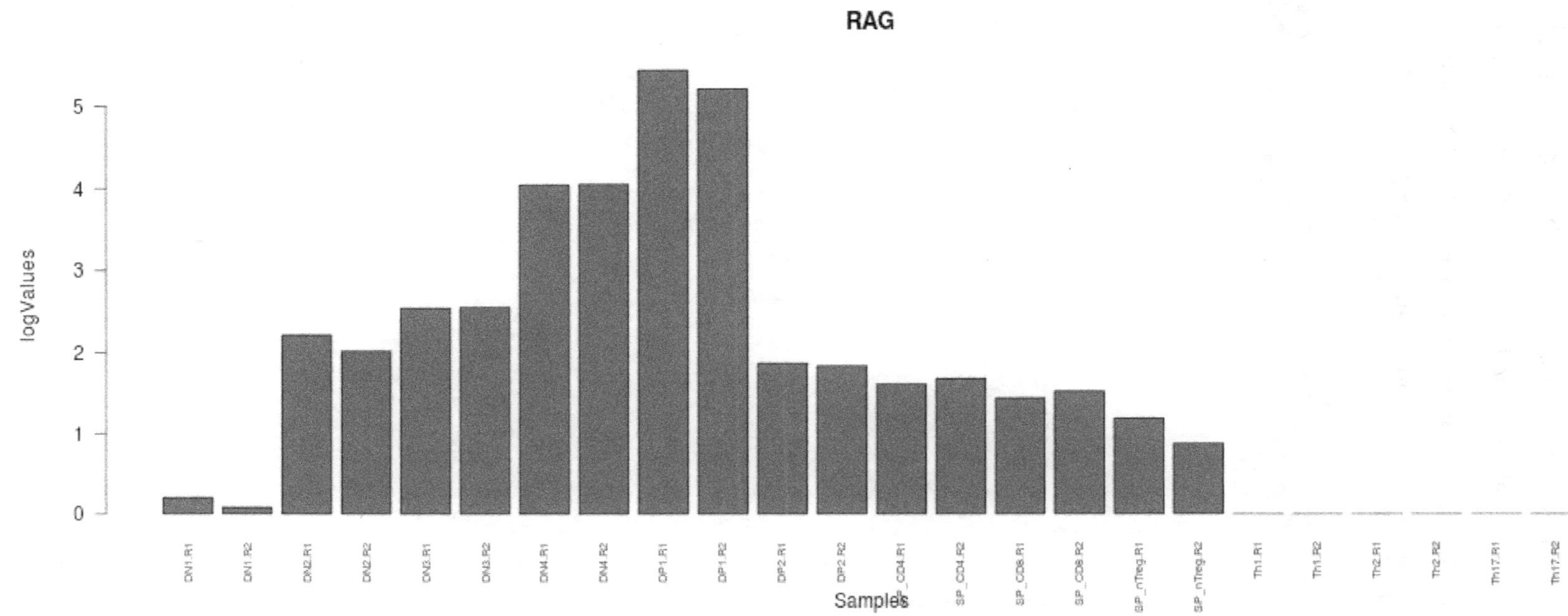

Figure 5.4: (A) RAG expression table across T cell development stages, B) A bar chart representing the normalized expression values in log scale

This table includes a search dialogue box where the user can search for one of the 17 miRNAs and obtain expression values specific to that miRNA. Further down is a heatmap of those miRNAs (**Figure 5.12 A and B**) and at the end is a Bar graph showing RAG1 expression across the 15 CLL patients and 48 T-ALL patients (**Figure 5.13 A and B**).

Normal miRNA Expression B-Cell stages

Show 10 entries

Search:

	miRNA_id	proB	preB	immatureB	matureB
1	mmu-miR-200a-3p	0.21	0.24	0.24	0.16
2	mmu-miR-382-3p	0.05	0.01	0.01	0
3	mmu-miR-92a-3p	644.24	1136.85	106.05	70.45
4	mmu-miR-92b-3p	1.31	0.19	0.89	0.01
5	mmu-miR-32-5p	0.1	0.14	0.07	0
6	mmu-miR-363-3p	13.38	18.33	9.94	0.04
7	mmu-miR-192-5p	37.21	102.43	57.85	0.8
8	mmu-miR-331-3p	5.95	6.39	5.26	0
9	mmu-miR-301a-3p	0.49	0.48	0.14	0
10	mmu-miR-301b-3p	0.32	0.14	0.07	0

Showing 1 to 10 of 29 entries   Previous 1 2 3 Next

Figure 5.5 A: Table representing mouse RAG1 miRNA expression across B cell development stages

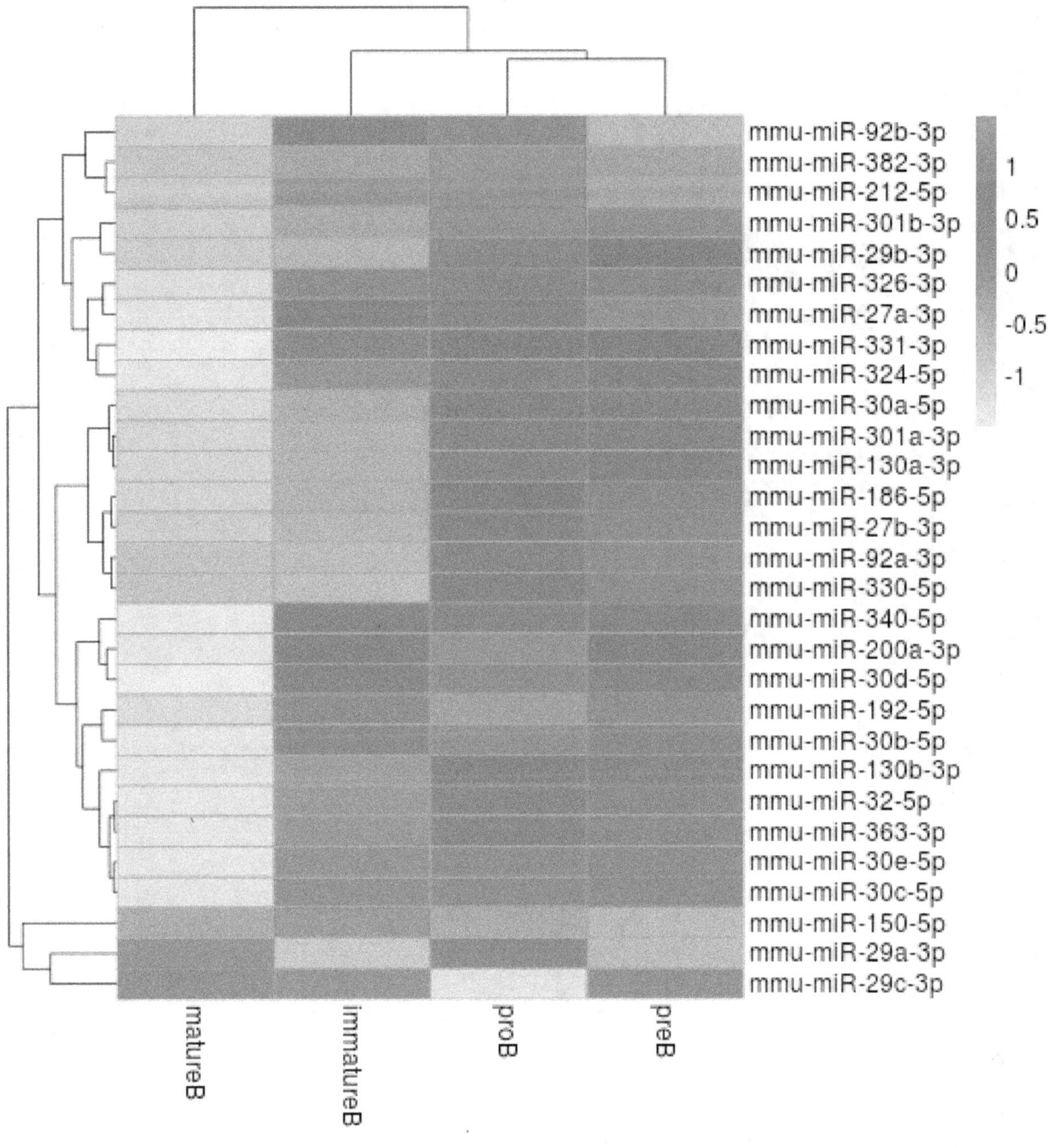

Figure 5.5 B: Heatmap corresponding to mouse RAG1 miRNA expression values across b cells stages

miRNA against RAG2 - Mouse B cells

Show 10 entries

Search:

	miR_id	proB	preB	immature	mature
1	mmu-miR-29a-3p	138.1978834	163.6038509	131.56	187.08
2	mmu-miR-29c-3p	0.548099037	1.167088727	1.11	1.53
3	mmu-miR-3535	0.170864882	0.615421369	0.64	1.5
4	mmu-miR-362-5p	0.308506037	0.651201681	0.66	0.7
5	mmu-miR-3962	0.0211547	0.623293038	7.16	0.63
6	mmu-miR-5114	1.634681338	3.645037981	3.56	2.33
7	mmu-miR-8094	0.060441999	0.141758189	0.09	0.14
8	mmu-miR-107-3p	106.748454	251.0645388	199.08	9.78
9	mmu-miR-130b-5p	0.750030261	1.319317692	1.09	0.01
10	mmu-miR-150-3p	2.000080696	10.73214199	57.61	0.05

Showing 1 to 10 of 19 entries

Previous 1 2 Next

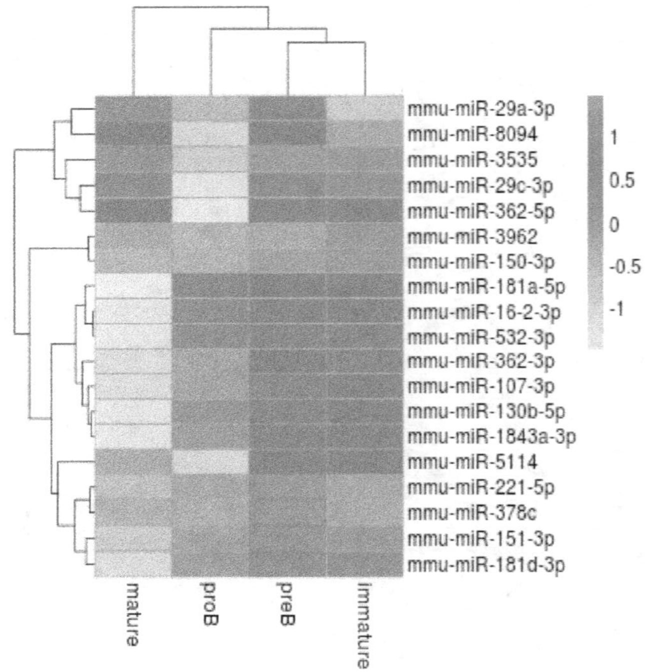

Figure 5.6: Tabulated expression values of miRNA against mouse RAG2 across B cell stages on the left, and heatmap showing the expression values of the same of miRNA against mouse RAG2 across B cell stages on the right.

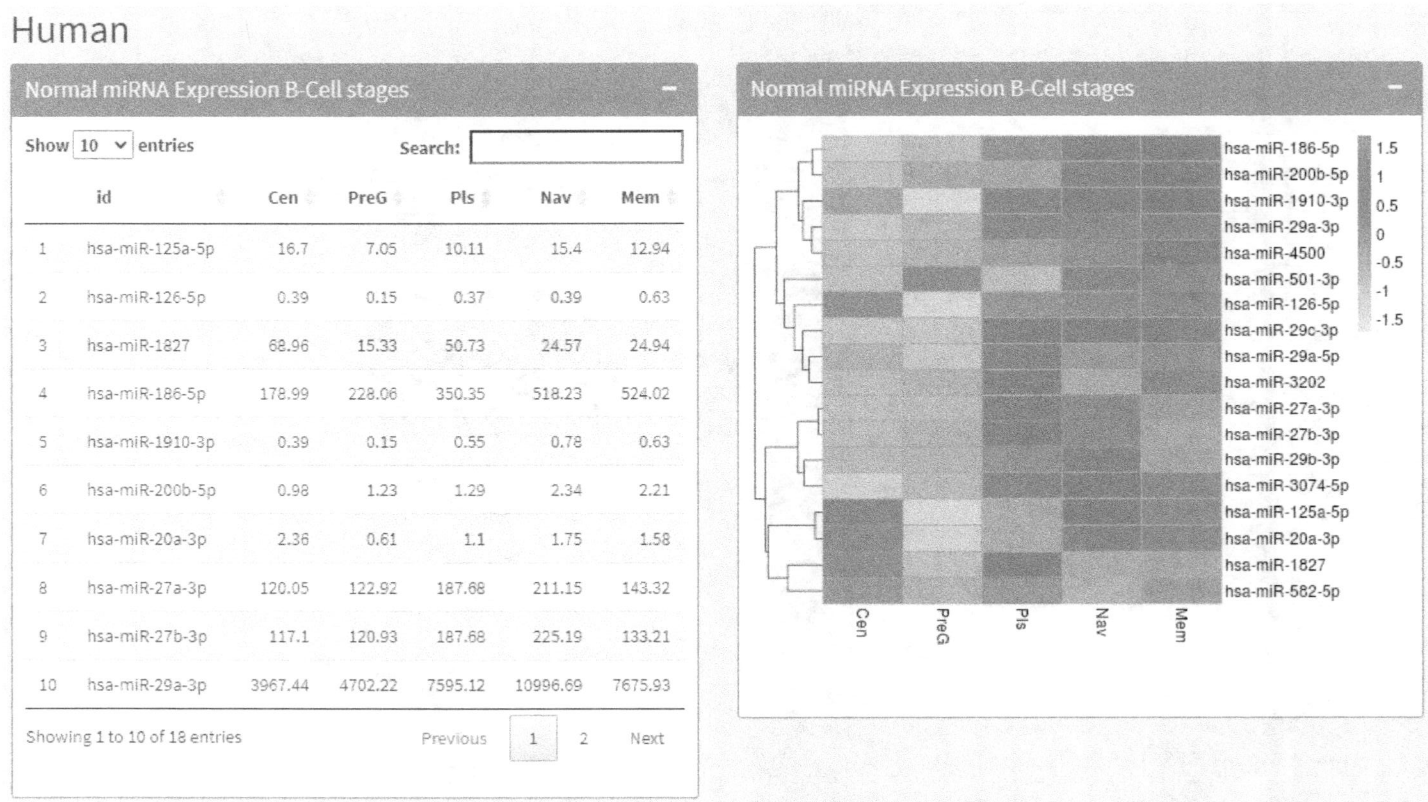

Human

Normal miRNA Expression B-Cell stages

Show 10 entries Search:

	id	Cen	PreG	Pls	Nav	Mem
1	hsa-miR-125a-5p	16.7	7.05	10.11	15.4	12.94
2	hsa-miR-126-5p	0.39	0.15	0.37	0.39	0.63
3	hsa-miR-1827	68.96	15.33	50.73	24.57	24.94
4	hsa-miR-186-5p	178.99	228.06	350.35	518.23	524.02
5	hsa-miR-1910-3p	0.39	0.15	0.55	0.78	0.63
6	hsa-miR-200b-5p	0.98	1.23	1.29	2.34	2.21
7	hsa-miR-20a-3p	2.36	0.61	1.1	1.75	1.58
8	hsa-miR-27a-3p	120.05	122.92	187.68	211.15	143.32
9	hsa-miR-27b-3p	117.1	120.93	187.68	225.19	133.21
10	hsa-miR-29a-3p	3967.44	4702.22	7595.12	10996.69	7675.93

Showing 1 to 10 of 18 entries Previous 1 2 Next

Figure 5.7: (A) Tabulated expression values of miRNA against Human RAG1 across B cell stages, **B)** heatmap showing the expression values of the same of miRNA against human RAG1 across B cell stages.

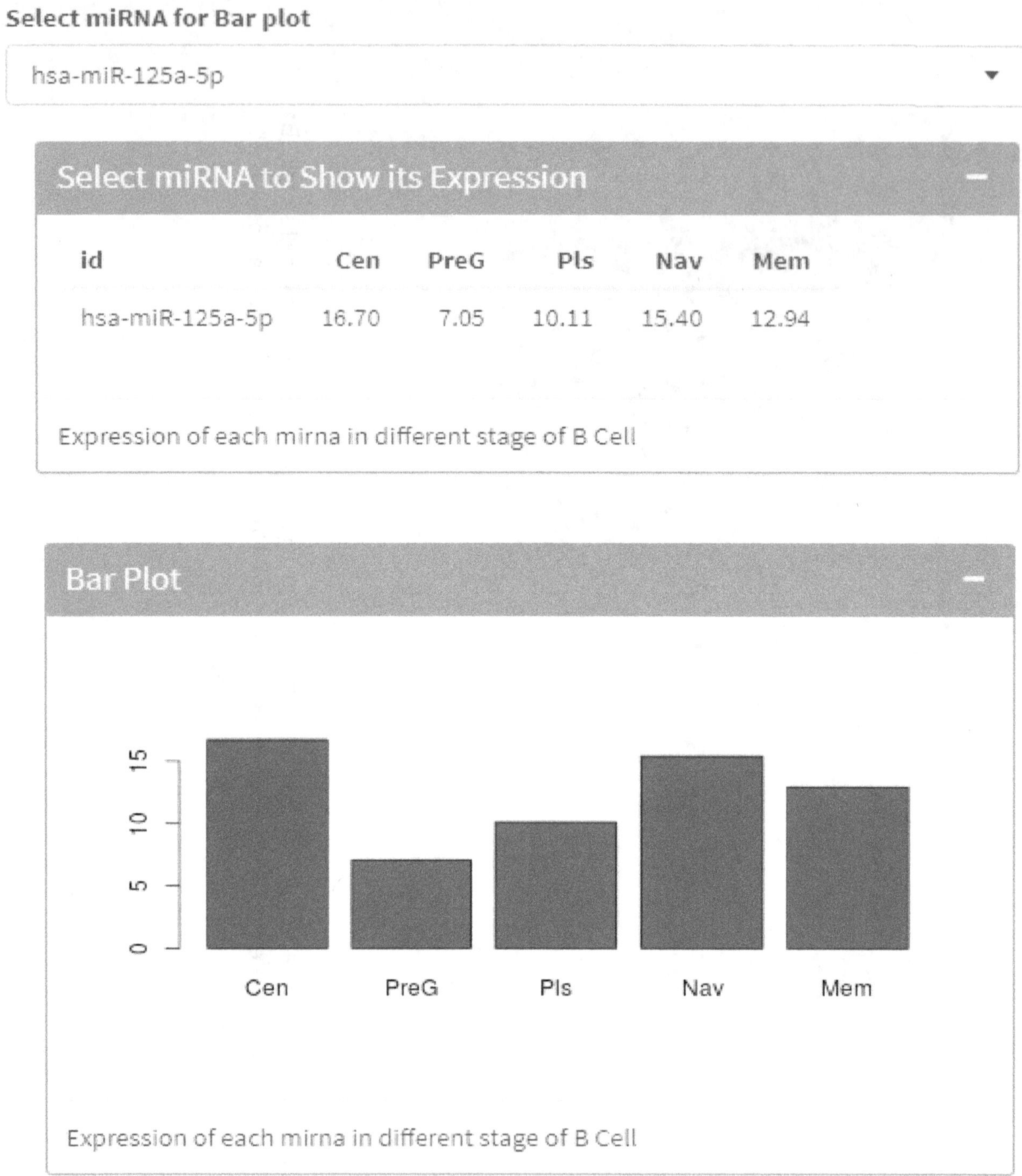

Figure 5.8 A): A dropdown menu of miRNA for the user to select to display the expression values, B) A bar graph displaying the expression pattern of chosen miRNA in human B cell stages

Normal miRNA Expression B-Cell Stages

Show 10 entries Search:

	id	Cen	PreG	Pls	Nav	Mem
1	hsa-miR-125a-5p	16.7	7.05	10.11	15.4	12.94
2	hsa-miR-126-5p	0.39	0.15	0.37	0.39	0.63
3	hsa-miR-1827	68.96	15.33	50.73	24.57	24.94
4	hsa-miR-186-5p	178.99	228.06	350.35	518.23	524.02
5	hsa-miR-1910-3p	0.39	0.15	0.55	0.78	0.63
6	hsa-miR-200b-5p	0.98	1.23	1.29	2.34	2.21
7	hsa-miR-20a-3p	2.36	0.61	1.1	1.75	1.58
8	hsa-miR-27a-3p	120.05	122.92	187.68	211.15	143.32
9	hsa-miR-27b-3p	117.1	120.93	187.68	225.19	133.21
10	hsa-miR-29a-3p	3967.44	4702.22	7595.12	10996.69	7675.93

Showing 1 to 10 of 18 entries Previous 1 2 Next

Figure 5.9: A table of human miRNA expression values across B cell stages

5.2.5. Expression Profiles of RAG1 and its interacting partners

Based on the literature study, we prepared a list of genes known to regulate and interact with RAG1 (POU2F2, E2A, FOXP1, MYB, BCL11A, FOXO1, EBF1, IKAROS, and PAX5). We identified the expression profiles of these genes in human and mouse B cell development data and T cell development data. The RAG regulators page displays these expression values in a tabular format (**Figure 5.14**) followed by a heatmap showing the same (**Figure 5.15**).

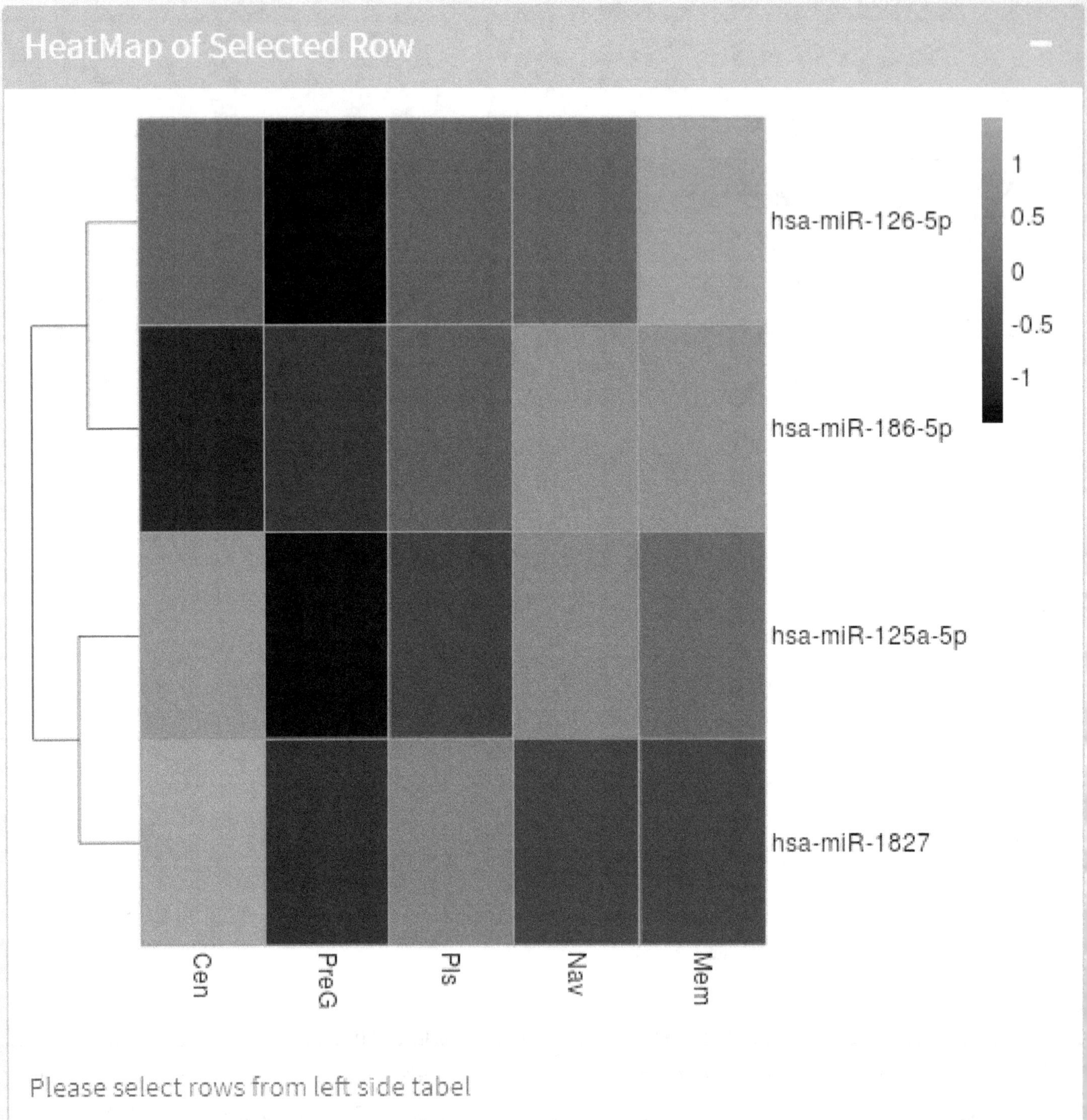

Figure 5.10: A Heatmap of the selected miRNA from Figure 5.9

miRNA against RAG2 - Human B cells

Show 10 entries   Search:

	miR_id	Centro_rpm	pre_GCB	Plasma	Naive	Me
1	hsa-miR-6728-5p	0.2	0.15	0	0	
2	hsa-miR-4781-3p	0.59	0.46	0.37	0.97	
3	hsa-miR-186-5p	178.99	228.06	350.35	518.23	
4	hsa-miR-7852-3p	0.39	0.92	0.18	0.39	
5	hsa-miR-6736-5p	0.2	0.15	0.18	0.19	
6	hsa-miR-9-3p	5.3	1.38	2.94	0.19	
7	hsa-miR-5187-5p	4.91	5.21	4.6	4.87	
8	hsa-miR-3121-3p	2.36	1.53	0.18	0.97	

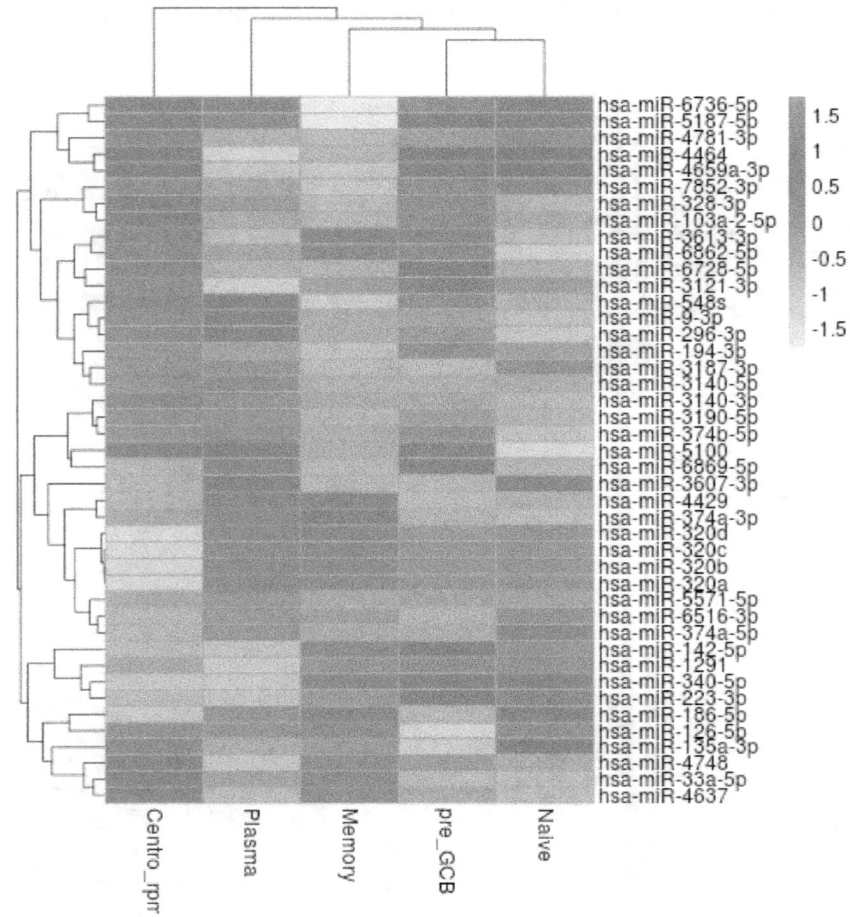

Figure 5.11: (A) Tabulated expression values of miRNA against Human RAG2 across B cell stages, **B)** heatmap showing the expression values of the same of miRNA against human RAG2 across B cell stages.

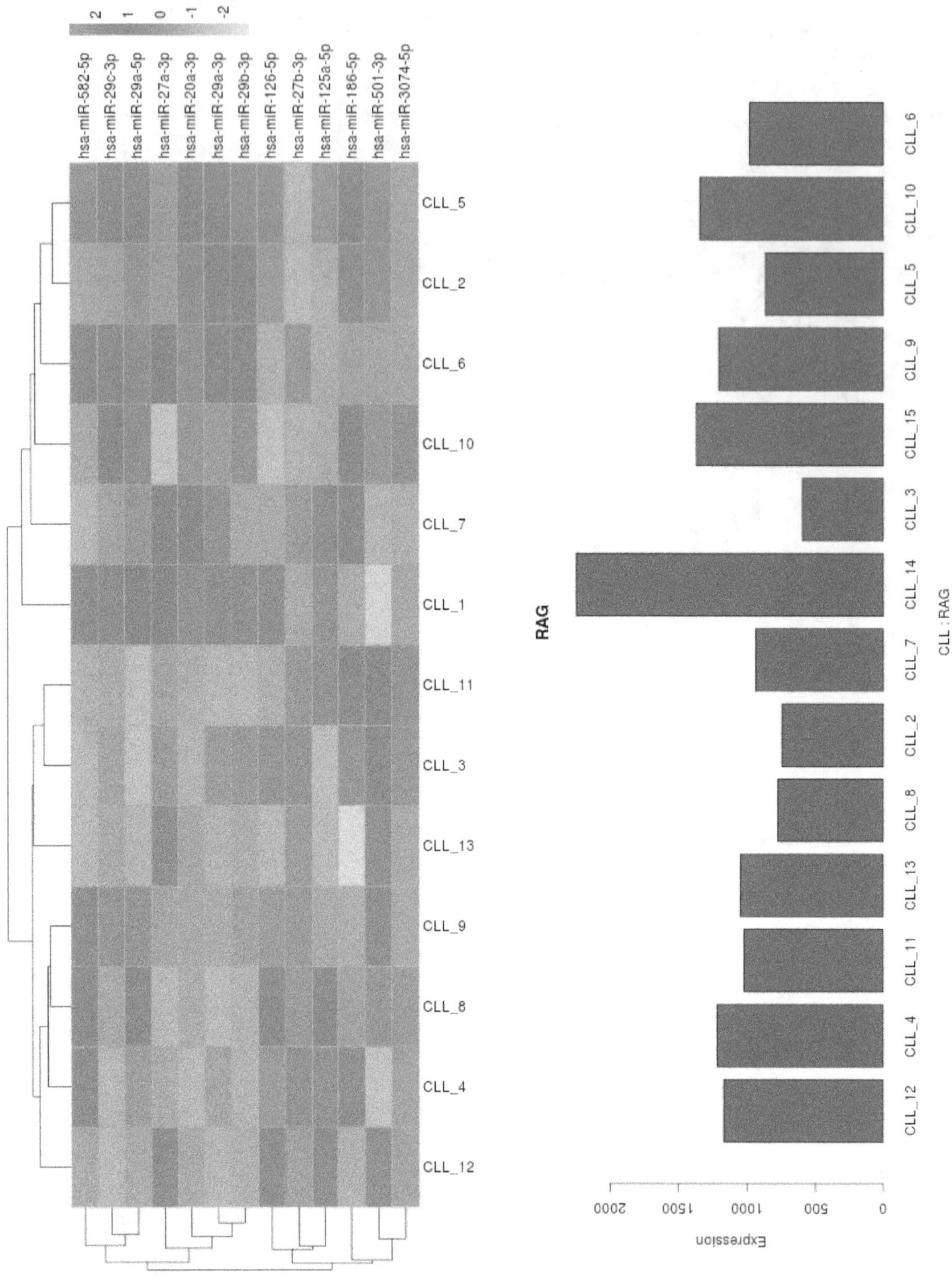

Figure 5.12: (A) Heatmap representing the expression values of miRNA against RAG1 in CLL patients, B) A bar graph representing RAG1 expression values in the same CLL patients

After that, the expression levels of genes known for RAG1 degradation and localization in B (**Figure 5.16**) and T cell development (**Figure 5.17**) data have been shown in a tabular as well as heatmap format. The next section shows expression data of RAG2 regulators in B and T cell development data across their development stages. The page ends with the Expression of RAG regulators in CLL condition (**Figure 5.18**).

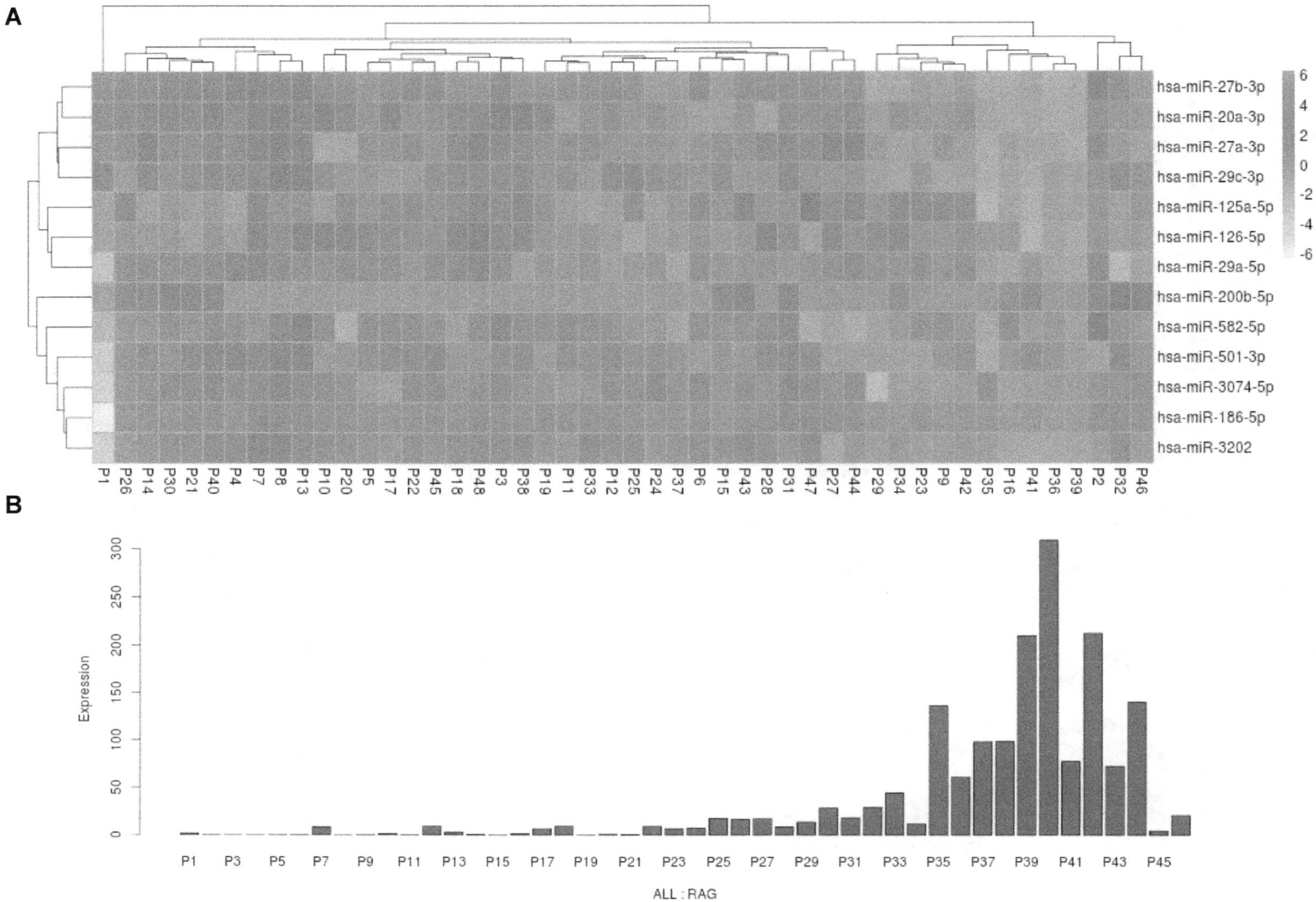

Figure 5.13: (A) Heatmap representing the expression values of miRNA against RAG1 in T-ALL patients, B) A bar graph representing RAG1 expression values in the same T-ALL patients

RAG1 Regulators

RAG Regulator and Expression in B-Cell stages

Show 10 entries Search:

	Ensemble_ID	Uniprot	EarlyB_1	EarlyB_2	ProB_1
1	POU2F2	P09086	24.62456566	17.6954804	8.115231658
2	E2A	Q6VGU4	237.0071753	207.1132303	1311.861327
3	FOXP1	Q9H334	69.41668475	52.17312609	112.5135156
4	MYB	P10242	488.819828	581.0396613	743.5296595
5	BCL11A	Q9H165	85.5029128	86.3082786	222.0501821
6	FOXO1	Q12778	17.81097225	18.26630235	224.9891095
7	EBF1	Q9UH73	12.0561327	4.052835834	307.9995866
8	RAG1	P15918	36.21962813	9.228288166	779.2328866
9	IKAROS	Q13422	271.092219	248.9164243	379.4629233
10	PAX5	Q02548	10.21185178	0.55179455	676.0101736

Showing 1 to 10 of 10 entries Previous 1 Next

Figure 5.14: Tabulated expression values of RAG1 regulators in B cell stages

5.2.6. Links to additional information about RAG1

The following two pages are curations of data from other resources with information specific to RAG1. Since a significant highlight of this database is the miRNA involved in RAG1, on the next page, we have cataloged all the circular RNAs that are known to make a sponge with every miRNA that we have mentioned in the previous pages. This instance presents the user with a drop-down list of miRNAs to choose from, resulting in a list of circRNA and its coordinates on the human genome, which might act as a sponge. Every circRNA has a corresponding UCSC genome browser link attached to it that displays the chromosomal location of the circRNA (**Figure 5.19**). Also, an MGI page of RAG1 with 158 mouse RAG1 MGI hyperlinks to the expression of RAG1 in various tissues. The table consists of the RAG1 MG1 ID, the genes symbol "Rag1", the link to the corresponding MGI database, the Assay type that determined the expression, the development stage of the mice at which the data was extracted, the tissue followed by the image id of the tissue expression data (**Figure 5.20**).

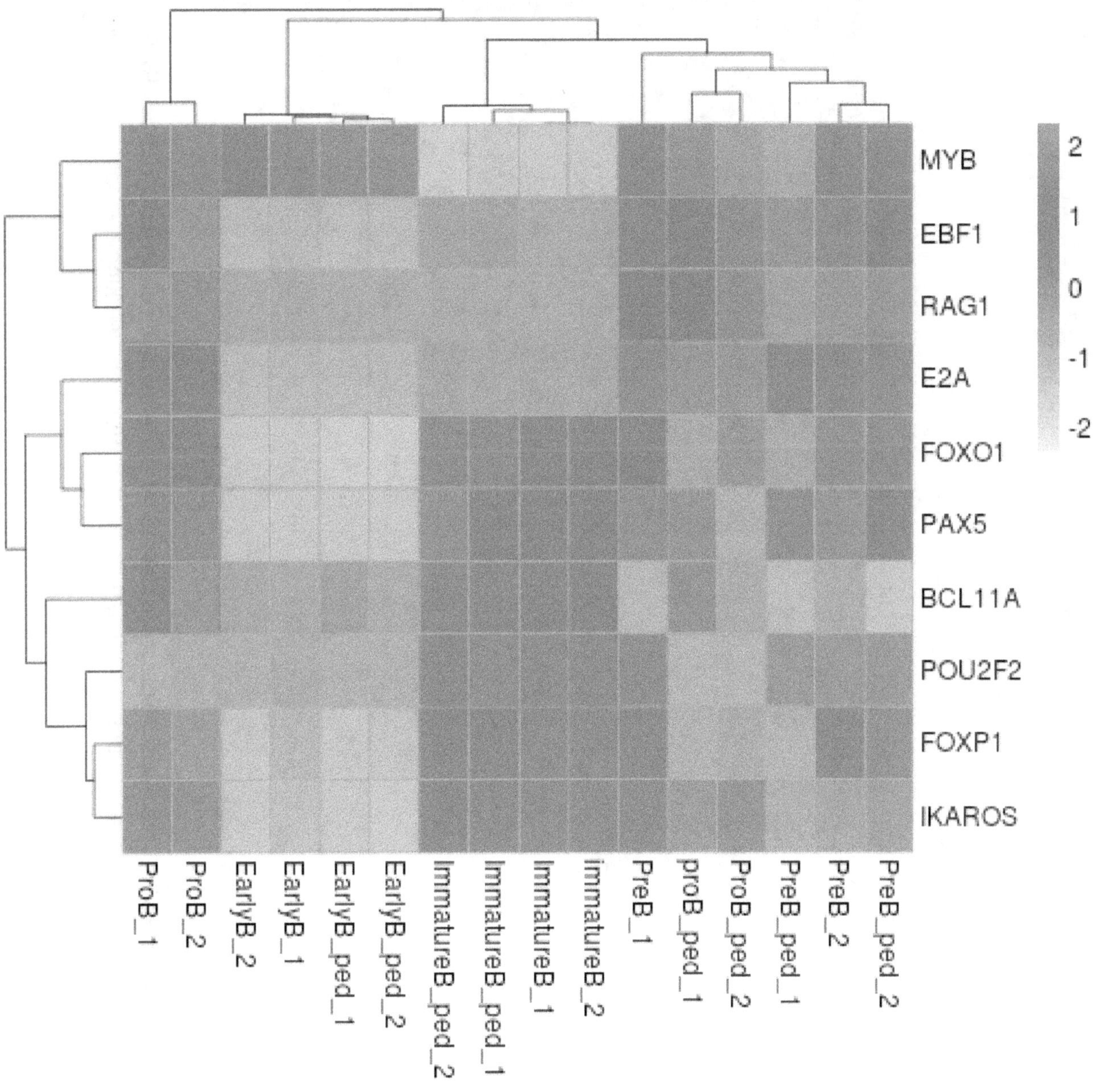

Figure 5.15: Heatmap representing expression values of RAG1 regulators in B cell stages

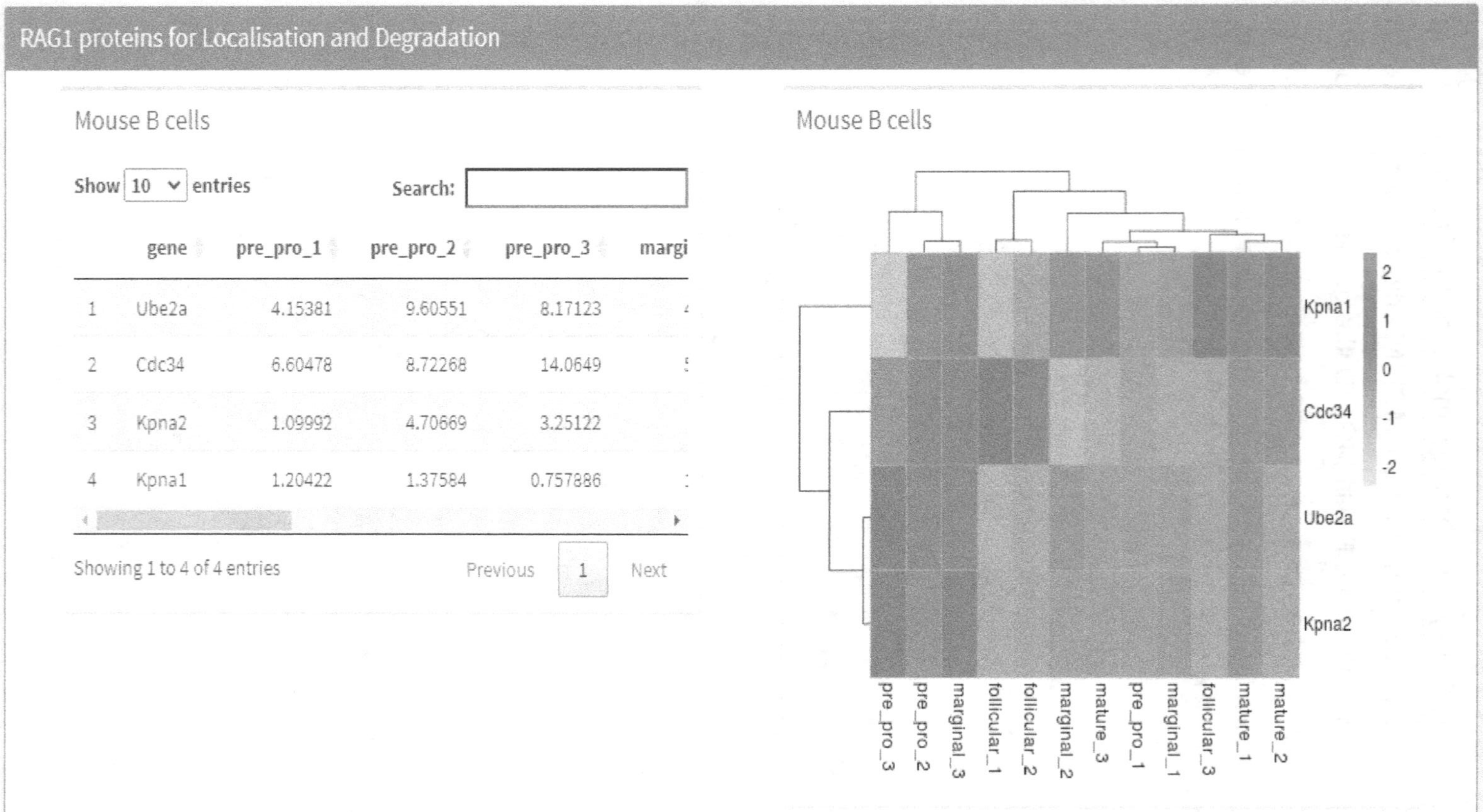

Figure 5.16: A table with expression values for proteins involved in mouse B cell RAG1 localization and Degradation on the left and a heatmap representing the same on the right

Mouse T cells

Show 10 entries Search:

	Gene	DN1_1	DN1_2	DN2_1	DN2_2	DN3_
1	Cdc34	21.38056	12.90906	41.79826	31.48751	42.67
2	Kpna1	64.70472	15.74524	72.6944	20.00945	74.32
3	Kpna2	5.49229	4.7891	6.30343	10.29298	10.98
4	Ube2a	26.82618	21.20949	33.75829	27.9403	33.71

Showing 1 to 4 of 4 entries Previous 1 Next

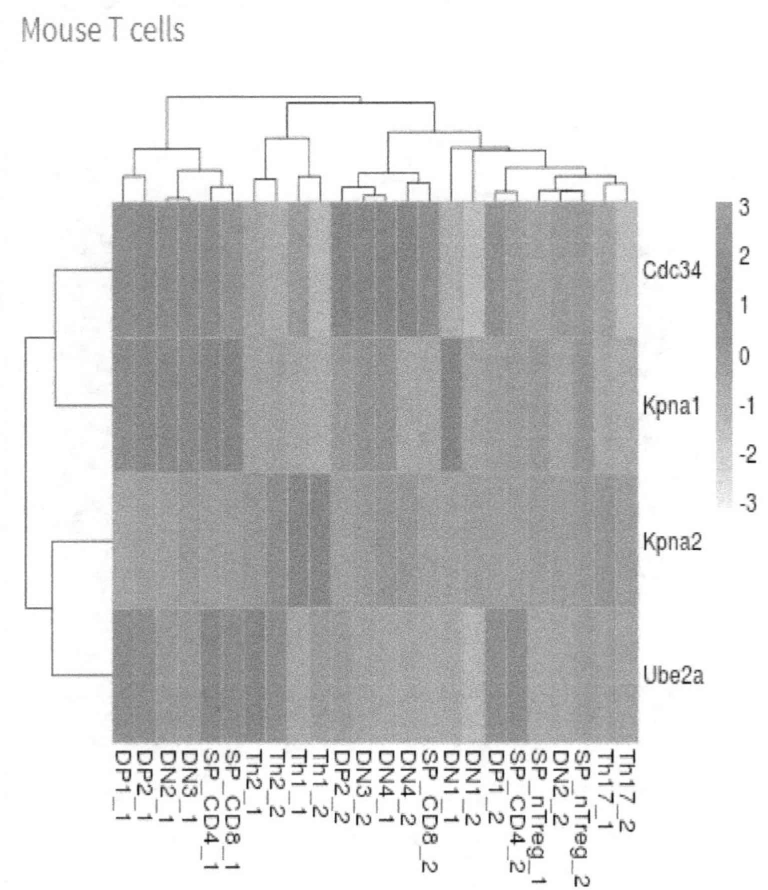

Figure 5.17: A table with expression values for proteins involved in mouse T cell RAG1 localization and Degradation on the left and a heatmap representing the same on the right

RAG Regulator and their Expression in CLL Patient Samples

Show 10 entries — Search:

	Gene	CLL_1	CLL_2	CLL_3	CLL_4	CLL_5	CLL_6	CLL_7	CLL_8	
1	FOXO1	60.343387825	91.6519173813	60.4915523175	74.7510300823	64.5897097185	52.6798943209	60.5289388366	58.1052283285	65.
2	FOXP1	202.1503492139	320.7817108347	406.6376572452	532.4857328087	284.8571813225	283.0253145867	424.6633486634	406.7365982997	559.
3	IKAROS	33.1888633038	51.2172479484	30.2457761587	77.519586752	46.3720992851	42.3505032776	61.4897156436	76.137885396	56.
4	PAX5	129.7382838238	138.8256983864	131.0650300212	171.6505135224	134.1478586461	158.0396829627	118.1755472525	172.3120564225	159.
5	RAG1	675.8459436404	746.6935621951	594.8335977884	1219.0877868982	866.1645687888	981.2921491146	938.6789403713	777.4078824644	1205.
6	E2A	208.1846879964	113.2170744122	77.2947612945	62.7539511802	149.0531762734	145.6444137107	150.8419586881	102.1850567157	111.

Showing 1 to 6 of 6 entries — Previous 1 Next

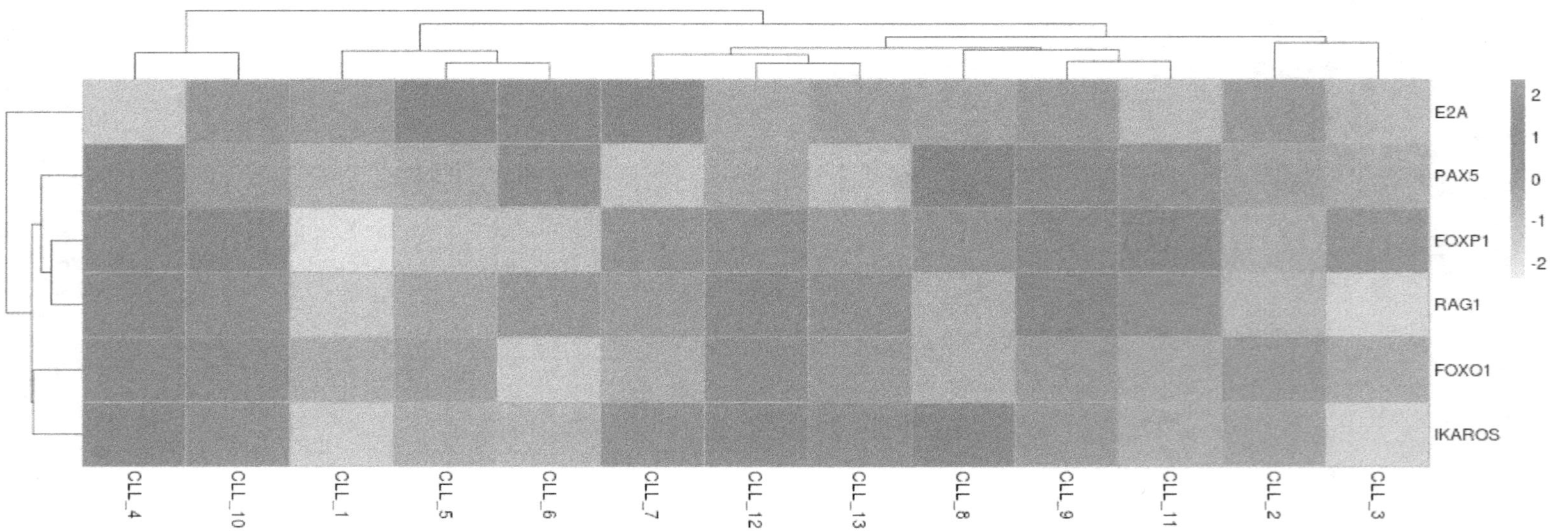

Figure 5.18: A) A table with expression values for proteins involved in RAG1 regulation in CLL patients and **B)** A heatmap representing expression values of RAG1 regulators in CLL patients

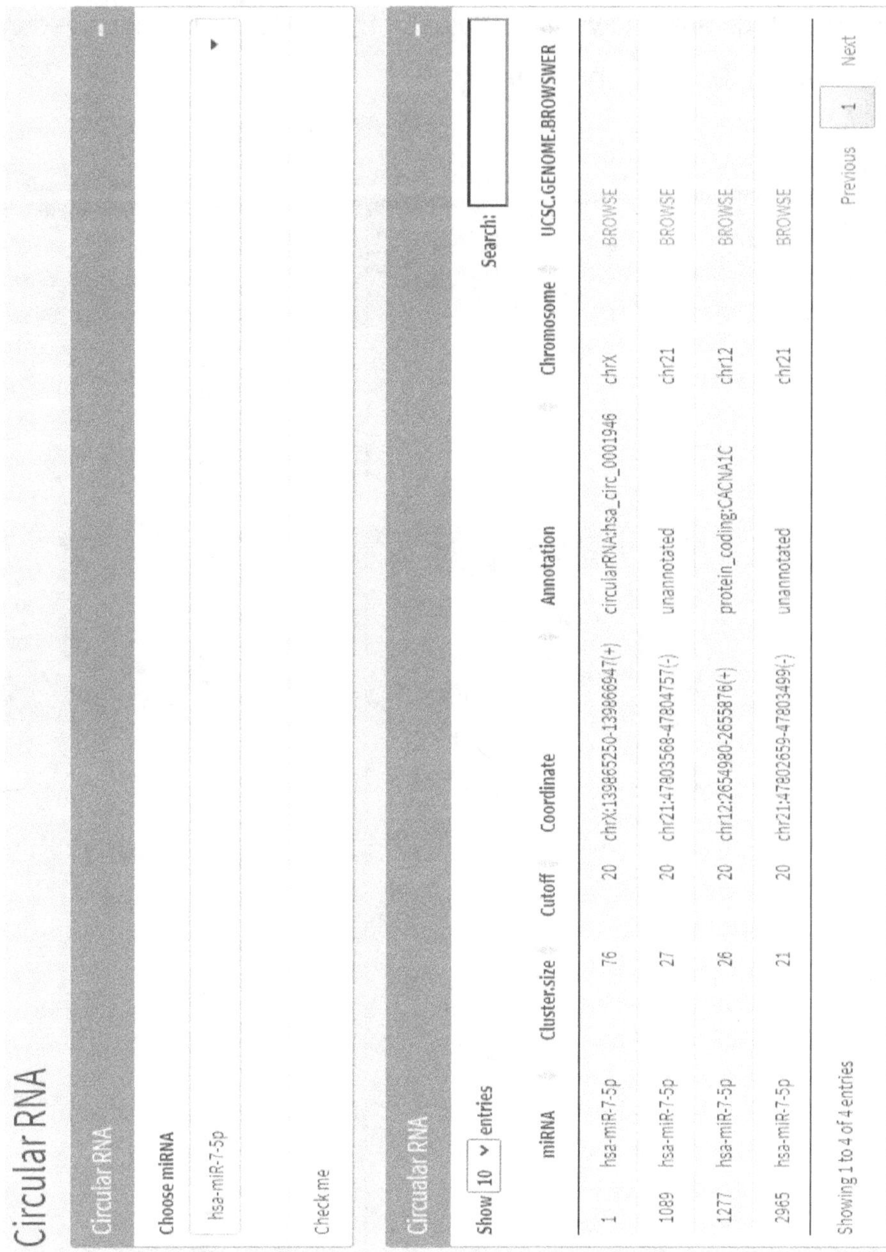

Figure 5.19: A dropdown menu of miRNA on the top followed by a list of circRNA sponges specific to the selected miRNA and UCSC genome browser links to the circRNA locations on the human genome

Interactive interphases for the user

The following two utilities are highly user-friendly. The first is a Download section where all the data displayed on the database can be downloaded by the user with three available options, mouse data, human data, or all the files together (**Figure 5.21**). One of the most exciting utilities comes next: the page where users can upload their data and visualize it by adhering to the following steps. 1) It starts by asking you to upload a file of your choice in a tabular format by clicking on the "Browse button", 2) If your input file has a header, you check the "Header" box followed by 3) choosing the separator that is present in your file (Comma, Semicolon or Tab) (**Figure 5.21**). Once all these three steps are followed, the values of your file will be displayed in a tabular format followed by a heatmap depicting the same.

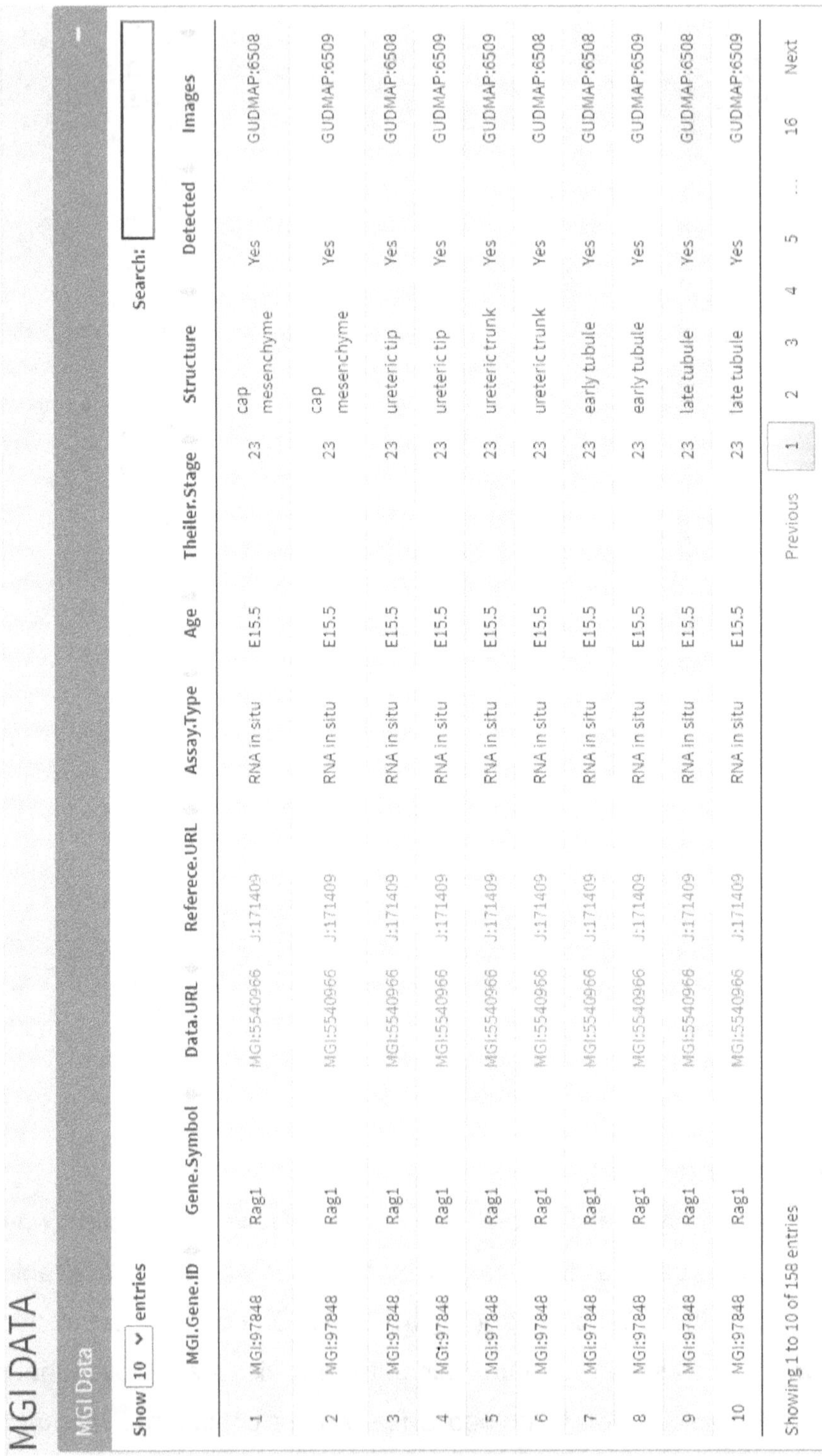

MGI DATA

MGI Data

Show 10 entries Search:

	MGI.Gene.ID	Gene.Symbol	Data.URL	Referece.URL	Assay.Type	Age	Theiler.Stage	Structure	Detected	Images
1	MGI:97848	Rag1	MGI:5540966	J:171409	RNA in situ	E15.5	23	cap mesenchyme	Yes	GUDMAP:6508
2	MGI:97848	Rag1	MGI:5540966	J:171409	RNA in situ	E15.5	23	cap mesenchyme	Yes	GUDMAP:6509
3	MGI:97848	Rag1	MGI:5540966	J:171409	RNA in situ	E15.5	23	ureteric tip	Yes	GUDMAP:6508
4	MGI:97848	Rag1	MGI:5540966	J:171409	RNA in situ	E15.5	23	ureteric tip	Yes	GUDMAP:6509
5	MGI:97848	Rag1	MGI:5540966	J:171409	RNA in situ	E15.5	23	ureteric trunk	Yes	GUDMAP:6509
6	MGI:97848	Rag1	MGI:5540966	J:171409	RNA in situ	E15.5	23	ureteric trunk	Yes	GUDMAP:6508
7	MGI:97848	Rag1	MGI:5540966	J:171409	RNA in situ	E15.5	23	early tubule	Yes	GUDMAP:6508
8	MGI:97848	Rag1	MGI:5540966	J:171409	RNA in situ	E15.5	23	early tubule	Yes	GUDMAP:6509
9	MGI:97848	Rag1	MGI:5540966	J:171409	RNA in situ	E15.5	23	late tubule	Yes	GUDMAP:6508
10	MGI:97848	Rag1	MGI:5540966	J:171409	RNA in situ	E15.5	23	late tubule	Yes	GUDMAP:6509

Showing 1 to 10 of 158 entries — Previous 1 2 3 4 5 … 16 Next

Figure 5.20: A table displaying MGI hyperlinks to the expression pages of RAG1 in various tissues.

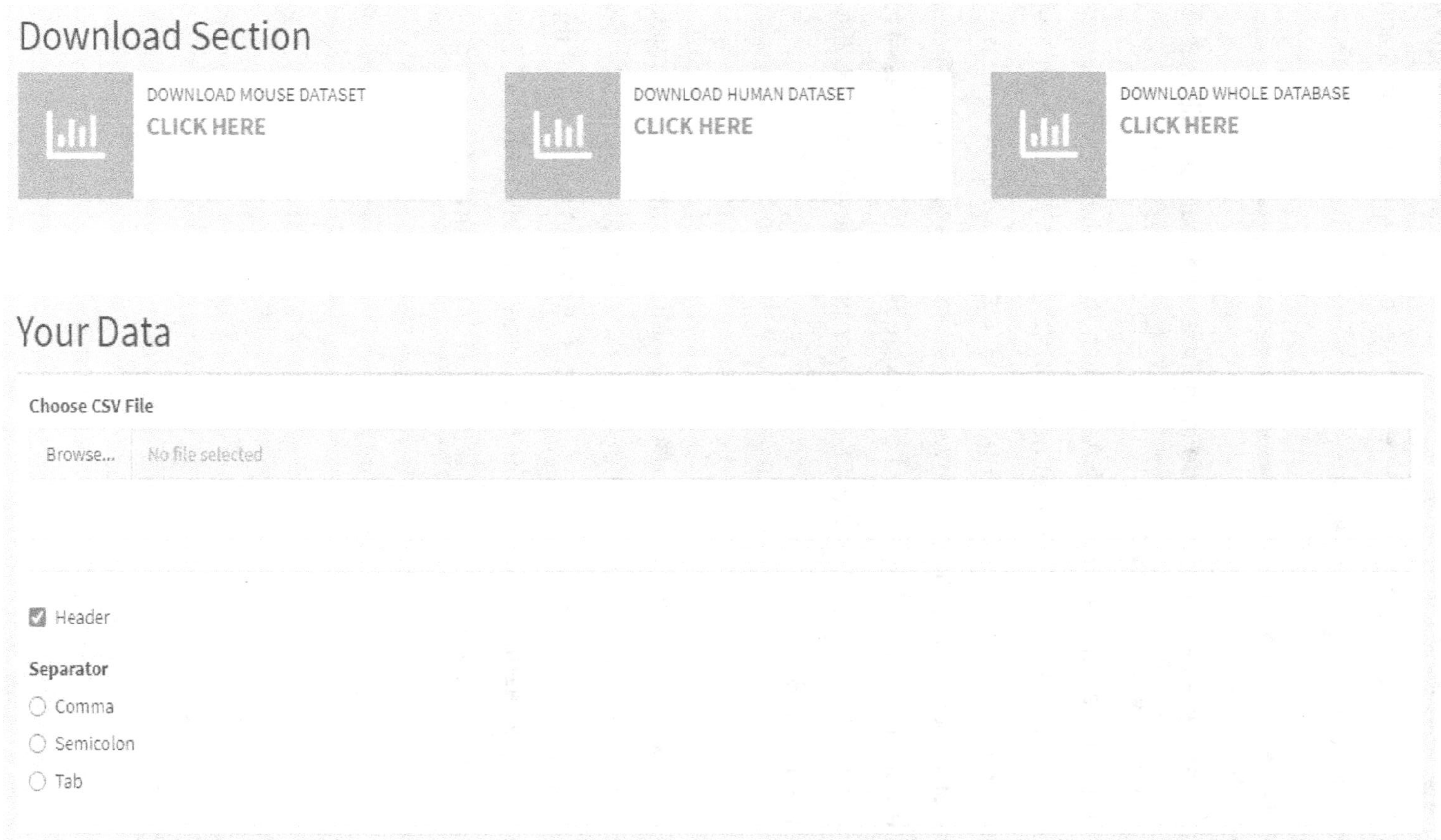

Figure 5.21: The image top shows the page where all the data from the database can be downloaded and the bottom image represents the interactive utility where the users have an option to visualize their data by uploading expression files.

5.2.7. Comparison of miRNA expression across various conditions.

Since our database deals with the expression of miRNA against RAGs in various conditions (aberrant and normal), we have also incorporated a page where the user can compare expression profiles of miRNA across different conditions of the database.

5.2.8. Advantages of the database

Using the database, miRNAs against RAG regulators can be identified, and their significance in regulating genomic integrity be studied. As an example, we would like to draw focus on miR-29c-3p. When gathering and analyzing expression data of miRNAs known to regulate RAG1 across B cell developmental stages for the database, we came across miR-29c-3p. We observed that the expression of this miRNA is negligible in the preB and proB cell stages, while it increases drastically in the mature stages of B cells, indicating an inverse pattern of expression. These findings were validated experimentally using knockdown and overexpression studies. It was also seen that in 87% of CLL patients and 79% of T-ALL patients, the expression levels of miR-29c-3p and RAG1 were inversely correlated [26].

5.2.9. RAGs in AML samples

To check for the expression of RAG1 and RAG2 in AML, we used the AML transcriptome samples from Chapter 4 and profiled the expression of RAGs in all the samples. Although a generally low expression profile was seen for the genes, it was seen that for RAG1, 51% (56 samples) of the samples had expression higher than the median value (0.039 TPM), and similarly for RAG2 51% of the samples had a higher expression value than the media (0.61 TPM) (**Figure 5.22**).

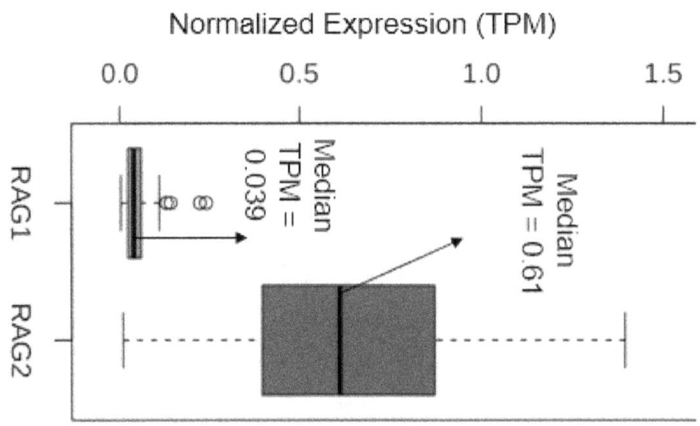

Figure 5.22: Average expression of RAG1 and RAG2 across AML samples

5.3. DISCUSSION

RAG1 is a well-characterized and well-studied nuclease complex protein that is involved in DNA damage and repair mechanisms in more ways than one[29,30]. Specifically expressed in the early stages of B and T cell development, RAG1 primarily initiates the process of V(D)J recombination[9,12,15,31]. Aberrant RAG expression, via various non-physiological mechanisms, leads to translocations that in turn lead to leukemias and lymphomas[15,19,32,33]. Aberrant RAG can be blocked using certain means, such as microRNAs and regulatory transcription factors[26,34]. It is only imperative that these expression profiles be collated and studied to derive therapeutic gains from them. Here we present a database specific to RAG1 that provides regulatory information in an NGS data analysis context. It is the first of its kind where information on transcription regulation in terms of miRNA and transcription factors has been represented under the same umbrella (remove). Immgen provides information on the gene regulatory networks involved in the differentiation and function of hematopoietic stem cells[35].

Gathering such information into one single resource can prove to be of much relevance. One example is the recently published study that highlights the role of miR-29c-3p in RAG1 expression in a stage-specific manner and CLL and T-ALL patients[26]. miRAGDB further explores the factors involved in regulating RAG1.

The database contains information from Human and Mouse samples as well. The sequencing data available from mice is much more than that in humans. From mice, miRNA expression data were available for both B and T cell developmental stages, whereas only the B cell stages have been found for humans. miRAGDB offers data visualization in a heatmap form and the form of individual bar graphs. The Human page even allows users to add and remove miRNA based on which miRNAs' expression profiles they might want to study. Not only miRNA but as discussed earlier, transcription factors and other proteins are responsible for a gene's regulation; therefore, we have incorporated a page that lets the users understand the expression profiles of RAG1 regulators in the conditions mentioned earlier. It is always important to be able to understand the expression profile and subsequently the possible function of a gene in the aberrant conditions; once the same is known in a normal scenario and hence the database also hosts expression profiles of transcription factors associated with RAG1 and miRNA known to regulate it in CLL and T-ALL patients. We also looked for expression patterns of RAG1 and RAG2 in AML samples and found that in both the cases half of the samples have a relatively higher expression value. We are in the process of updating the database and adding information related to RAGs in AML samples.

Another valuable and unique featurette is the page where users are allowed to upload their expression matrices and visualize whichever data they like. This database is only the first version. We will incorporate it in the upcoming versions as we gather more information from various B and T cell sequencing experiments and other leukemia and lymphoma conditions. Meanwhile, this utility where one's data can be uploaded can be used extensively by the users to view expression profiles from any experiment as they please, in the form of a comprehensive heatmap. Lastly, the database has links to MGI and UCSC genome browsers where information on alternate RAG1 transcripts in mice, mouse RAG1 phenotypes, associated circular RNA, etc. is available.

5.4. REFERENCES

1. Schatz DG, Oettinger MA, Baltimore D. The V(D)J recombination activating gene, RAG-1. Cell. 1989. pp. 1035–1048. doi:10.1016/0092-8674(89)90760-5

2. Dreyer WJ, Bennett JC. The molecular basis of antibody formation: a paradox. Proc Natl Acad Sci U S A. 1965;54: 864–869.

3. Lederberg J. Genes and antibodies. Science. 1959;129: 1649–1653.

4. Nishana M, Raghavan SC. Role of recombination activating genes in the generation of antigen receptor diversity and beyond. Immunology. 2012;137: 271–281.

5. Yuan M, Wang Y, Qin M, Zhao X, Chen X, Li D, et al. RAG enhances BCR-ABL1-positive leukemic cell growth through its endonuclease activity in vitro and in vivo. Cancer Sci. 2021;112: 2679–2691.

6. Thomson D, Shahrin H, Wang P, Wadham C, Hughes TP, Schreiber A, et al. High Recombination Activating Gene (RAG) Expression and RAG Mediated Recombination Is Associated with Oncogenic Rearrangement Observed with Tyrosine Kinase Inhibitor Resistant CML. Blood. 2018. pp. 3001–3001. doi:10.1182/blood-2018-99-111212

7. Weinstock DM, Jasin M. Alternative pathways for the repair of RAG-induced DNA breaks. Mol Cell Biol. 2006;26: 131–139.

8. Lieber MR. The Mechanism of Double-Strand DNA Break Repair by the Nonhomologous DNA End-Joining Pathway. Annual Review of Biochemistry. 2010. pp. 181–211. doi:10.1146/annurev.biochem.052308.093131

9. Gellert M. V(D)J recombination: RAG proteins, repair factors, and regulation. Annu Rev Biochem. 2002;71: 101–132.

10. Schatz DG, Oettinger MA, Baltimore D. The V(D)J recombination activating gene, RAG-1. Cell. 1989;59: 1035–1048.

11. Schatz DG, Swanson PC. V(D)J recombination: mechanisms of initiation. Annu Rev Genet. 2011;45: 167–202.

12. Schatz DG, Baltimore D. Uncovering the V(D)J recombinase. Cell. Elsevier BV; 2004. pp. S103–6, 2 p following S106.

13. Schatz DG, Ji Y. Recombination centres and the orchestration of V(D)J recombination. Nat Rev Immunol. 2011;11: 251–263.

14. Lewis SM. The mechanism of V(D)J joining: lessons from molecular, immunological, and comparative analyses. Adv Immunol. 1994;56: 27–150.

15. Roth DB. Restraining the V(D)J recombinase. Nat Rev Immunol. 2003;3: 656–666.

16. Nambiar M, Goldsmith G, Moorthy BT, Lieber MR, Joshi MV, Choudhary B, et al. Formation of a G-quadruplex at the BCL2 major breakpoint region of the t(14;18) translocation in follicular lymphoma. Nucleic Acids Research. 2011. pp. 936–948. doi:10.1093/nar/gkq824

17. Nambiar M, Raghavan SC. Mechanism of Fragility at BCL2 Gene Minor Breakpoint Cluster Region during t(14;18) Chromosomal Translocation. Journal of Biological Chemistry. 2012. pp. 8688–8701. doi:10.1074/jbc.m111.307363

18. Raghavan SC, Swanson PC, Wu X, Hsieh C-L, Lieber MR. A non-B-DNA structure at the Bcl-2 major breakpoint region is cleaved by the RAG complex. Nature. 2004. pp. 88–93. doi:10.1038/nature02355

19. Mills KD, Ferguson DO, Alt FW. The role of DNA breaks in genomic instability and tumorigenesis. Immunol Rev. 2003;194: 77–95.

20. Rommel PC, Oliveira TY, Nussenzweig MC, Robbiani DF. RAG1/2 induces genomic insertions by mobilizing DNA into RAG1/2-independent breaks. J Exp Med. 2017;214: 815–831.

21. Alt FW, Zhang Y, Meng F-L, Guo C, Schwer B. Mechanisms of programmed DNA lesions and genomic instability in the immune system. Cell. 2013;152: 417–429.

22. Raisch J. Role of microRNAs in the immune system, inflammation and cancer. World Journal of Gastroenterology. 2013. p. 2985. doi:10.3748/wjg.v19.i20.2985

23. Chen C-Z, Li L, Lodish HF, Bartel DP. MicroRNAs modulate hematopoietic lineage differentiation. Science. 2004;303: 83–86.

24. Johnston RJ, Poholek AC, DiToro D, Yusuf I, Eto D, Barnett B, et al. Bcl6 and Blimp-1 are reciprocal and antagonistic regulators of T follicular helper cell differentiation. Science. 2009;325: 1006–1010.

25. Liston A, Papadopoulou AS, Danso-Abeam D, Dooley J. MicroRNA-29 in the adaptive immune system: setting the threshold. Cell Mol Life Sci. 2012;69: 3533–3541.

26. Kumari R, Roy U, Desai S, Nilavar NM, Van Nieuwenhuijze A, Paranjape A, et al. MicroRNA miR-29c regulates RAG1 expression and modulates V(D)J recombination during B cell development. Cell Rep. 2021;36: 109390.

27. Wu S, Huang S, Ding J, Zhao Y, Liang L, Liu T, et al. Multiple microRNAs modulate p21Cip1/Waf1 expression by directly targeting its 3′ untranslated region. Oncogene. 2010. pp. 2302–2308. doi:10.1038/onc.2010.34

28. Peter ME. Targeting of mRNAs by multiple miRNAs: the next step. Oncogene. 2010;29: 2161–2164.

29. Coster G, Gold A, Chen D, Schatz DG, Goldberg M. A Dual Interaction between the DNA Damage Response Protein MDC1 and the RAG1 Subunit of the V(D)J Recombinase. Journal of Biological Chemistry. 2012. pp. 36488–36498. doi:10.1074/jbc.m112.402487

30. Lee GS, Neiditch MB, Salus SS, Roth DB. RAG proteins shepherd double-strand breaks to a specific pathway, suppressing error-prone repair, but RAG nicking initiates homologous recombination. Cell. 2004. pp. 171–184.

31. Schatz DG, Swanson PC. V(D)J Recombination: Mechanisms of Initiation. Annual Review of Genetics. 2011. pp. 167–202. doi:10.1146/annurev-genet-110410-132552

32. Raghavan SC, Kirsch IR, Lieber MR. Analysis of the V(D)J Recombination Efficiency at Lymphoid Chromosomal Translocation Breakpoints. Journal of Biological Chemistry. 2001. pp. 29126–29133. doi:10.1074/jbc.m103797200

33. Nussenzweig A, Nussenzweig MC. Origin of chromosomal translocations in lymphoid cancer. Cell. 2010;141: 27–38.

34. Kuo TC, Schlissel MS. Mechanisms controlling expression of the RAG locus during lymphocyte development. Curr Opin Immunol. 2009;21: 173–178.

35. Heng TSP, The Immunological Genome Project Consortium, Painter MW, Elpek K, Lukacs-Kornek V, Mauermann N, et al. The Immunological Genome Project: networks of gene expression in immune cells. Nature Immunology. 2008. pp. 1091–1094. doi:10.1038/ni1008-1091

Chapter 6: Identify variants associated with Acute Leukemia specific to the Indian population

6.1. INTRODUCTION

India is the 3rd largest contributor in terms of Leukemia Incidence rates worldwide, with a median survival rate of 35.5%[1,2]. Out of all the cancers, blood cancers account for 9.5% in men and 5.5% in women[3]. Of the two major classes of leukemias, Myeloid leukemias are more common in India than lymphoid ones in the west[3]. Amongst the subtypes of AML, the Indian population has M2 as the most common subtype[4,5]. Childhood leukemias are the most studied in India, and the median age of incidence is 40 years which is a significant departure from what is known in developed countries[1,4].

The Genomic Landscape of AML in India is significantly different[6]. Amongst the most commonly known mutated genes in AML, the prevalence of NPM1 is as high as 45%, whereas the frequency in western populations is 20-40%, and the NPM1 and FLT3 mutations are linked to poor prognosis[5,7,8]. DNMT3A mutations are rare in the Indian population than in Caucasians. The occurrence of cytogenetic abnormalities is also a differentiating factor. The translocations t (8;21) and inv(16) are common in the Indian population

In terms of neutropenia, Indian studies have focused more on Febrile Neutropenia (FN), an infection-related reduction of neutrophils in AML patients. It has been reported that almost 90% of AML patients develop FN during induction[9].

In this study, we have performed matched WGS and transcriptome sequencing and analysis of 10 Indian patient samples from a hospital in Bangalore. We performed fusion detection in all the samples and found novel fusion HOXD11-AGAP3 in 3 of the patients. We performed variant analysis and identified novel mutations in genes implicated in Leukemia. On performing Differential expression analysis, we observed that neutrophil degranulation and differentiation of myeloid differentiation pathways were downregulated, a typical phenotype of AML. Immune profiling using CIBRSORTx revealed differences in the immune profile of the Indian patients compared to the Caucasian population.

6.2. RESULTS

6.2.1. Subjects for the study

Peripheral blood samples were collected from patients diagnosed with Acute Leukemia at the Healthcare Global Enterprises Ltd, Bengaluru, Karnataka, India. We obtained 1 ALL sample and 9 AML samples. The institutional review board approved the protocol of HCG and the Institute of Bioinformatics and Applied Biotechnology. The details of all the patients are given in Table 6.1. Informed consent was obtained from all the participants. Most of the patients had a complex karyotype except for one being BCR-ABL translocation and one having RUNX1-RUNX1T1 translocation.

6.2.2. Identification of novel variants specific to the Indian population

We performed variant analysis on 10 whole-genome sequencing samples. The average number of reads per sample was 15 million reads, with a read length of 150 bases. On aligning to the hg38 reference genome, we obtained an average of >80% alignment. Post variant calling and filtering of reads based on depth and 1000genome variants, the average number of mutations per sample was 0.1million.

On analyzing the mutation profiles of genes known to be implicated in AML, it was seen that important transcription factors like RUNX1, KMT2A, ABL1, GATA1, NOTCH1, ASXL1, , IKZF1, MN1 and CEBPA had deleterious missense mutations that were unique to the Indian samples(Figure 6.1). All the coding mutations were uploaded onto the ENSEMBL VEP database. Along with the genes mentioned above, there were deleterious mutations in PSMA2, PSMA3, and DPF2 genes. The Granulocyte differentiation pathway and the Regulation of the hematopoietic progenitor cell differentiation pathway are enriched in deleterious mutations. Amongst the genes involved in granulopoiesis/neutropenia, there was a missense variant only in the HLA-DRB5 gene.

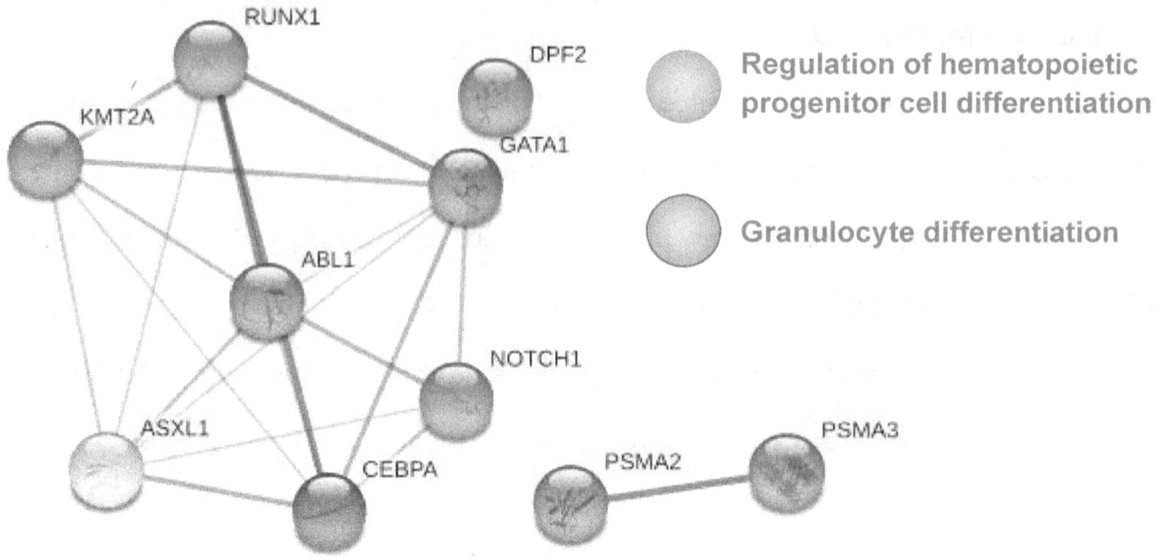

Figure 6.1: STRINGdb network of the deleterious genes showing enrichment of Granulocyte differentiation pathway and Regulation of hematopoietic progenitor cell differentiation pathway.

6.2.3. SLX4 and RAD1 show 3'UTR mutations that modify miRNA binding sites

The mutational landscape for DNA damage and repair genes was plotted in a waterfall plot for all the patients. It was seen that SLX4, a gene of the Fanconi anemia pathway, had the highest mutation frequency. Amongst all the DDR pathways, the Fanconi Anemia pathway and the HR pathway were the two most mutated pathways (Figure 6.2). Out of the 15 genes with 3'UTR mutations, only SLX4 and RAD1 had mutations that altered miRNA binding sites. Interestingly, SLX4 has two kinds of 3;UTR variants, one loses an miRNA binding site for miR-211-5p, and one gains an miRNA binding site for miR-6832-5p (Figure 6.3)

Figure 6.2: Mutation frequency of DNA Damage and Repair genes in the Indian Acute Leukemia cohort

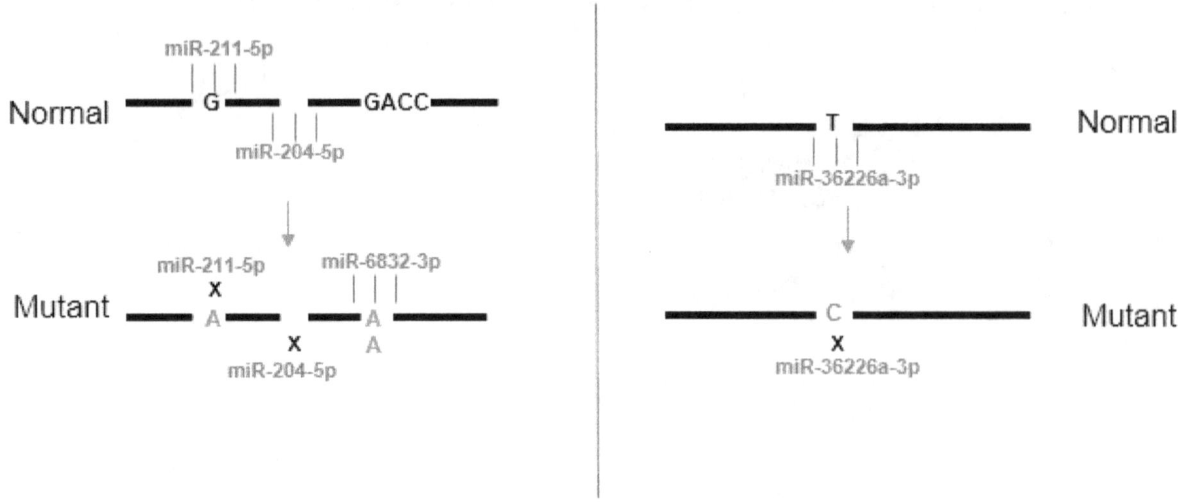

Figure 6.3: UTR mutations in SLX4 and RAD1 altering miRNA binding sites

6.2.4. PCA analysis of AML samples

We obtained two normal whole blood samples as controls. The samples consisted of 9 AML and 1 ALL sample. A quantile normalization was performed for the raw reads, and the samples were normalized using voom normalization method. We performed PCA analysis, and the plot was generated using the online ClustViz tool. All the AML samples clustered together and separated from 2 control and an ALL sample, indicating similarity among AMl samples and differences in the Control and ALL sample gene expression (Figure 6.4).

Further AML samples were subjected to PCA analysis. Three clusters were obtained (TL_1, TL_5 and TL_7), (TL_9, TL_8, TL_3, P3) and (TL_2 and TL_6), indicating differences among the three clustered groups in gene expression (Figure 6.5). We performed fusion transcript analysis using transcriptome to check if the differences obtained were representative of the translocations.

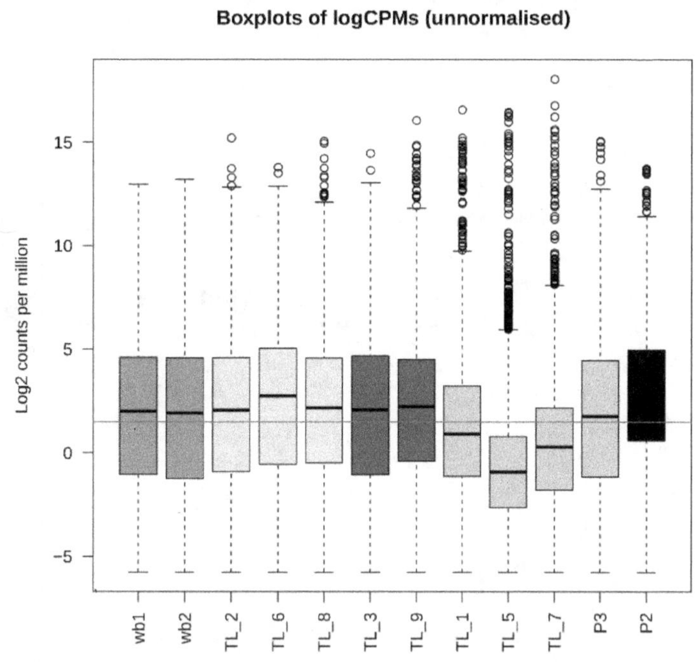

Figure 6.4: Un-normalized boxplot of Transcriptome libraries – average log transformed CPM (counts per million) read counts

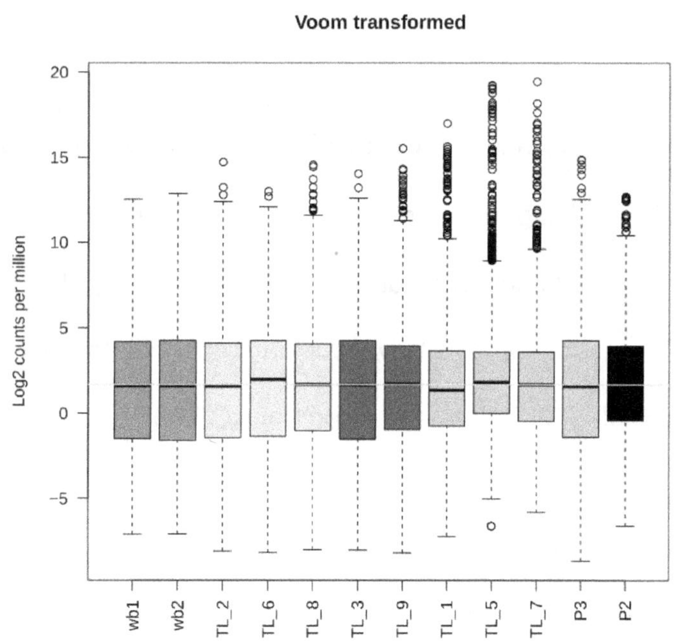

Figure 6.5: Voom normalized boxplot of Transcriptome libraries average log transformed CPM (counts per million) read counts.

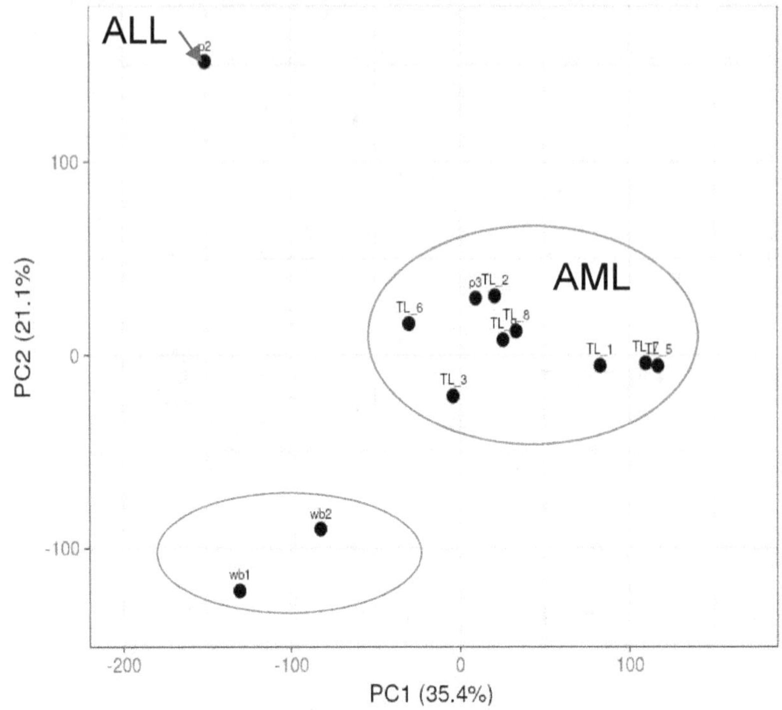

Figure 6.6: PCA plot showing Indian Acute Leukemia clusters, with ALL being significantly far away from the AML patient cluster

6.2.5. Transcriptome analysis reveals novel Fusion gene HOXD11-AGAP3

We obtained three different fusions by performing fusion detection using the STAR-Fusion tool. The first was BCR-ABL1 fusion in 4 out of 10 samples, TL_2, TL_6, TL_8, and P2 (ALL) (Table 6.2). Secondly, we observed a novel fusion transcript formed between Exon 1 of HOXD11 on chr2 at position 176972344 and Exon1 of AGAP3 on chr7 at position 150783928, resulting in a chr2:chr7/HOXD11-AGAP3 fusion in samples TL-3, TL-6, and TL-9 (Figure 6.8). Additionally, TL-9 showed a KMT2A-MLLT3 fusion. To further validate the presence of these fusion transcripts, we ran the FusionInspector tool as a part of the STAR-Fusion output. We observed that all three fusions, BCR-ABL1, KMT2A-MLLT3, and HOXD11-AGAP3, had a significant number of reads spanning the respective junctions (Figure 6.9). Interestingly, it was also seen that for all the fusion transcripts detected, the translocation breakpoints in the participating genes occurred in the exonic regions.

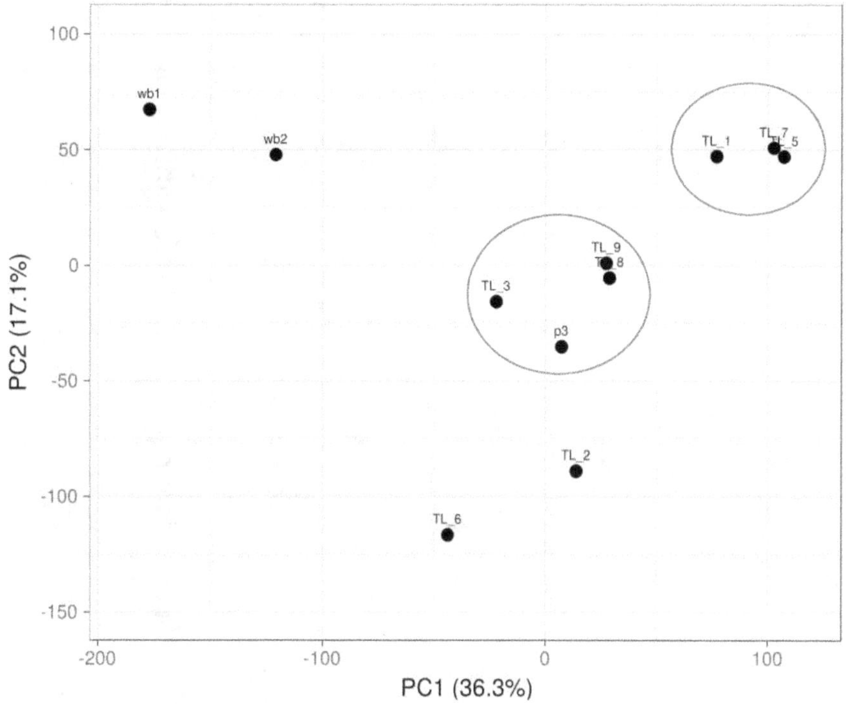

Figure 6.7: PCA plot with Indian Acute Leukemia clusters without the ALL sample.

TL-1	--
TL-2	BCR;ABL1
TL-3	HOXD11;AGAP3
TL-5	--
TL-6	BCR;ABL& HOXD11;AGAP3
TL-7	--
TL-8	BCR;ABL1
TL-9	KMT2A;MLLT3& HOXD11;AGAP3
P2	BCR-ABL1
P3	--

Table 6.2: Fusion genes detected in Indian Acute Leukemia Samples

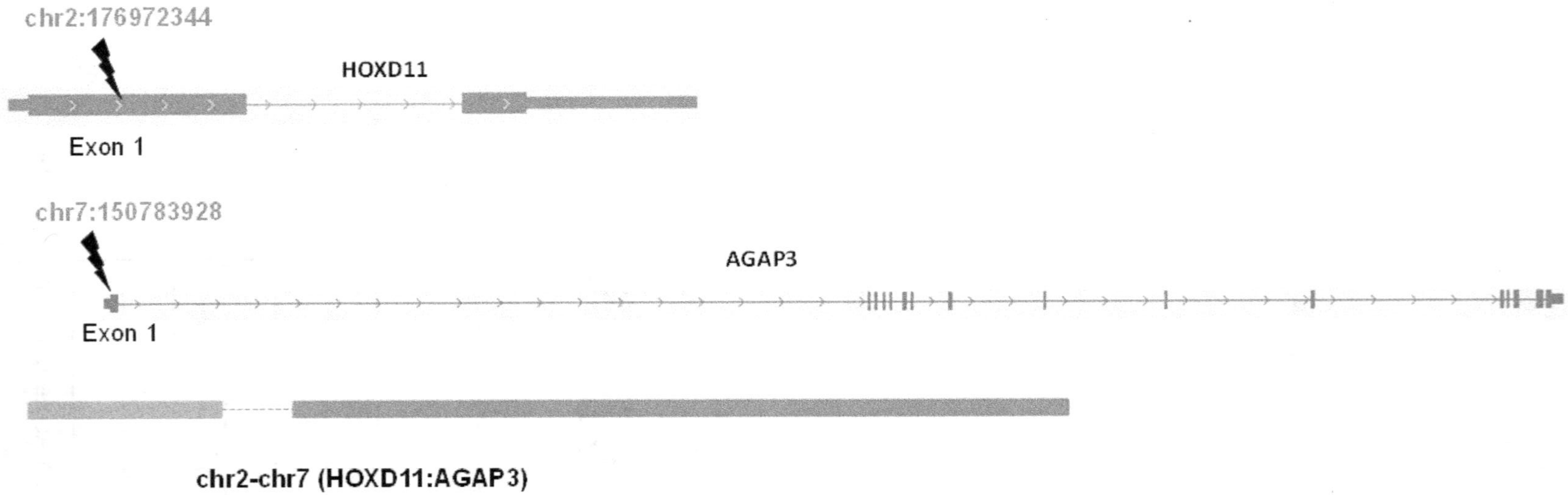

Figure 6.8: A diagrammatic representation of HOXD11-AGAP3 fusion from chr2 and chr7 respectively at the reported locations of Exon 1 in each gene

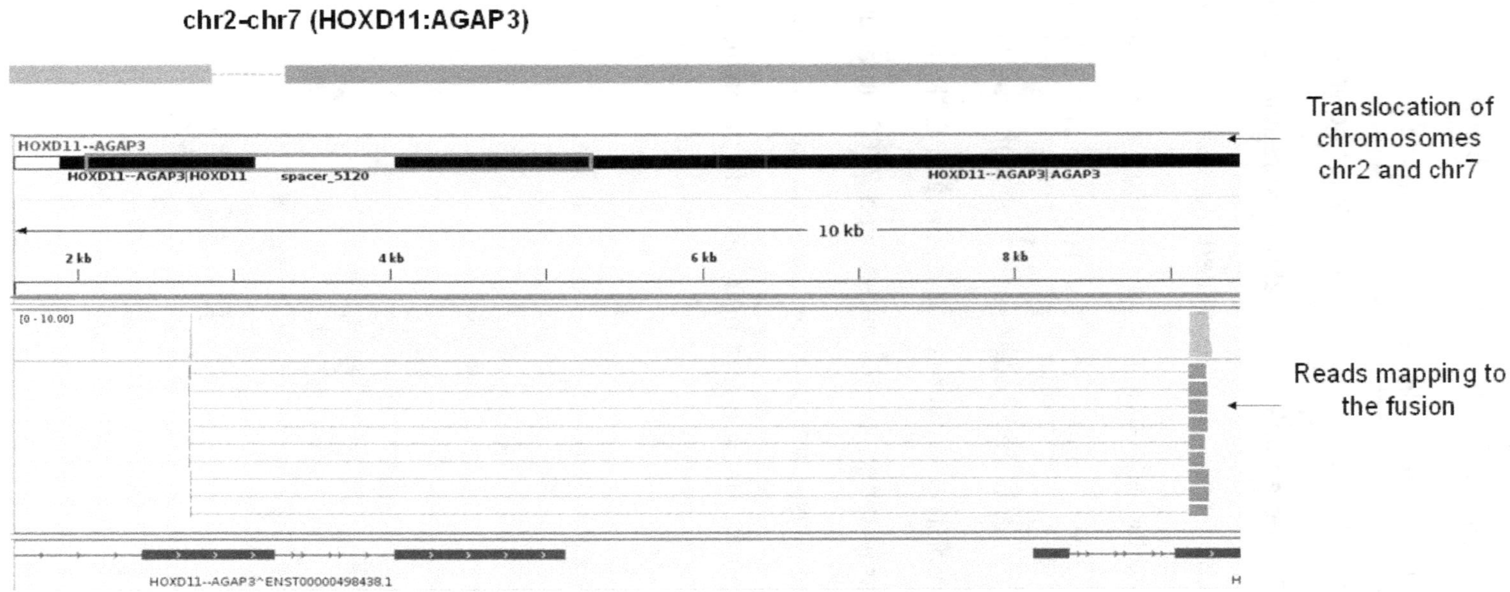

Figure 6.9: An IGV snapshot showing the HOXD11-AGAP3 fusion transcript with reads from the alignment file mapping to the junction.

6.2.6. Differential Expression analysis reveals pathways uniquely enriched in samples with similar fusion genes

Differential expression analysis was performed using DeSeq2 for the acute leukemia sample groups against the whole blood control samples. Differentially expressed genes were filtered based on a p-value cut off of <0.05 and log2FC >2 for upregulated and <-2 for downregulated genes. For the BCR-ABL group, we obtained 1634 upregulated and 1286 downregulated genes. Furthermore, pathway analysis was performed. Enriched upregulated pathways belong to neutrophil degranulation, cytokine signalling, and the adaptive immune system, whereas PI3K-AKT and TGFband JAK-STAT were downregulated(Figure 6.10). The HOXA11-AGAP3 group showed 1797 upregulated genes and 2598 down-regulated genes, and their pathway analysis revealed upregulated NF-kB, NOD and TNF signalling, whereas cell cycle and ECM receptor were downregulated (Figure 6.11). The samples without any fusion showed 7766 upregulated and 1377 downregulated genes and the pathways which were upregulated are cell-cell communication, ECM degradation and collagen trimerization and neutrophil degranulation and IRAK4 deficiency (Figure 6.12).

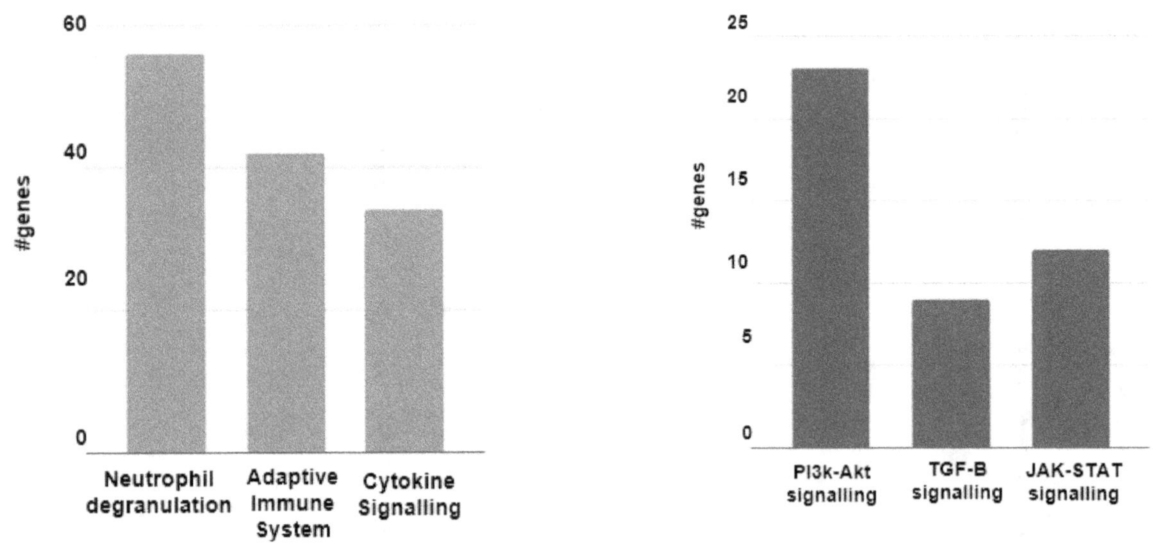

Figure 6.10: Pathways enriched in BCR-ABL group: A) Upregulated, B) Downregulated

We also performed a differential expression analysis of all the AML samples vs control samples and we saw that, pathways like Cell migration, Receptor Tyrosine kinase signaling, and Hemoglobin complex were upregulated while T cell differentiation, Neutrophil degranulation, and Regulation of myeloid differentiation pathways were downregulated

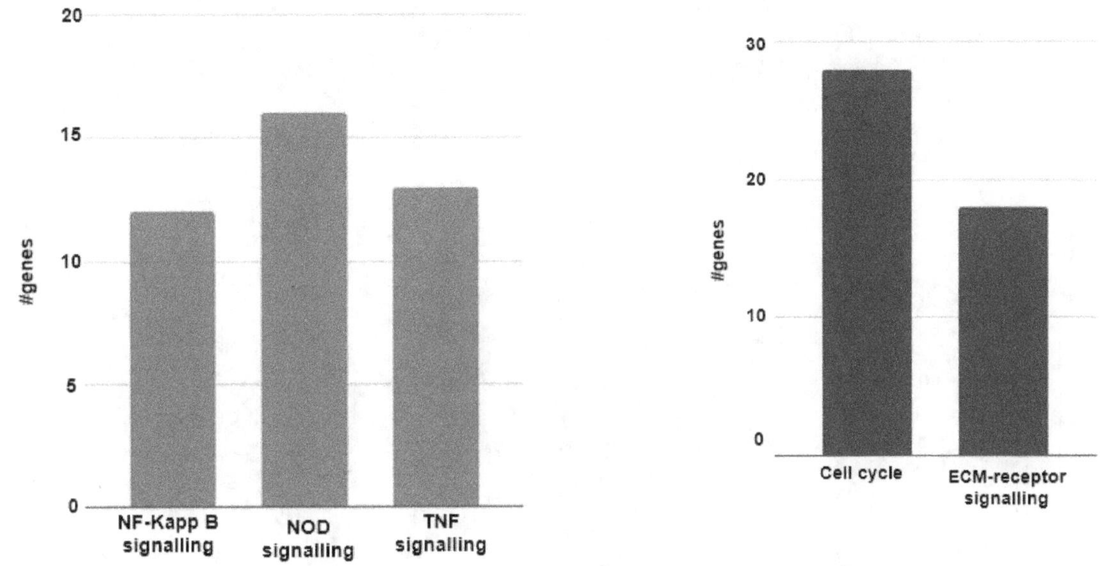

Figure 6.11: Pathways enriched in HOXA11-AGAP3 group: A) Upregulated, B) Downregulated

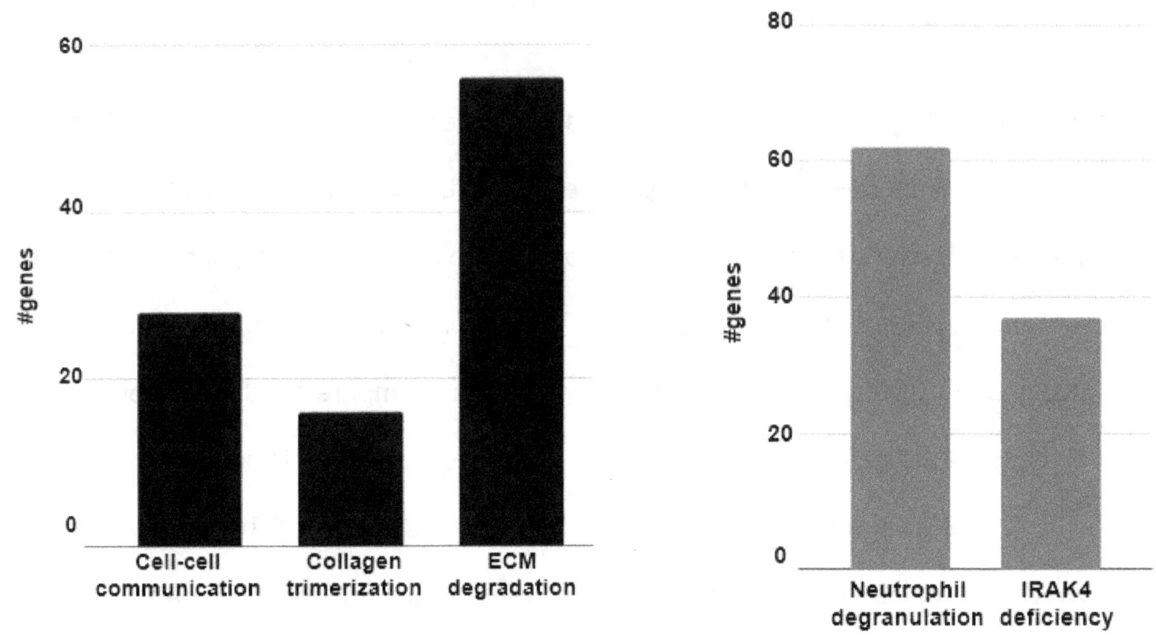

Figure 6.12.: Pathways enriched in the group where no fusion was detected: A) Upregulated, B) Downregulated

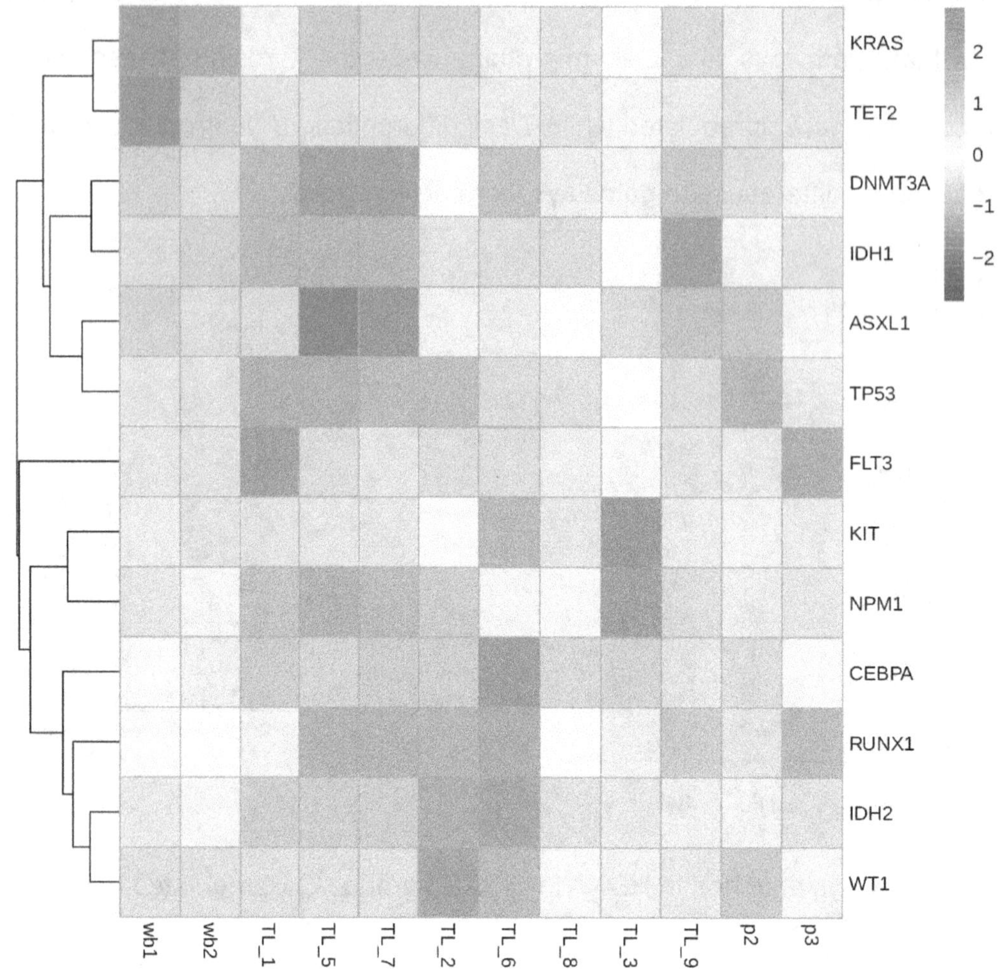

Figure 6.13: Expression profiles of genes implicated in AML in the Indian cohort

6.2.7. Expression Analysis of genes implicated in AML in an Indian cohort

A heatmap was plotted for genes known to be implicated in AML and neutropenia. On comparing the samples amongst each other based on the AML expression profiles, it was seen that the genes KRAS and TET2 were consistently downregulated as compared to the control whole blood samples. The rest of the genes showed that TL-1, TL-5 and TL-7 had similar expression profiles, except for FLT3 being upregulated in the TL-1 sample. TL-2 and TL-6 had similar expression profiles, while TL-3 and TL-8 had the same profile, with the exceptions of KIT and NPM1 being higher in TL-3. TL-9, P2, and P3 had unique expression profiles (Figure 6.13). These sample similarities based on expression profiles were corroborated in the case of neutropenia genes, with certain obvious exceptions. One striking example is MPO and ELANE genes, which are highly upregulated in TL_6 and TL_9 samples (Figure 6.14).

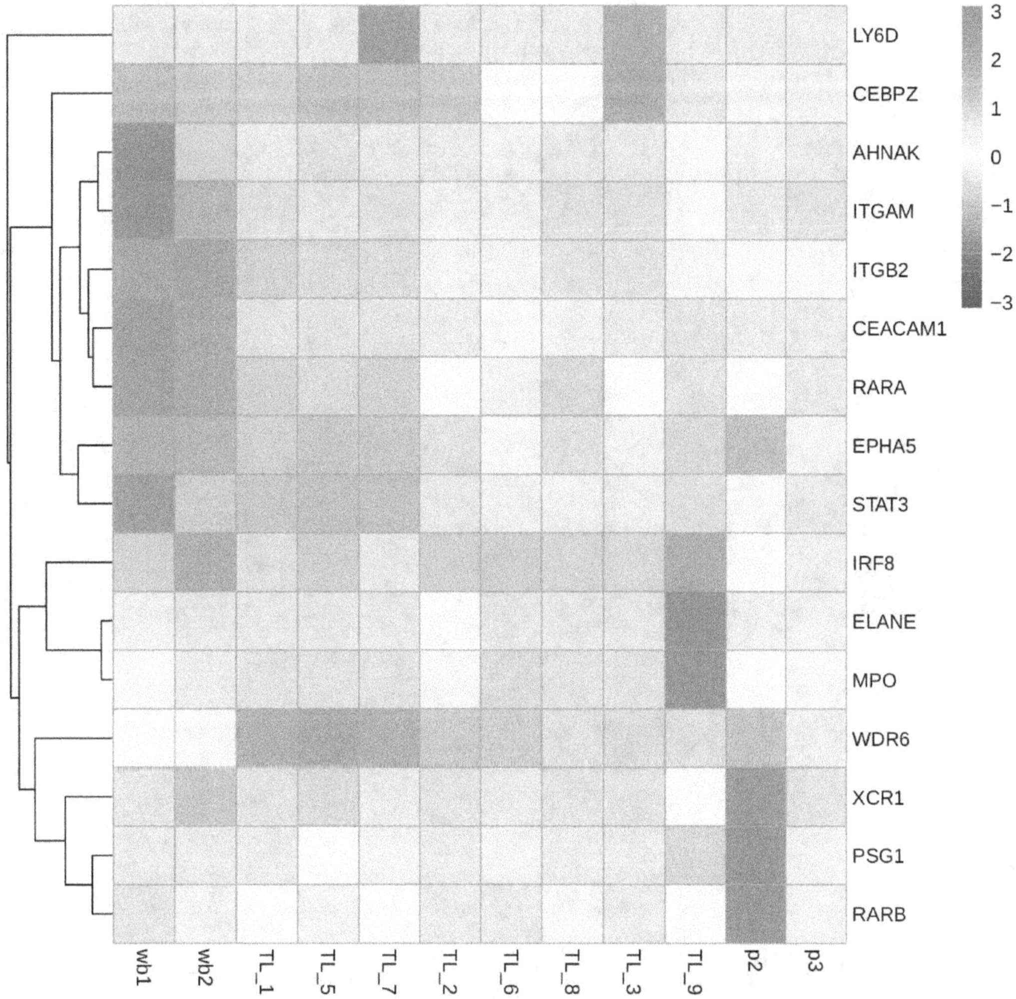

Figure 6.14: Expression profiles of genes implicated in Granulopoiesis in the Indian cohort

6.2.8. Analysis of DDR pathways reveals pathway specific signatures

We have explored the mutation profiles of DDR genes in a previous section, and in continuation, we investigated the expression profiles of DDR pathways. The first two pathways that we analysed were HR (Figure 6.15 top) and NHEJ (Figure 6.15 bottom). One again TL_1, 5 and 7 showed a similar downregulation across all the genes. Based on the cummulative gene expression profile, as compared to the whole blood control samples, the TL_2 and TL_6 have a similar

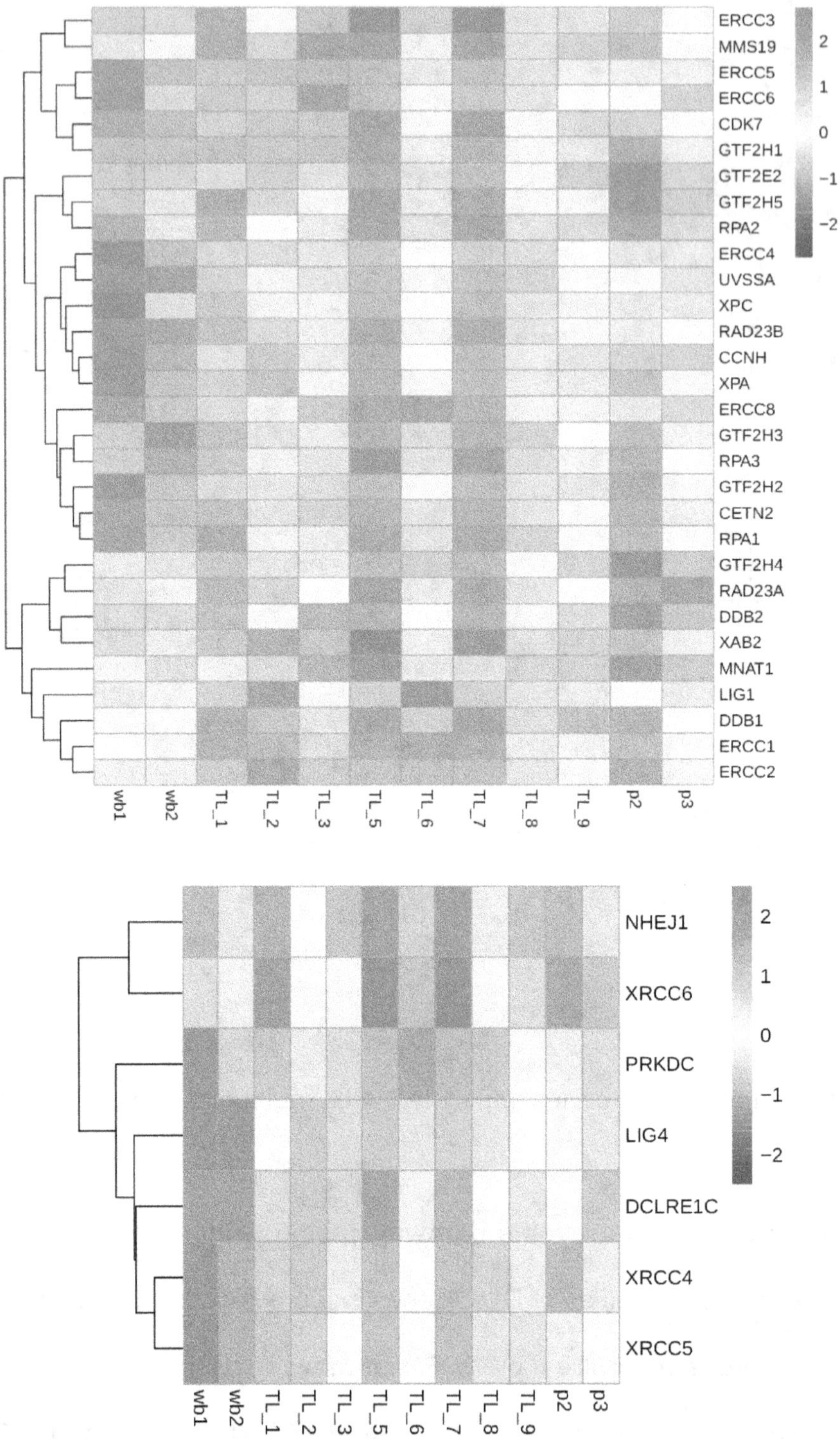

Figure 6.15: Expression profiles of genes in (top) HR pathway and (bottom) NHEJ pathway

expression profile for one set of genes (RAD51 and its interactors, RAD54L/B, EME1, DMC1, XRCC2-3, SHLD1, SLX genes, SWASP1, BRCA1, GEN1), but for the rest of the genes, TL_2 is downregulated. NHEJ shows a general down regulation in all the Acute Leukemia samples, except the ALL sample. Some exceptions are as follows, PRKDC is upregulated in TL_6, XRCC6 was seen to be upregulated in P3 and TL_6, while NHEJ1 is also upregulated in TL_6 and TL_3 (Figure 6.15). Considering the NER and BER pathways (Figure 6.16 A and B), once again TL_1, 5 and 7 fall into one category and TL_2 and TL_6, into one and TL_3 and TL_8 into another. As expected, P2 and P3 show a unique profile once again. In terms of the whole blood

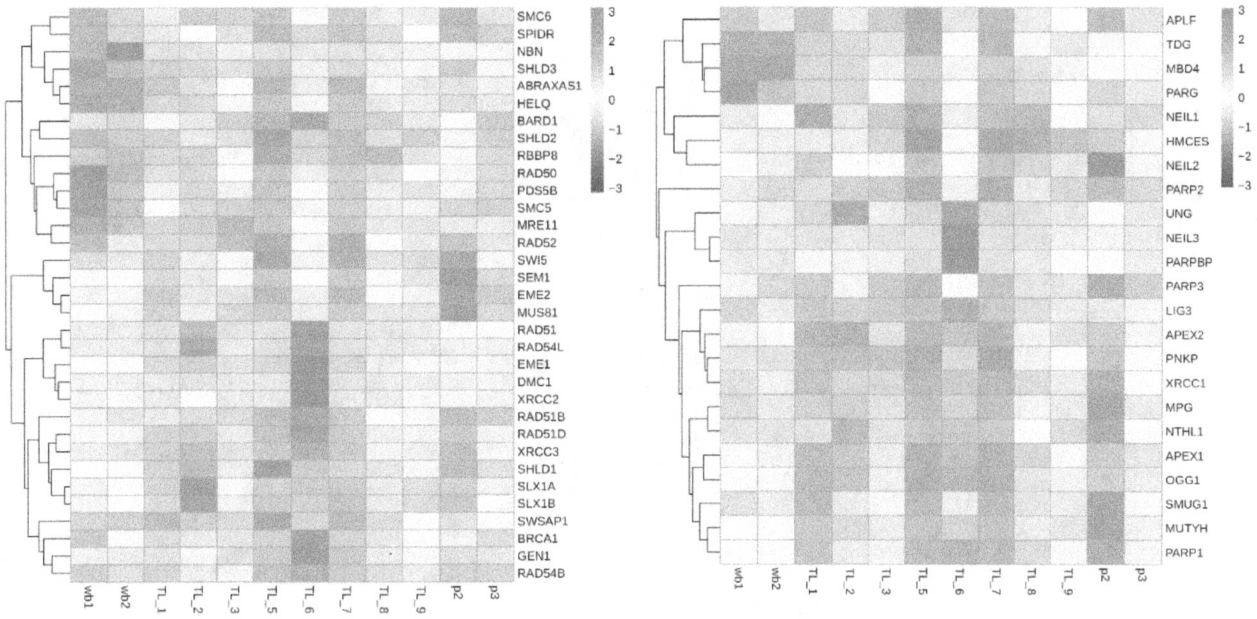

Figure 6.16: Expression profiles of genes in A) NER pathway and B) BER pathway

control samples, there is a distinct upregulation in one part of the NER genes, while in the part with GTF2H4, RAD23B, DDB2, XAB2, MNAT1, LIG1, ERCC1/2, the contorls are downregulated on an average (Figure 6.16 A). Having ontained a mutational signature for Fanconi Anemia genes, we additionally profiled their expression pattern (Figure 6.17). Apart from, obtaining similar expression patterns across fusion gene groups, the most intriguing part was that SLX4 was significantly upregulated in the samples that contained the interupting mutation, samples TL_2 and TL_6.Interestingly it can also be observed that TL_6 is upregulated in DDR genes.

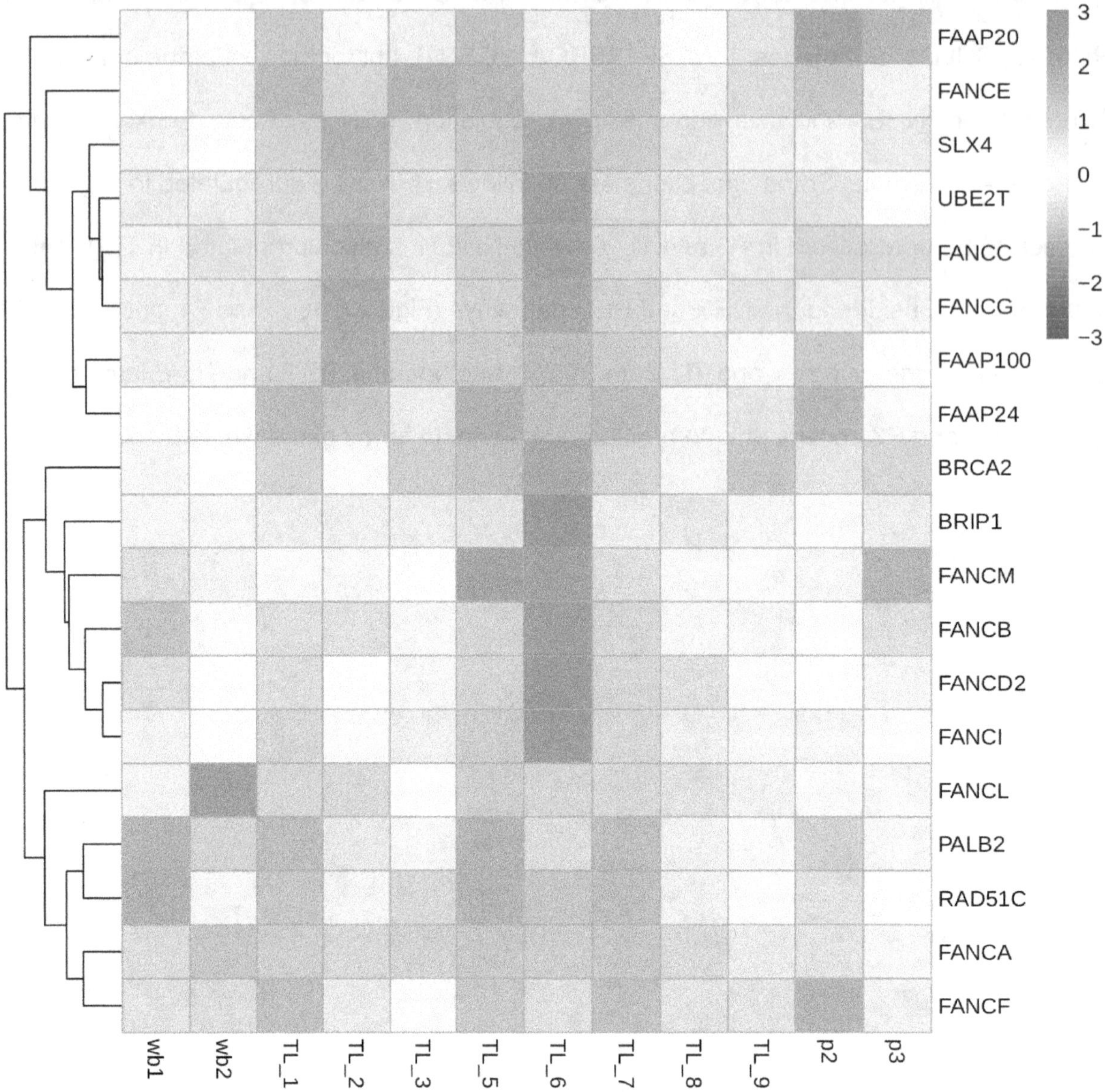

Figure 6.17: Expression profiles of genes in Fanconi Anemia pathway

6.2.9. Immune cell profiling of Indian patient samples revealed

We evaluated the immune cell profiles with CIBERSORTx. All the acute leukemia samples had a very different immune profile compared to the whole blood controls. We checked for the immune profile in 3 different groups depending on the fusion transcripts. Among the groups with no fusion transcript (TL_1, TL_5, TL_7, and P3), TL_1 and TL_7 showed a very similar distribution of immune fractions with high mast cell and negligible neutrophil fractions (Figure 6).

TL_5 was the only one with a significantly high fraction of neutrophils (45%) compared to the negligible levels in others (Figure 6.18). In the group with BCR-ABL1 fusion (TL_2, TL_6, and TL_8), TL_2 and TL_6 were similar with a higher fraction of Mast cells, Tregs, Macrophage M0, and CD8 cells, while TL_8 had a higher fraction of activated dendritic cells. In the subgroup HOXD11:AGAP3 fusion, all three TL_3, TL_6, and TL_9 were dissimilar in immune fractions, which could be due to the presence/absence of additional fusion in those samples. TL_3, the only sample with just the HOXD11-AGAP3 fusion, had a high frequency of resting CD4 cells and NK cells, followed by CD4 naive and CD8 cells. TL_6's immune profile was closer to the TL_2 samples than as compared to TL_3 and TL_9. TL_9 showed the highest M0 and M2 macrophage fractions and a relatively high fraction of CD8 cells, indicating patient-specific immune cell fractions.

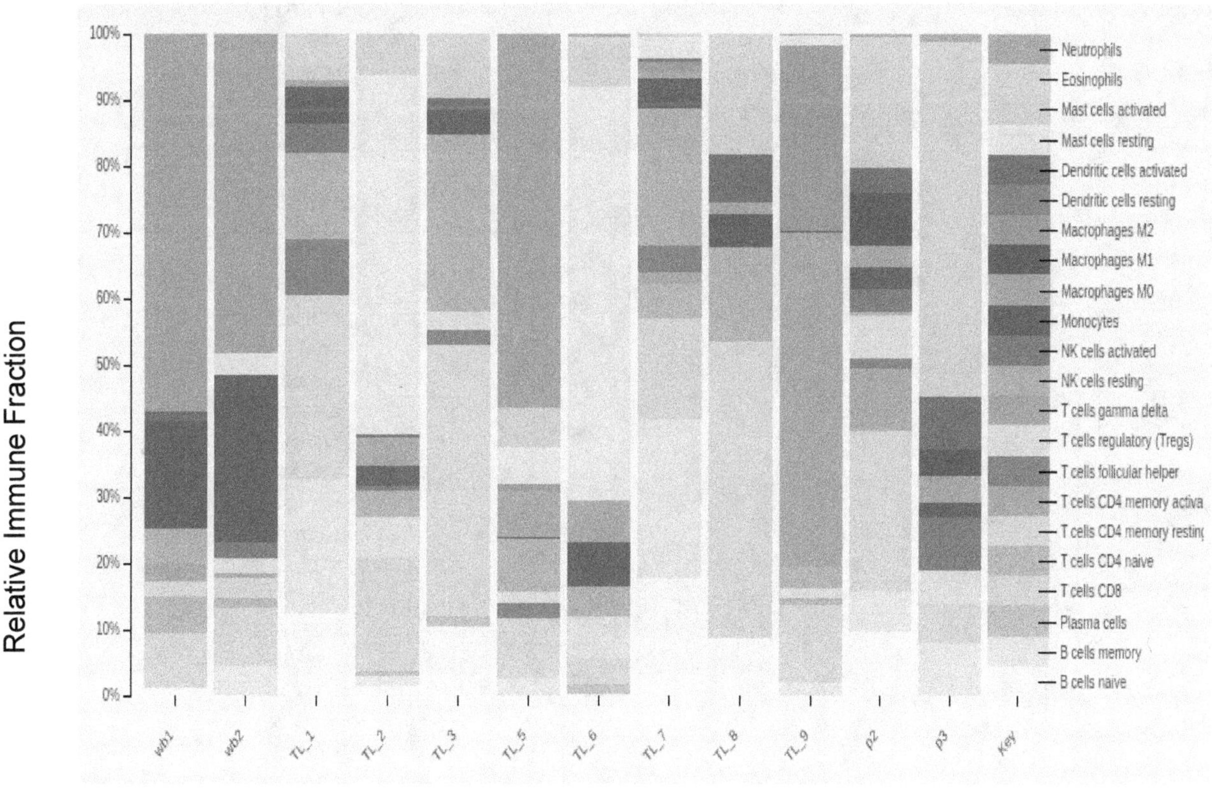

Figure 6.18: Immune profiles of Indian Acute Leukemia samples as compared to whole blood controls in terms of relative fraction of immune cell

6.2.10. WGCNA using differential lincRNA and mRNA in an Indian cohort.

To profile long noncoding RNA and understand if there was subtype specificity, differential expression of long noncoding RNA was performed as described in chapter4. We selected

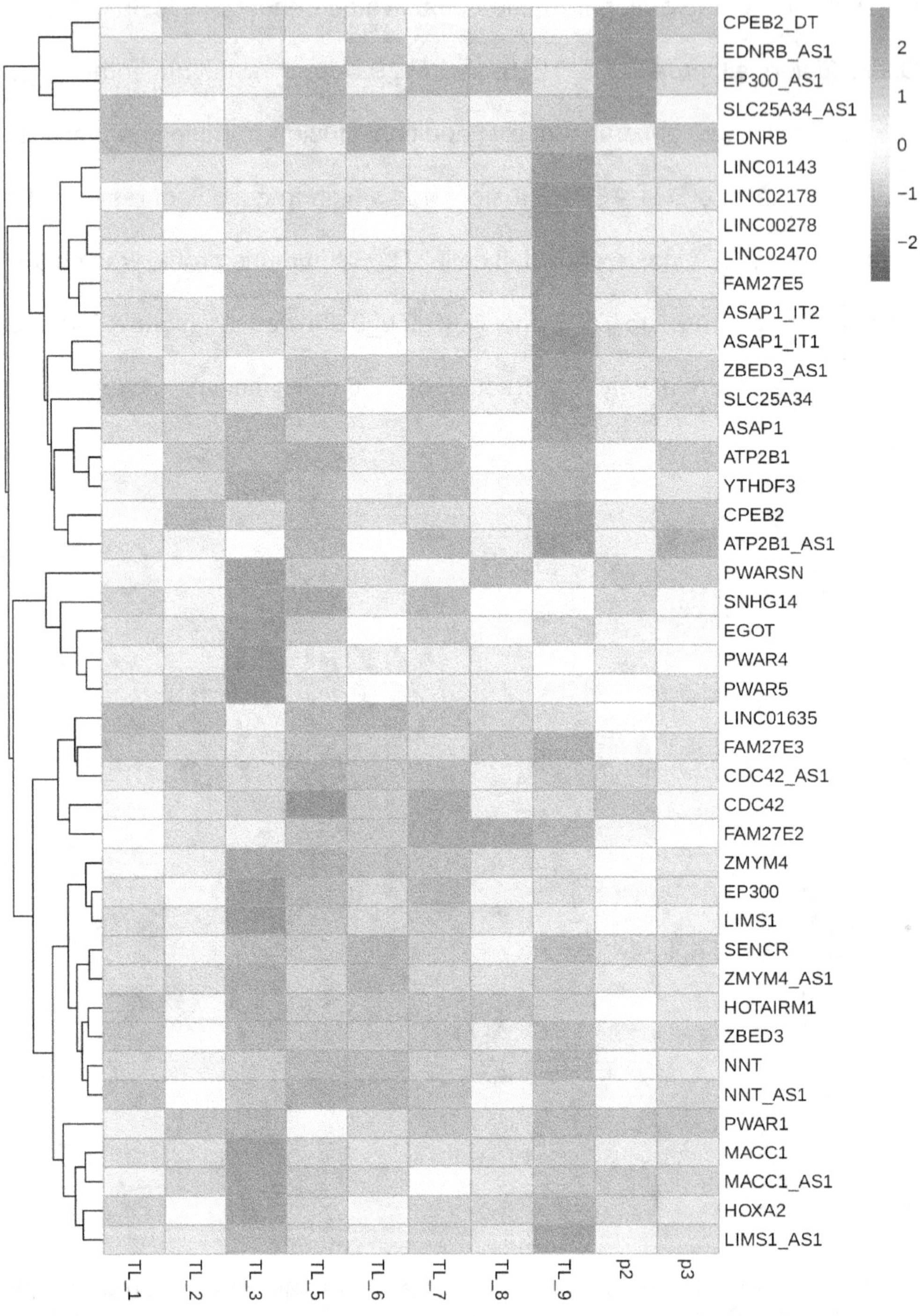

Figure 6.19: Expression profiles of lncRNA-mRNA profiles in Acute leukemia samples

subtypes based on fusion transcripts1) TL-1, TL-5, TL-7, P3 - no translocation detected, 2) TL-2, TL-8 and P2 - BCR-ABL1, and 3) TL-3, TL-6, TL-9 - HOXD11-AGAP3 as traits and performed a correlational analysis of mRNA-linc RNA. We selected only lincRNA-mRNA pairs in the vicinity of each other and simultaneously checked for the lncRNA and mRNA expression (Figure 6.19). Following the WGCNA analysis we also performed a pathway analysis. WGCNA results revealed a significant correlation (r=0.87, p-value=0.001) between the fusion gene category and co-expression of lncRNA and mRNA in the "green-yellow" module with 213 transcripts containing mRNA and lncRNA (Figure 6.20). The pathways regulated were HOX gene activation and FOXO signalling pathway (Figure 6.21). Based on the vicinity of locations between the transcripts, we found 27 mRNA-lncRNA pairs present within 2000 bases of each other and plotted a heatmap (Figure 6.19). Analysis revealed TL-1, TL-5, TL-7, and P3 - no translocation had most of the lincRNA, mRNA pair downregulated, whereas TL-3, TL-6, TL-9 - HOXD11-AGAP3, showed most of it to be upregulated with TL9 showiiing higher level of both lincRNA and mRNA pair. TL-2, TL-8 and P2 - BCR-ABL1 showed low expression of both lincRNA and mRNA than the HOXD11-AGAP3 group and higher than no fusion group. All three groups had a distinct pattern of lincRNA-mRNA expression. (Figure 6.19). In the HOXD11-AGAP3 group, HOTAIR and the gene next to it, HOXA2, were both upregulated, whereas they were downregulated in the other 2 groups. Many such lincRNA-mRNA pairs are observed, which might be regulated by the fusion gene product of HOXD11 and AGAP3. To get a better understanding of the immune system-related effect of HOXD11-AGAP3, we screened for additional signatures and amongst the chemokines, we obtained CCL28 and DOCK2 to be highly expressed in HOXD11-AGAP3 samples as compared to the rest (Figure 6.21).

6.3. DISCUSSION

To highlight the differences between the mutational profiles of the Indian and Caucasian populations, we profiled the mutations in the 10 patients. We observed that critical transcription factors like RUNX1, ASXL1, NOTCH1, and CEBPA had deleterious missense mutations. When comparing the two populations, RUNX1, ASXL1, and CEBPA genes were common, with

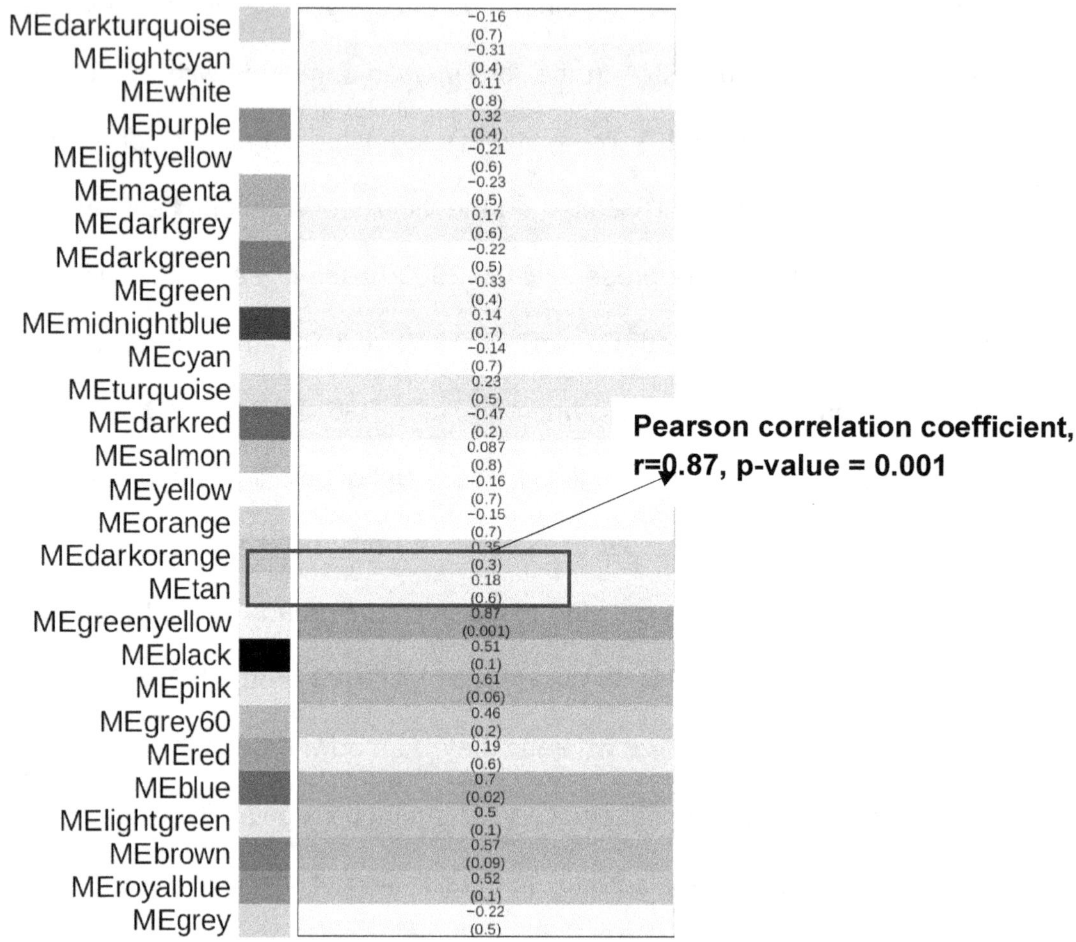

Figure 6.20: Module trait relationship between co-expression of lncRNA-mRNA and presence of fusion genes

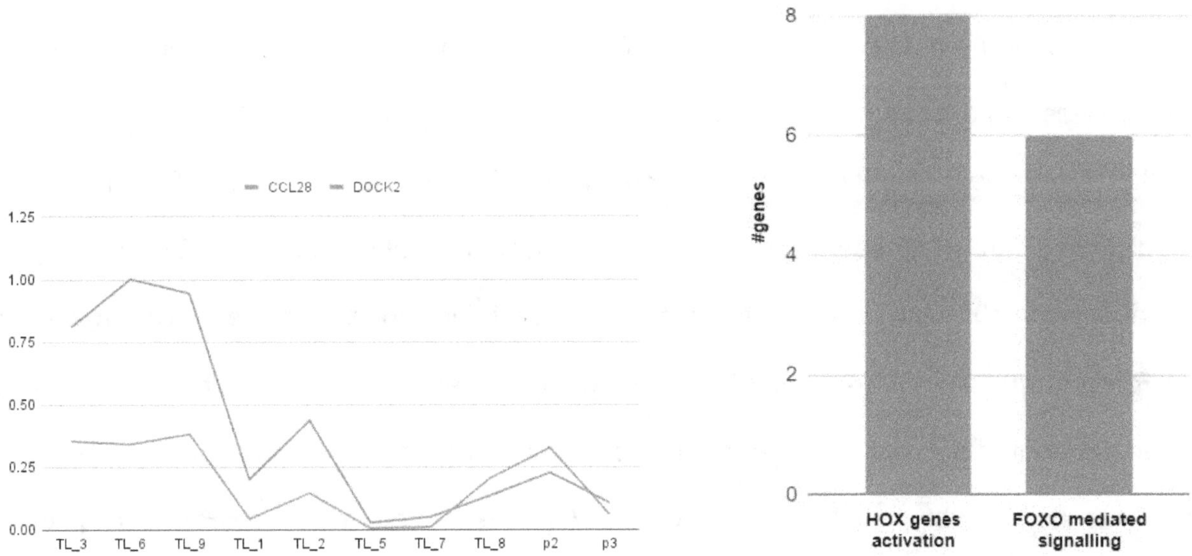

Figure 6.21: (Right) Pathways enriched from lncRNA-mRNA WGCNA analysis (left) Expression profiles of CCL28 and DOCK2

population-specific mutations. The ASXL1 mutation was a frameshift variant (rs750318549) and is considered to be pathogenic. Pathogenic mutations in ASXL1 are associated with a high frequency in the M5 subtype of AML[10]. The mutation in CEBPA is an inframe deletion (rs746430067), suspected to be associated with Acute myeloid leukemia. A previous study has shown that CEBPA mutations are more common in the Asian cohort than in the Caucasian population.

In that context, CEBPA mutations have been reported in 18% of south Indian AML patients[11,12]. In the caucasian data analyzed, only 3 out of 109 patients (2%) showed a mutation in CEBPA. A novel germline RUNX1 mutation in Indian myeloid malignancy was reported[13]. Interestingly, the RUNX1 mutation (novel and deleterious) found in the analyzed cohort was probably a somatic mutation different from the one reported[13]. Other transcription factors that had novel deleterious mutations unique to the Indian cohort were GATA1, KMT2A, and NOTCH1. A previous study has reported NOTCH1 mutations in ALL favouring better outcomes, but there has been no report of NOTCH1 mutations in AML in India[14]. KMT2A is a key player in AML translocations, and its rearrangements and somatic mutations have been linked to outcome predictions in AML[15,16]. Our study found no mutations in the caucasian population for KMT2A, but a novel deleterious mutation was found in the Indian cohort. As expected, pathway analysis of all the novel deleterious mutations revealed alterations in the Regulation of hematopoietic cell differentiation and granulocyte differentiation pathways. These results were also obtained from WGCNA analysis of the caucasian cohort through investigation of transcriptome profiles. Of the 15 DDR genes with 3'UTR mutations, only SLX4 and RAD1 harbored those that affected miRNA binding sites and is a clear departure from the caucasian population analysis where 3'UTR mutations were signature, specific to the M1 subtype in MRE11A and UBE2A genes that are from the HR and ubiquitination pathways, while in this population, SLX4 and RAD1 are from the Fanconi anemia and general DDR pathway genes. In the case of SLX4, 5' UTR variants have been associated, at low prevalence, with breast cancer[17].

Among the genes known to be implicated in AML, KRAS and TET2 were the only ones downregulated across all the samples in the Indian cohort. KRAS overexpression leads to adverse prognosis in AML patients, so its downregulation in these samples could suggest a better prognosis in the Indian population. TET2, a putative tumor suppressor, is known to be significantly underexpressed in AML samples, and our result corroborates that observation[18]. The genes associated with neutropenia had an expression profile similar to the caucasian population. MPO and ELANE are two co-expressed hub genes in an AML network analysis that correlate with significant prognosis[19].

Interestingly, MPO and ELANE were upregulated in TL-6 and TL-9 genes. The MPO expression status suggests that TL-6 and TL-9 could belong to M1, M2, M3, or M4 subtypes, and the rest of the samples could be M0, M5, M6, or M7[20]. In continuation to the mutation profiles of DDR genes, we also catalogued their transcriptome profiles. Most of the DDR pathways displayed expression patterns similar to those obtained previously, except NHEJ, which shows a general downregulation across all the AML samples. In normal individuals, NHEJ is highly active[21], and it has been shown that in BCR-ABL malignancies, NHEJ is low because of the downregulation of LIG4[22]. Our data also showed downregulation of LIG4 in all the samples, including BCR-ABL samples. The ALL sample shows an upregulation of NHEJ genes, which is well established[23]. RAD1, a component of the DNA repair complex, was expressed high in samples where 3'UTR had mutation with no coding variants, suggesting it is a wild-type complex and could be a reason for chemoresistance. The overexpression of RAD1 was associated with genomic instability and replication stress(http://dx.doi.org/10.1586/17474086.2016.1141673).

SLX1-SLX4 is important for cleaving branched structures formed during homologous recombination and interstrand crosslink repair[25]. In the Indian cohort, overexpression of SLX4 might enhance DNA repair in karyotypically defective cells. Mutations in SLX4 are associated with cancer predisposition. DDR activation in the patients can be targeted in these individuals keeping pathways altered due to the activation of different genes in DDR.

CIBERSORTx analysis showed a distinct pattern of immune cells across the individuals and did not follow fusion gene patterns indicating the fusion products might not influence them. However, mild similarities between the patients were observed, indicating the heterogeneity of AML. TL-5 has a significantly high (45%) neutrophil content which was not observed in any of the samples of the caucasian population. It has been observed that the neutrophil to lymphocyte ratio in the pretreatment group has a better prognosis than NLR high [26]. It is possible that the high neutrophil count in the TL-5 sample could be due to an infection and may indicate a bad prognosis. We could categorize the patients into three groups based on fusion genes and differential gene expression. We detected BCR-ABL fusion in TL-2, TL6, and TL8, which suggests that these samples could have a CML origin in with primary blast crisis, which is the case with TL-2, or they could belong to the recently discovered new category of AML, which are BCR-ABL positive[27,28]. P2, an ALL sample, also showed BCR-ABL, and it is known that 30% of the ALL samples can have this fusion[29]. In three samples, TL-3, TL-6, and TL-9, we detected a novel fusion gene pair, HOXD11-AGAP3. This fusion gene has been reported in neuroblastoma but not reported in AML cases[30]. AGAP3 is an NMDA receptor signaling complex; its fusion gene could be altering the GTPase signaling[31]. Additionally, we were able to detect the KMT2A-MLLT3 fusion gene in TL-9. TL-9 also showed a positive MPO status; hence, these results suggest TL-9 could be the M1 subtype.

In the Indian cohort, we did not see the pattern of immune cells anywhere close to that observed in the Caucasian cohort. The monocyte fraction which characterized the blood of Caucasian individuals was not observed in the Indian cohort. Altered CCL28 expression, which shows a significant effect on survival in AML samples (GEPIA), has been associated with chemokine responsiveness in AML patients. DOCK2, which is expressed only in hematopoietic tissue, is known to be of prognostic value in AML patients.

Long noncoding RNA in AML has been reviewed thoroughly[32]. Long noncoding RNA regulates gene expression by binding to the DNA, RNA or protein and directing the localization of the protein. They have been used as diagnostic and prognostic indicators of disease progression, especially cancer. lincRNA is known to regulate cell proliferation and apoptosis of cancer cells(presented in the literature review). One of the lincRNA HOTAIRM1 (present in HOXA gene cluster) overexpression has a well-known impact on prognosis in a myeloid cell differentiation manner in AML[33,34]. WGCNA analysis revealed HOTAIRM1 - HOXA2 lncRNA-mRNA pair overexpression in the HOXD11-AGAP3 positive samples. Interestingly, HOTAIRM1 was downregulated in the M1 subtype of the Caucasian cohort, whereas it was upregulated in HOXD11-AGAP3 samples in the Indian cohort and absent from other AML subtypes. WGCNA analysis of the Indian cohort revealed enrichment of genes associated with HOX gene activation and FOXO signalling pathways. Studies have shown that HOX genes are activated in AML samples having MLL fusion protein[35]. Interestingly, our samples revealed a novel HOXA11-AGAP3 fusion, and one of the samples showed co-occurrence of KMT2A-MLLT3 fusion, suggesting that the MLL fusion driven HOX gene activation.

6.4. CONCLUSION

A comparison has been drawn between the Indian cohort and the caucasian population samples at every stage of this study. There are unique mutation signatures and expression profile signatures, pointing to a different etiology and the need for novel approaches to treatment regimes. Novel fusion genes were also discovered, which have an immune system related functional impact on the patients, and it is clear that blood-based diagnostics need to be used for biomarkers discovery and therapeutic targets. The sample size for the Indian cohort was small, which warrants further investigation into the leukemia genetics of the Indian subcontinent.

6.5. REFERENCES

1. Philip C, George B, Ganapule A, Korula A, Jain P, Alex AA, et al. Acute myeloid leukaemia: challenges and real world data from India. Br J Haematol. 2015;170: 110–117.

2. Bahl A, Sharma A, Raina V, Kumar L, Bakhshi S, Gupta R, et al. Long-term outcomes for patients with acute myeloid leukemia: a single-center experience from AIIMS, India. Asia Pac J Clin Oncol. 2015;11: 242–252.

3. Ahirwar DR, Ahirwar R, Professor A, Department of Pathology, RKDF Medical College, Bhopal, et al. A study of leukemias Profile in central India. Tropical Journal of Pathology and Microbiology. 2018. pp. 181–187. doi:10.17511/jopm.2018.i02.12

4. Namratha Udupa MS, Babu KG, Suresh Babu MC, Lakshmaiah KC, Lokanatha D, Jacob AL, et al. Clinical profile, cytogenetics and treatment outcomes of adult acute myeloid leukemia. J Cancer Res Ther. 2020;16: 18–22.

5. Bhattacharyya J, Nath S, Saikia KK, Saxena R, Sazawal S, Barman MP, et al. Prevalence and Clinical Significance of FLT3 and NPM1 Mutations in Acute Myeloid Leukaemia Patients of Assam, India. Indian J Hematol Blood Transfus. 2018;34: 32–42.

6. Dalal HY, Damodar S, Veldore VH, Coral MK, Prabhu S, Chawla M, et al. A Prospective Analysis of the Genomic Landscape of Patients with Acute Myeloid Leukemia and Its Impact on Clinical Outcomes - Data from a Tertiary Care Center in India. Blood. 2019. pp. 5163–5163. doi:10.1182/blood-2019-130000

7. Ghosh K, Swaminathan S, Garg S, Madkaikar M, Gupta M, Jijina F. FLT3 and NPM-1 mutations in a cohort of acute promyelocytic leukemia patients from India. Indian Journal of Human Genetics. 2014. p. 160. doi:10.4103/0971-6866.142884

8. DiNardo CD, Cortes JE. Mutations in AML: prognostic and therapeutic implications. Hematology. 2016. pp. 348–355. doi:10.1182/asheducation-2016.1.348

9. Mishra K, Kumar S, Ninawe S, Bahl R, Meshram A, Singh K, et al. The clinical profile, management, and outcome of febrile neutropenia in acute myeloid leukemia from resource constraint settings. Ther Adv Infect Dis. 2021;8: 20499361211036592.

10. Rose D, Haferlach T, Schnittger S, Perglerová K, Kern W, Haferlach C. Subtype-specific patterns of molecular mutations in acute myeloid leukemia. Leukemia. 2017;31: 11–17.

11. Su L, Shi Y-Y, Liu Z-Y, Gao S-J. Acute Myeloid Leukemia With CEBPA Mutations: Current Progress and Future Directions. Frontiers in Oncology. 2022. doi:10.3389/fonc.2022.806137

12. Sarojam S, Raveendran S, Vijay S, Sreedharan J, Narayanan G, Sreedharan H. Characterization of CEBPA Mutations and Polymorphisms and their Prognostic Relevance in De Novo Acute Myeloid Leukemia Patients. Asian Pac J Cancer Prev. 2015;16: 3785–3792.

13. Rajpal S, Jain A, Jamwal M, Jain N, Sachdeva MUS, Malhotra P, et al. A novel germline *RUNX1* mutation with co-occurrence of somatic alterations in a case of myeloid neoplasm with familial thrombocytopenia: first report from India. Leukemia & Lymphoma. 2019. pp. 2568–2571. doi:10.1080/10428194.2019.1587756

14. Natarajan V, Bandapalli OR, Rajkumar T, Sagar TG, Karunakaran N. NOTCH1 and FBXW7 mutations favor better outcome in pediatric South Indian T-cell acute lymphoblastic leukemia. J Pediatr Hematol Oncol. 2015;37: e23–30.

15. Issa GC, Zarka J, Sasaki K, Qiao W, Pak D, Ning J, et al. Predictors of outcomes in adults with acute myeloid leukemia and KMT2A rearrangements. Blood Cancer J. 2021;11: 162.

16. Bill M, Mrózek K, Kohlschmidt J, Eisfeld A-K, Walker CJ, Nicolet D, et al. Mutational landscape and clinical outcome of patients with de novo acute myeloid leukemia and rearrangements involving 11q23/. Proc Natl Acad Sci U S A. 2020;117: 26340–26346.

17. Garibay GR de, de Garibay GR, Díaz A, Gaviña B, Romero A, Garre P, et al. Low prevalence of SLX4 loss-of-function mutations in non-BRCA1/2 breast and/or ovarian cancer families. European Journal of Human Genetics. 2013. pp. 883–886. doi:10.1038/ejhg.2012.268

18. Zhang T-J, Zhou J-D, Yang D-Q, Wang Y-X, Wen X-M, Guo H, et al. TET2 expression is a potential prognostic and predictive biomarker in cytogenetically normal acute myeloid leukemia. J Cell Physiol. 2018;233: 5838–5846.

19. Chen S, Chen Y, Lu J, Yuan D, He L, Tan H, et al. Bioinformatics Analysis Identifies Key Genes and Pathways in Acute Myeloid Leukemia Associated with DNMT3A Mutation. Biomed Res Int. 2020;2020: 9321630.

20. Béné MC, Nebe T, Bettelheim P, Buldini B, Bumbea H, Kern W, et al. Immunophenotyping of acute leukemia and lymphoproliferative disorders: a consensus proposal of the European LeukemiaNet Work Package 10. Leukemia. 2011. pp. 567–574. doi:10.1038/leu.2010.312

21. Scully R, Panday A, Elango R, Willis NA. DNA double-strand break repair-pathway choice in somatic mammalian cells. Nat Rev Mol Cell Biol. 2019;20: 698–714.

22. Sallmyr A, Tomkinson AE, Rassool FV. Up-regulation of WRN and DNA ligase IIIalpha in chronic myeloid leukemia: consequences for the repair of DNA double-strand breaks. Blood. 2008;112: 1413–1423.

23. Chiou S-S, Huang J-L, Tsai Y-S, Chen T-F, Lee K-W, Juo S-HH, et al. Elevated mRNA transcripts of non-homologous end-joining genes in pediatric acute lymphoblastic leukemia. Leukemia. 2007;21: 2061–2064.

24. Bret C, Viziteu E, Kassambara A, Moreaux J. Identifying high-risk adult AML patients: epigenetic and genetic risk factors and their implications for therapy. Expert Rev Hematol. 2016;9: 351–360.

25. Payliss BJ, Patel A, Sheppard AC, Wyatt HDM. Exploring the Structures and Functions of Macromolecular SLX4-Nuclease Complexes in Genome Stability. Front Genet. 2021;12: 784167.

26. Zhang Q, Yang Q, Weng Y, Huang Z, Chen R, Zhu Y, et al. Neutrophil-to-lymphocyte ratio correlates with prognosis and response to chemotherapy in patients with non-M3 de novo acute myeloid leukemia. Translational Cancer Research. 2021. pp. 1013–1024. doi:10.21037/tcr-20-2179

27. Neuendorff NR, Burmeister T, Dörken B, Westermann J. BCR-ABL-positive acute myeloid leukemia: a new entity? Analysis of clinical and molecular features. Ann Hematol. 2016;95: 1211–1221.

28. Pastoret C, Houot R. “Chronic myelogenous leukemia in primary blast crisis” rather than “de novo -positive acute myeloid leukemia.” Clin Case Rep. 2017;5: 757–760.

29. Mariotti B, Meconi F, Palmieri R, De Bellis E, Lavorgna S, Ottone T, et al. Acute Myeloid Leukemia with Concomitant BCR-ABL and NPM1 Mutations. Case Rep Hematol. 2019;2019: 6707506.

30. Wu W, Xu WJ, Liu JB, Sun J, Huang YM, Lv ZB. Exome sequencing identifies predisposing and fusion gene in ganglioneuroma, ganglioneuroblastoma and neuroblastoma. Math Biosci Eng. 2019;16: 7217–7229.

31. Nagashima S, Takeda K, Shiiba I, Higashi M, Fukuda T, Tokuyama T, et al. Critical role of CRAG, a splicing variant of centaurin-γ3/AGAP3, in ELK1-dependent SRF activation at PML bodies. Sci Rep. 2019;9: 20107.

32. Ng M, Heckl D, Klusmann J-H. The Regulatory Roles of Long Noncoding RNAs in Acute Myeloid Leukemia. Frontiers in Oncology. 2019. doi:10.3389/fonc.2019.00570

33. Zhang X, Weissman SM, Newburger PE. Long intergenic non-coding RNA HOTAIRM1 regulates cell cycle progression during myeloid maturation in NB4 human promyelocytic leukemia cells. RNA Biol. 2014;11: 777–787.

34. Gao J, Wang F, Wu P, Chen Y, Jia Y. Aberrant LncRNA Expression in Leukemia. J Cancer. 2020;11: 4284–4296.

35. Slany RK. The molecular biology of mixed lineage leukemia. Haematologica. 2009. pp. 984–993. doi:10.3324/haematol.2008.002436

Chapter 7:
Summary and Highlights

Summary and Highlights

This study explored the variants and expression of the genes implicated in AML and identified novel mutations in the 3'UTR of the DNA repair genes and correlated the expression with survival using public data and inhouse sequenced whole genome and RNA seq of Indian Acute Leukemia samples.

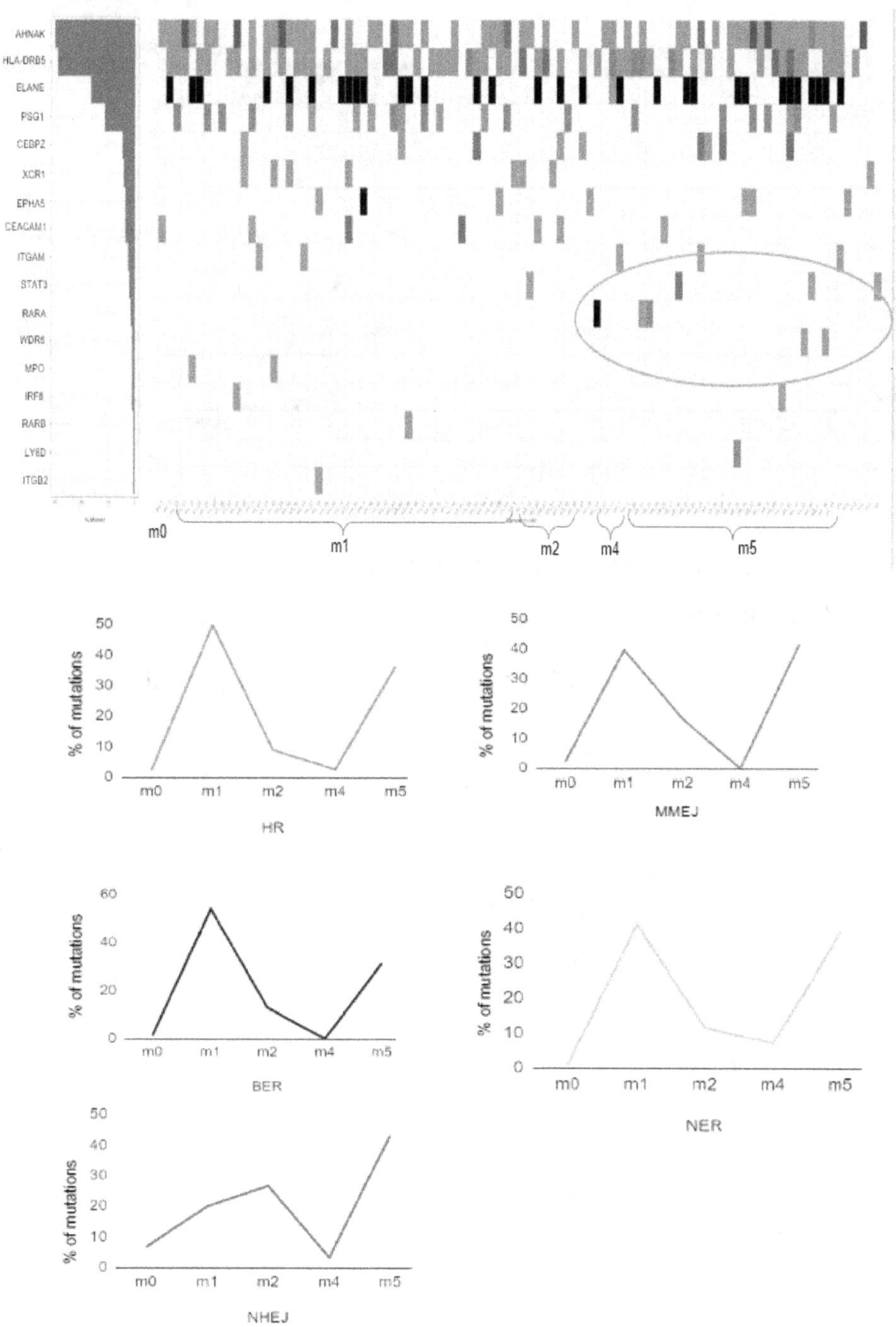

Figure 7.1: Haematological malignancies are governed by Subtype specific variant signatures in granulopoiesis and DDR pathways

- We Identified M5 subtype specific variants in granulopoiesis transcription factors.
- M1 subtype was enriched in HR and BER pathways, and M5 subtypes was enriched in NER, HR and MMEJ pathways

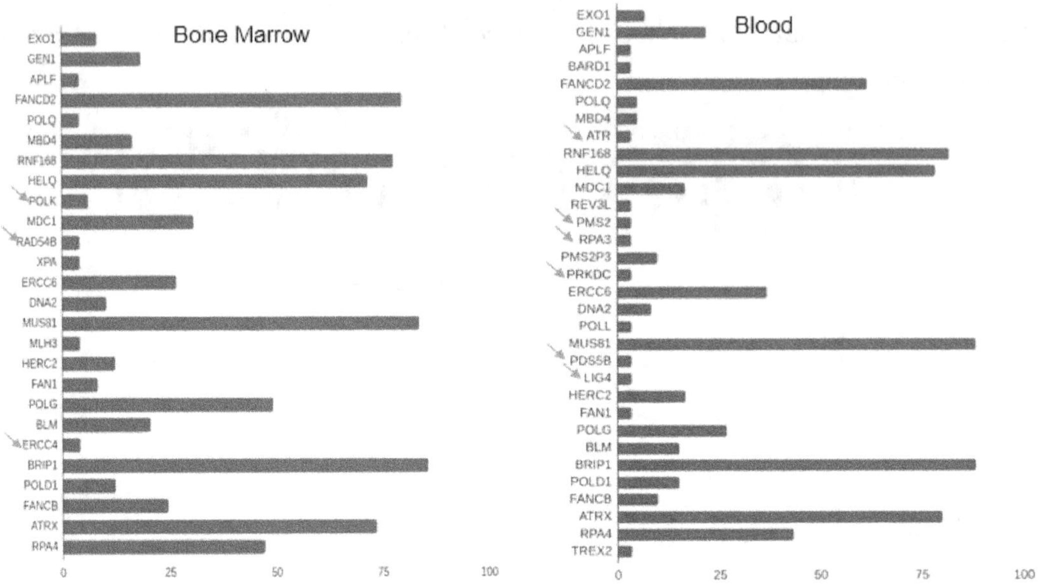

Figure 7.2: Signatures/variants unique to bone marrow and blood

- 63% of the mutations present in Bone marrow are also observed in Blood with 11% unique to Bone Marrow and 26% unique to Blood
- Bone marrow samples were enriched with unique mutations in the HR pathway
- Peripheral blood samples were enriched with unique mutations in the NHEJ pathway

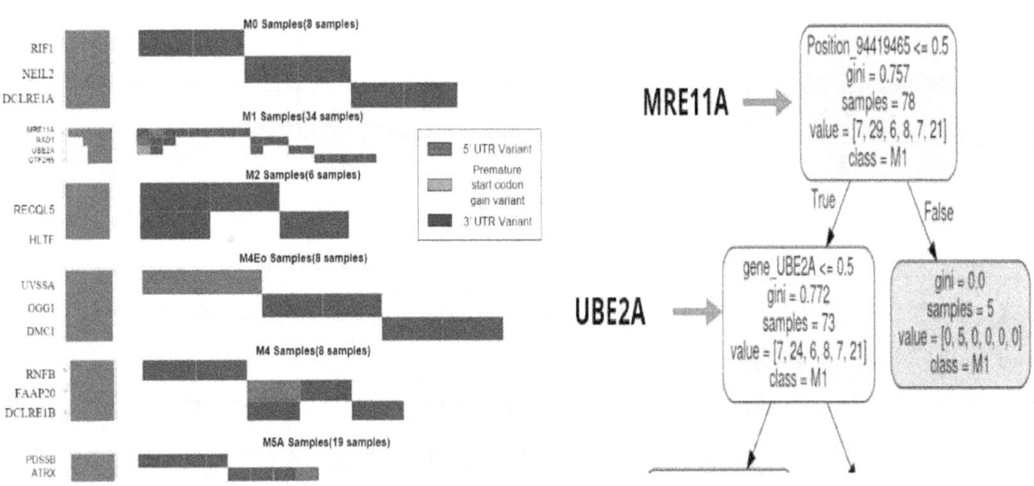

Figure 7.3: Subtype specific 3'UTR variant signatures in DDR genes of which MRE11A and UBE2A were validated using machine learning

➢ Subtype specific 3'UTR variant signatures were identified; M0 - RIF1, NEIL2, DCLRE1A; M1- MRE11A, RAD1, UBE2A, and GTF2H5; M2- RCQI5 and HLTF; M4Eo- OGG1 and DMC1; RNFB and DCLRE1B; M5A PDS5B and ATRX

➢ Using machine learning methods MRE11A and UBE2A were validated as M1 specific 3'UTR variant signatures, with a model accuracy of 80%

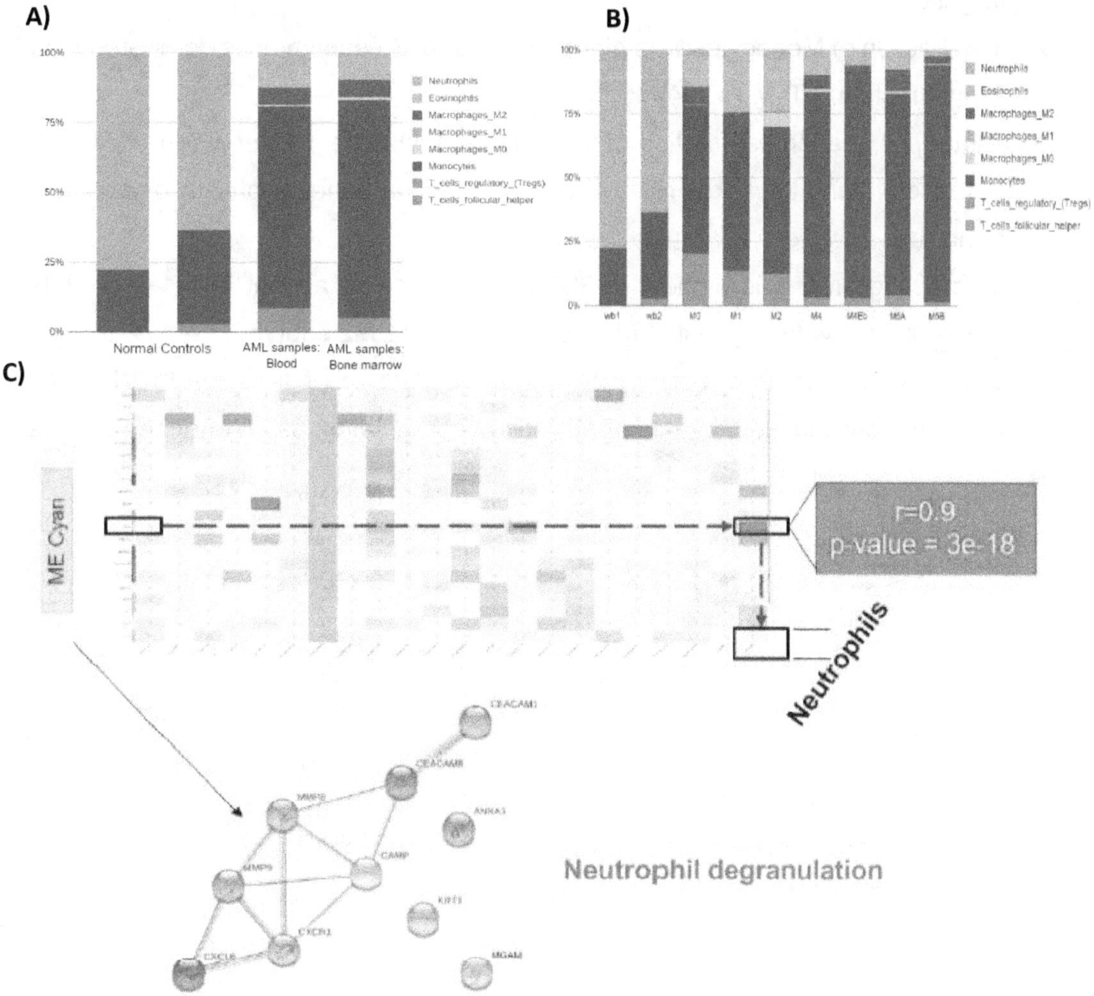

Figure 7.4: A) Immune cell profiles between blood and bone marrow tissue types B) Immune cell profiles across AML subtypes C) Significant correlation of the Cyan module with neutrophils. Pathway analysis of genes of the significantly correlated module shows neutrophil degranulation

- Immune cell profiles revealed a higher fraction of Macrophage M0 in bone marrow samples (t-test: t-value -1.5, p-value=0.06) vs a higher fraction of T-regulatory cells in blood samples (t-test: t-value 2.12, p-value=0.017).
- There was a higher neutrophil fraction in Bone marrow samples.
- The monocyte fraction was the largest among all immune cell fractions in bonemarrow and blood of AML compared to the control blood, where the neutrophil fraction was the largest.
- The fraction of Monocytes was higher in M4 and M5 subtypes as compared to M0-M2, Tregs fraction: M0-M2 > M4-M5
- Neutrophil, the largest fraction of immune cells, was negligible/absent in M1, M4, and M5, and M0 and M2 had a relatively higher fraction of neutrophils but not comparable to normal.
- Macrophage Mo was highest in M2, low in M0, and absent in M1 and M4Eo. M2 macrophages were highest in M5A and least in the M2 subtype.
- WGCNA analysis of correlation between co-expression of genes and AML subtypes of bone marrow samples revealed neutrophil degranulation as an enriched pathway.

Subtype	Module colour	Correlation value	P-value	Pathways
M0	Black	0.36	2e-04	SREBP signalling
M1	Pink	0.29	0.03	GPCR signalling
M2	Dark grey	0.4	3e-05	TLR signalling, NK-cell signalling
M4Eo	Steel blue	0.47	4e-07	Cell-cell communication
M4	Light pink4	0.3	0.002	Olfactory signalling
M5A	Grey	0.62	2e-12	ECM receptor signalling
M5B	Yellow	0.62	1e-12	IRAK4 and MyD88 deficiency, Innate Immune system

- WGCNA analysis reveals subtype pathways

Figure 7.5: Subtype specific significantly correlated genes modules from WGCNA. The first column has AML subtypes, the second column contains the correlated gene, the 3rd column shows the Pearson correlation coefficient, the 4th column shows the significance values and the last column contains their corresponding pathways.

- 3'UTR variant analysis revealed somatic mutations in miRNA binding sites in UBE2A and MRE11A.

➢ Significant expression differences were seen between samples with and without the 3/UTR variants in UBE2A and MRE11A

➢ Combined survival data of MRE11A and UBE2A builds an accurate prognostic prediction model with 61% accuracy.

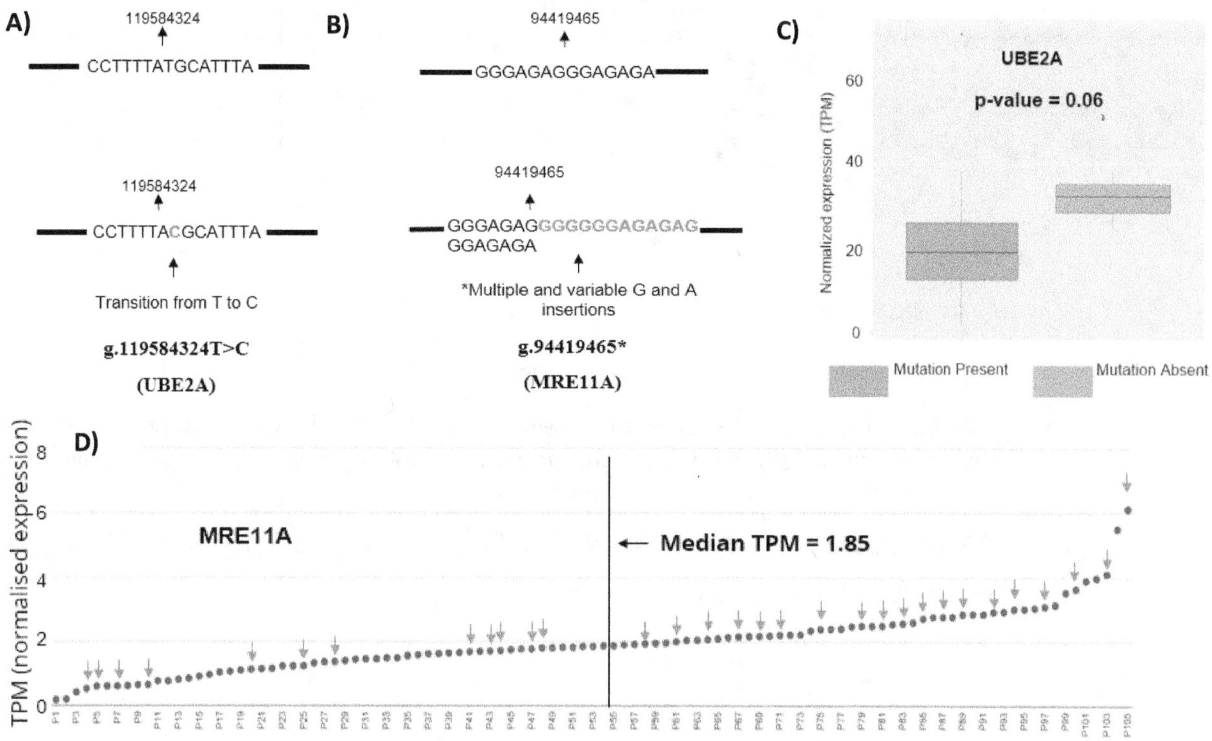

Figure 7.6: 3'UTR variants in A) UBE2A and B) MRE11A which interrupts miRNA binding sites. C) Significant difference in expression between samples with and without 3'UTR variant in UBE2A and D) in MRE11A

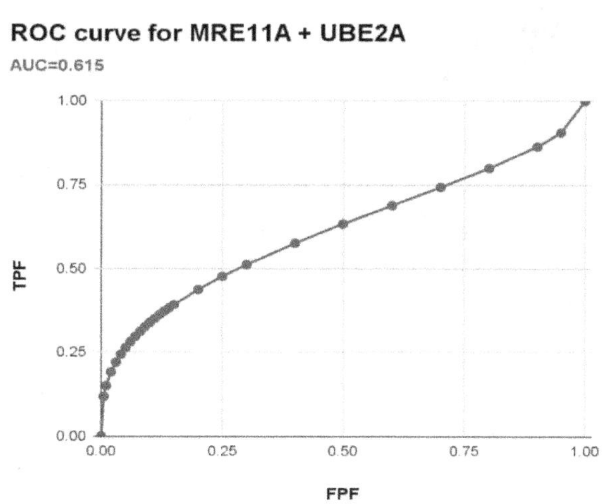

Figure 7.7: Combined ROC curve for UBE2A and MRE11A with 61% accuracy

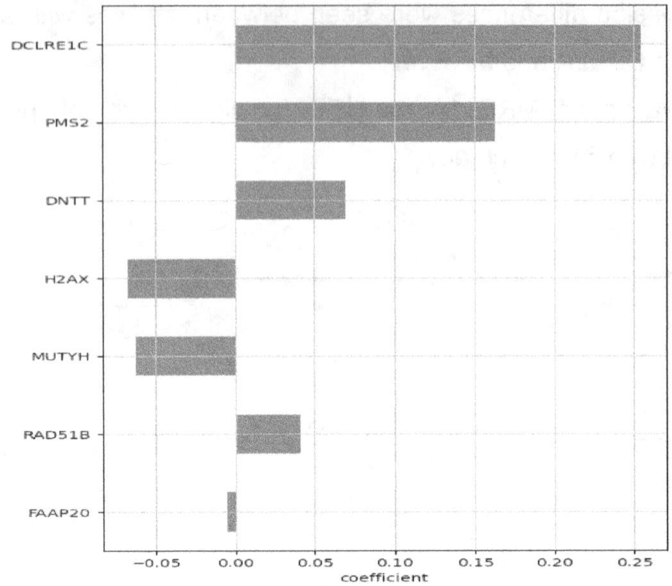

Figure 7.8: Lasso regression model for genes with discernible Regression coefficients. Negative coefficients signify dead signatures and positive coefficients signify alive signatures

➤ LASSO regression was run on survival and expression data from TARGET database revealing alive and dead DDR gene signatures.

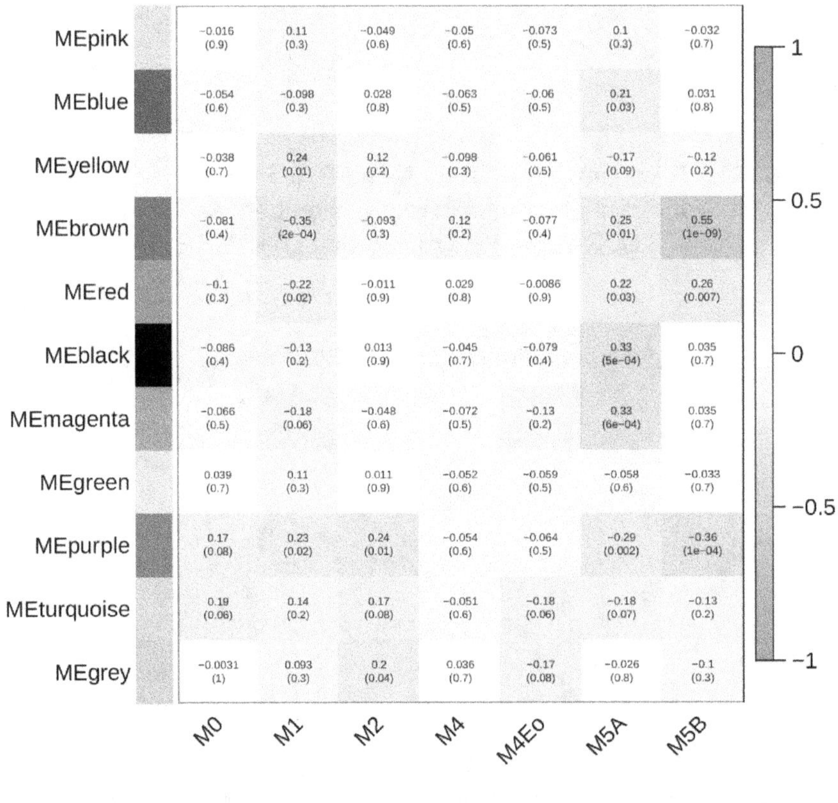

Figure 7.9: Module-trait correlation heatmap between lncRNA-mRNA co-expression and AML subtypes.

➢ WGCNA analysis of lncRNA-mRNA co-expression revealed unique subtype specific signalling pathways, not represented by mRNA analysis.

➢ CASC15, a known oncogenic lincRNA in AML showed binding to the miR-642a-5p and miR-125a-3p, whose binding sites gets interrupted by the 3'UTR variant in the MRE11A gene

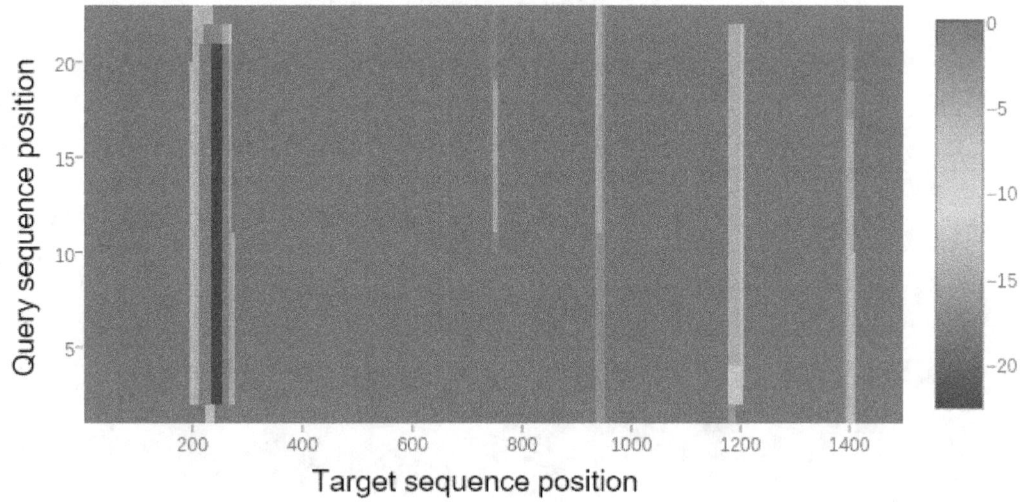

Figure 7.10: Heatmap representing the binding of miR-642a-5p onto the target sequence from CASC15 lincRNA. The intensity of the blue colour corresponds to the strength of binding

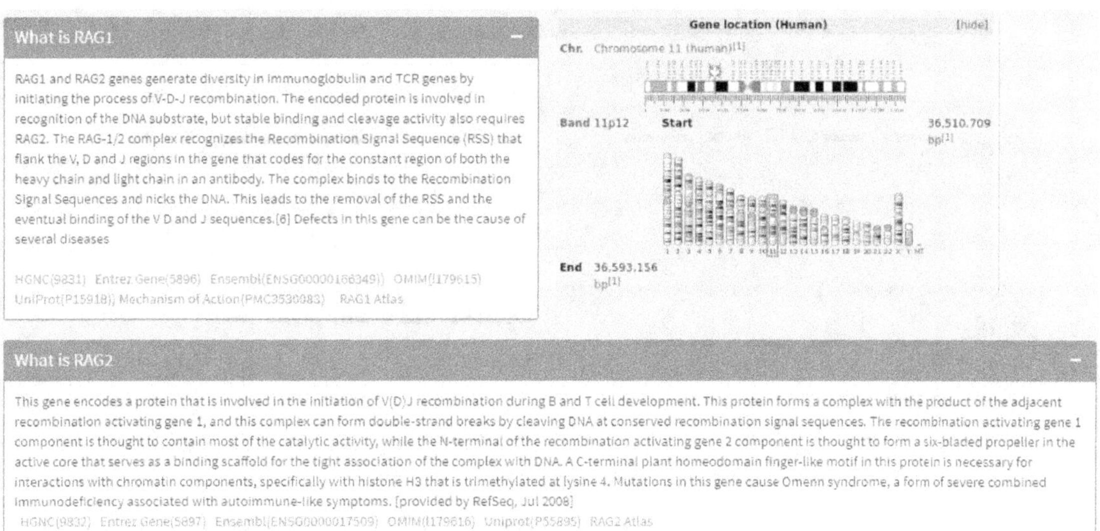

Figure 7.11: The home page from miRAGDB database

➢ As an offshoot of the transcriptome analysis, we developed a database of RAG regulators in normal and aberrant B and T cell conditions.

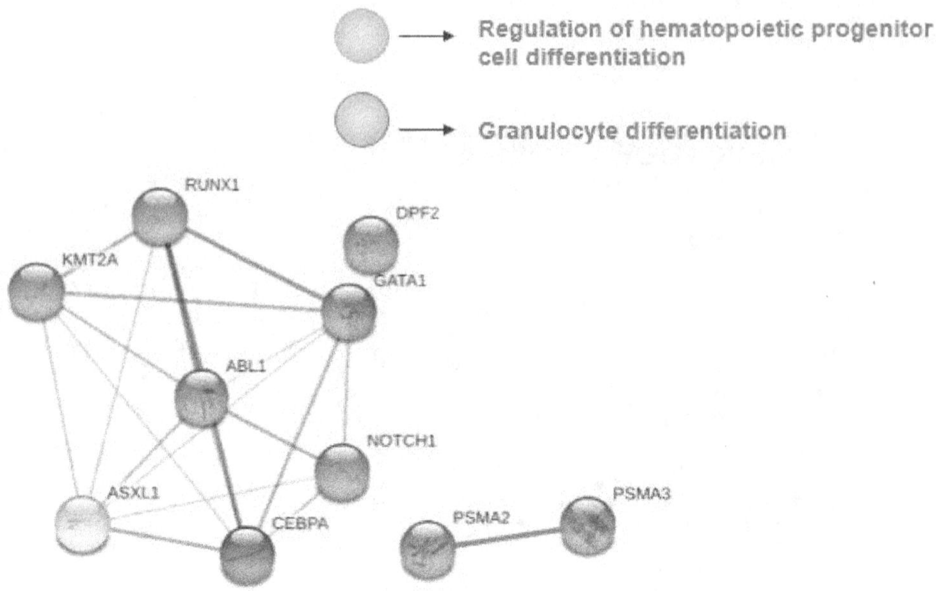

Figure 7.12: STRINGdb network of the deleterious genes showing enrichment of Granulocyte differentiation pathway and Regulation of hematopoietic progenitor cell differentiation pathway

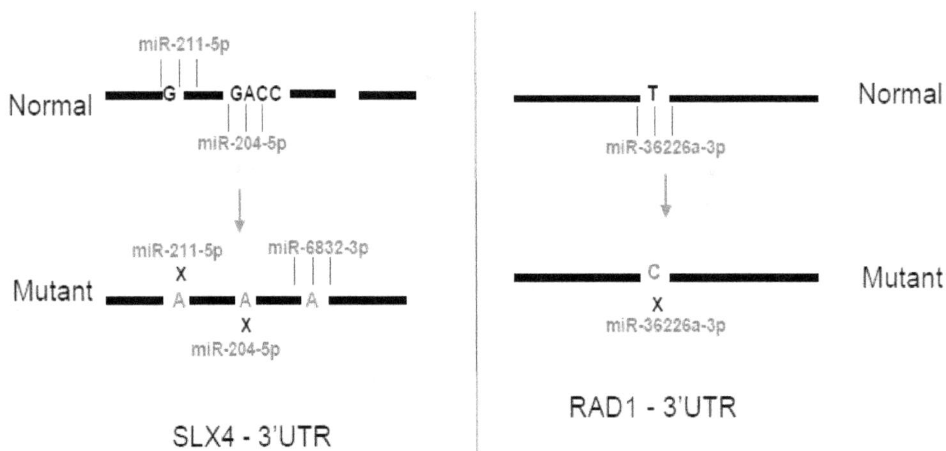

Figure 7.13: UTR mutations in SLX4 and RAD1 altering miRNA binding sites

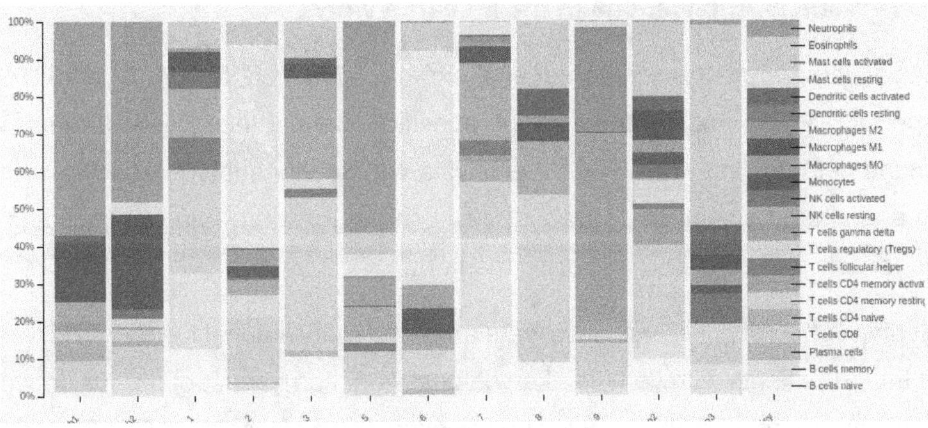

Figure 7.14: Immune profiles of Indian Acute Leukemia samples as compared to whole blood controls in terms of relative fraction of immune cell

- WGS analysis revealed novel deleterious variants unique to the Indian population
- SLX4 and RAD1 showed 3'UTR variants specific to the Indian population that alter miRNA binding sites.
- Transcriptome analysis revealed distinct immune cell signature specific to the Indian population and a novel fusion transcript HOXA11-AGAP3 in 3 out of 10 samples

Patient ID	Fusion Gene Detected
TL-1	--
TL-2	BCR;ABL1
TL-3	HOXD11;AGAP3
TL-5	--
TL-6	BCR;ABL1, HOXD11;AGAP3
TL-7	--
TL-8	BCR;ABL1
TL-9	KMT2A; MLLT3, HOXD11;AGAP3
P2	BCR-ABL1
P3	--

Figure 7.15: Fusion genes detected in Indian Acute Leukaemia Samples

Conclusion – Clinical Applications of the research work:

In conclusion, integrated transcriptome and exome, identified MRE11A and UBE2A as subtype specific 3'UTR variants and subtype specific potential therapeutic targets. With the aid of immune cell profiling and WGCNA analysis we identify subtype specific neutropenia signatures and altered signalling pathways. We also highlight the role of noncoding RNA in AML pathogenesis and as subtype specific markers.

From the Indian cohort specific study, we were able to identify a novel fusion HOXD11-AGAP3 in three of the 10 patients with complex karyotypes. Function impact of the fusion was found to be immune system related, via sample specific expression of cytokines CCL28 and DOCK2, which are seen to be of prognostic significance in the Caucasian population. Additionally, by drawing focus on AGAP3 and its interactors, we found TTYH3 to be of a potential therapeutic and prognostic target

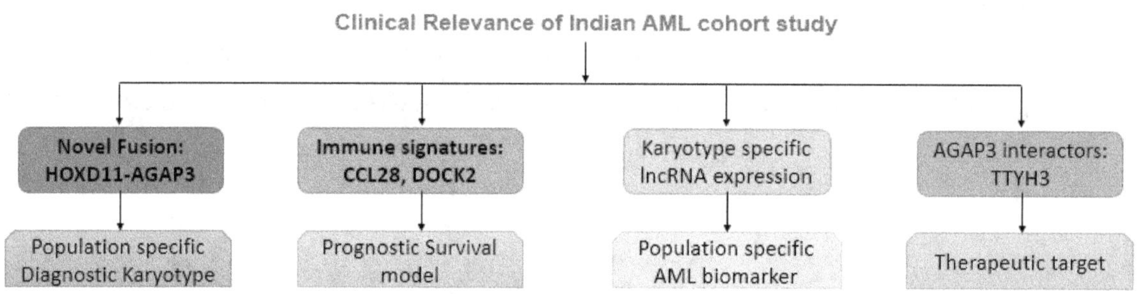

Appendix

Appendix I

Python Code for Calculating TPM for an input file with read counts

```
import pandas as pd
import numpy as np

samples=[line.rstrip() for line in open("lncSamplesNew")]
header=["chrom", "start", "end", "gene"]+ samples            #adding headers

df=pd.read_csv("lncforTPM.tsv", names=header, sep="\t")            #headers applied in the csv
file
print(df)

df=df.sort_values("gene")                              #sorting the values wrt gene
print(df)

df=df.drop_duplicates(subset=["gene"], keep="last")            #taking out all the duplicates from
the df
print(df)

gene_length=(df['end']-df['start']).tolist()             #calculating gene length (end-start)=length
and adding it to list

onlyGenes={'Genes':df["gene"].tolist()}                  #only genes from the dataframe is loaded
in TPM_df
TPM_df=pd.DataFrame(onlyGenes)
print(TPM_df)

for col_name in samples:
   reads=df[col_name].tolist()                          #read count from the sample added to list
   A_val=[]
   A_val=[((x*1000)/gene_length) for x, gene_length in zip(reads, gene_length)]       #formula
for calculating A
   sum_A=sum(A_val)                                     #taking sum of A_val
   print(sum_A)
   TPM=[]                                      #creating a list TPM
   TPM=[A*(1/sum_A)*1000000 for A in A_val]            #tpm formula
   TPM_df[col_name]=TPM                                  #TPM_df and calculated tpm values stored
in TPM
TPM_df=TPM_df.round(4)                                   #TPM values rounded upto 4 places
print(TPM_df)
TPM_df.to_csv("Lnc_tpm.tsv", sep="\t")                    #saving in csv file
```

Appendix II

1. DNA lysis Buffer(100ml)

   584.4 mg NaCl

   5ml 10%SDS

   100µl Triton X-100

   200µl 0.5M EDTA

   1ml 1M TrisCl pH-8

   5µg/µl Proteinase K

2. 1X PBS (pH 7.4)

   137mM NaCl

   2.7mM KCl

   8mM Na2HPO4

   2mM KH2PO4

3. 1X TE (pH 8.0)

   10mM Tris-HCl

   1mM EDTA•Na2

www.ingramcontent.com/pod-product-compliance
Lightning Source LLC
LaVergne TN
LVHW080045210926
848481LV00011B/3285